RADICAL ACTS

ALSO BY MARTIN DUBERMAN

Martin Duberman is Distinguished Professor of History Emeritus at Lehman College and the Graduate School of the City University of New York and was the founder and first director of the Center for Lesbian and Gay Studies at the CUNY Graduate School. He has authored over twenty books, including *James Russell Lowell,* finalist for the National Book Award; *Black Mountain: An Exploration in Community; Paul Robeson,* the winner of several awards; *Stonewall;* the memoir *Cures: A Gay Man's Odyssey;* and, most recently, *The Worlds of Lincoln Kirstein,* runner-up for the Pulitzer Prize in biography. Duberman himself has received numerous awards, including the Bancroft Prize, the Lambda Book Award, the George Freedley Memorial Award, and, in 2008, the American Historical Association's Lifetime Achievement Award for Distinguished Scholarship.

RADICAL ACTS

Collected Political Plays

MARTIN DUBERMAN

THE NEW PRESS

NEW YORK
LONDON

Requests for permission to reproduce selections from this book should be mailed to:
Permissions Department, The New Press, 38 Greene Street, New York, NY 10013.

Published in the United States by The New Press, New York, 2008
Distributed by W. W. Norton & Company, Inc., New York

LIBRARY OF CONGRESS CATALOGING-IN-PUBLICATION DATA

Duberman, Martin B.
Radical acts : collected political plays / Martin Duberman.
p.   cm.
ISBN 978-1-59558-407-6 (pbk.)
1. Political plays, American.   I. Title.
PS3554.U25R33   2008
812'.54—dc22   2008020425

The New Press was established in 1990 as a not-for-profit alternative to the large,
commercial publishing houses currently dominating the book publishing industry.
The New Press operates in the public interest rather than for private gain, and is
commited to publishing, in innovative ways, works of educational, cultural, and
community value that are often deemed insufficiently profitable.

www.thenewpress.com

Composition by dix!
This book was set in Perpetua

Printed in Canada

2   4   6   8   10   9   7   5   3

For Rosalyn Higgins
And fifty years of loving friendship

CONTENTS

PREFACE

Putting History on the Stage

Historians and playwrights usually regard each other as engaged in separate enterprises. The former explores life in the past, the latter life in the present; the one employs the written word, the other the spoken word. Yet I've long felt that each might profit from incorporating some of the distinctive qualities of the other—by combining the theater's emotional immediacy with history's revelations about the diversity through time of human experience.

Almost all marriages of history and theater have, to date, been made by dramatists—Shakespeare's *Richard II*, John Osborne's *Luther,* or Michael Frayn's *Copenhagen*, say—more given to an imaginative re-working of the historical record than to the sort of careful re-assemblage characteristic of the professional historian (though we're now fully aware that the historian's presumed objectivity is prey to all sorts of subtly concealed biases).

Over the years I myself have made various attempts to make theater and in particular political theater, out of historical materials, beginning with my first produced play, *In White America*, which opened off Broadway in 1963, had a long run, and is still performed.* In the succeeding four decades, that early, easy success proved difficult to duplicate—even as my view of *how* history might be put on the stage

* I've extensively revised the plays published here (except for *In White America*) during 2007–08, and as of this writing these new versions have not yet been publicly read or otherwise performed.

underwent considerable revision. With *In White America,* I thought—I now know better—that my role should and could be confined to that of the scrupulous documentarian, refusing to embellish the script with any words that didn't come directly from a primary source and confining my own contribution to writing brief "bridges" between scenes.

Yet even back then, a double consciousness was at work in me. One part of my brain knew perfectly well that "objectivity" was an unattainable goal, no matter how painstaking the effort to achieve it. In selecting some historical documents over others and in then trimming and shaping them for dramatic purposes, I was engaged in a subjective process that assuredly qualified as a variant form of invention—and I knew it. It was the same process, I felt, that characterized all historical writing.

As early as 1964, I even wrote an op-ed piece in the *New York Times* pointing out that the historical profession was remiss in failing to acknowledge that certain inherent features of attempts to re-create the past inevitably compromised claims to absolute objectivity. Only fragmentary traces, not the whole record of what happened, remains; and those traces heavily reflect the experiences of the most privileged sector of society. Moreover, the historian's personal experience, whether remembered or not, plus his or her ideological mindset, consciously held or not, meant that even the most meticulous practitioners would inevitably select, omit, and emphasize certain aspects of the historical record over others.

Despite my early recognition of the subjectivity of historical writing, I was still, at the time of *In White America*, wedded to the conviction that as a professional historian it was my duty to *try* and reconstruct the past as impartially as possible. I further believed that the documentary format would successfully minimize any opportunity or temptation to introduce my own voice. Even as I cut and spliced historical diaries, letters, newspaper accounts, and congressional debates into the scenes that make up *In White America*, I acted as if another virginal birth was at hand. Beyond what I accepted as an irreducible amount of minor tampering (such as a change in tense here or there), during rehearsals I allowed neither myself nor the actors any deviation from the purportedly immaculate text. Not since Von Ranke ("wie es eigentlich gewesen") had so rigid a sentinel stood guard over the (imagined) integrity of the historical record.

My literal-mindedness got me into a running battle with Fred Pinkard, one of the original cast members of *In White America*. It was Fred who was assigned the bridge material that introduced the John Brown scene in the play, and Fred didn't take kindly to the line, "John Brown . . . has alternately been called a saint and a madman." Fred, an African American, would have none of it. Throughout the rehearsal period he argued tenaciously with me over the line, insisting that the "saint/madman" phrase maligned a man who was a hero to black Americans. I tried to persuade Fred that Civil War historians (my own specialty at the time) did indeed divide in just that way in their verdict on Brown. Fred wanted to know how many of those historians were black. *Touché*, I thought—"not many," I sheepishly said. Fred shrugged, as if to say "case closed," and went back to omitting the offending line whenever I wasn't seated hawk-eyed in the theater.

In the years since *In White America*, I've loosened up considerably, letting my own imaginative needs and the requirements of the dramatic form in which I was working increasingly surface—partly in response, doubtless, to shifting cultural norms that for some time have insistently emphasized the difficulties, not the possibilities, of establishing a stable truth. I've never lost my ingrained sense that historical evidence must be respected, but I've happily welcomed its frequent absence as a blessed opportunity for freely inventing dialogue and exploring personality.

As a biographer (of Paul Robeson and Lincoln Kirstein, among others) I've been known for my meticulous treatment of evidence—all the more reason, probably, why I enjoyed the holiday from scrupulosity, welcomed the chance to flesh out in the plays interior lives and relationships for which the historical record was scant or blank. Should a flurry of unease erupt, I'd calm myself with the reminder that once I'd shifted from the documentary format of *In White America*, I'd entered a novelistic terrain in which the demands of narrative and character development took precedence over literal exposition.

In the course of writing both *Mother Earth* and *Visions of Kerouac* I've interwoven primary sources—a snippet from one of Emma Goldman's speeches, say, or from a Kerouac novel (her words available in "public domain," his by specific arrangement with the Kerouac estate)—with my own inventions. Most of the scenes and almost all of the characters in those two plays are based on actual episodes and people, but elaborated so fully as to constitute a synergistic collaboration. I sometimes found that a few lines or sometimes just a phrase from, say, a Goldman or Kerouac letter, would trigger in me some imagined dialogue or even a full-length scene—the end product becoming so tight an amalgam of my words and theirs that at this point I couldn't confidently separate the constituent parts.

With *Posing Naked* I've carried the process of fictionalization still further. The structure of the play adheres closely to the events and pivotal personalities involved in the 1960 arrest of the famed literary critic Newton Arvin on charges of running an interstate pornography ring. But none of Arvin's (or any of the other characters') own words have been incorporated into the script, and I've freely imagined most of the scenes and dialogue. The courtroom scene does include some bits from the trial record (and some phrases from Ralph Waldo Emerson's writings); that aside, the play contains no direct documentary quotation.

Except for *In White America*, which has had a large number of productions (including Paris and London), *Visions of Kerouac* is the only other play in this volume to have had anything like a professional production—three, in fact, though all of them were low-budget, limited-run affairs. Both *Kerouac* and *Mother Earth* (but not *Posing Naked*) have also had readings and an occasional workshop—*Kerouac* most recently at the Rattlestick Theater in New York City, *Mother Earth* at the New York Theatre Workshop.

But readings (this is less true of a full workshop) aren't often a very satisfying vehicle for refining a script. There's rarely enough rehearsal time (and sometimes none at all—the so-called "cold reading") for actors actually to learn lines or for directors to put a play "on its feet." Actors, moreover, are usually unpaid and often juggling a half dozen other commitments in order to "be seen"—and to put food on the table. Many young directors—few established ones will ever take on a reading, unless the script is already the subject of interest and hype—are these days video or film oriented: creating visual "stage pictures" seems to take precedence over helping actors explore their characters or playwrights their scripts.

Occasionally a reading *has* been helpful in re-working a script; but in the case of *Mother Earth* and *Visions of Kerouac*, other obstacles have then appeared. At the close of each successful reading or workshop of those two plays, the sponsoring management has always summed up its verdict in comparable language: "Though we greatly admire the writing, we've reluctantly concluded that it would be unwise to proceed to a full-scale production: the cast of the play is too large, the potential costs too great, the themes too politically radical, the serious-minded theater-going public currently too small, to warrant the risks."

I can sympathize with such a judgment. Certainly on Broadway the pursuit of laughs and the dispensing of easy comfort tend to hold iron sway. Plays that threaten to evoke pain or trouble the conscience are usually avoided, though occasionally one or two do get through the net. But whereas a multitude of lightly entertaining musicals will prosper despite middling reviews, the infrequent production of a serious, politically driven play, even if the critical reception is highly favorable, rarely has a sustained run. A large enough audience for challenging theater simply isn't there to offset the currently astronomical costs of production.

It wasn't always this way. Back in the 1960s, when the counter-cultural challenge to authority was at its height, the New York theater was alive with spirited provocation. The Open Theater, the Theater of the Ridiculous, the Negro Ensemble Company, and the Living Theater led the way, but they were hardly alone in bringing dangerous stage fare to audiences hungry for it. The hope is that this new generation—or to be more precise, the growing progressive segment of it that doesn't attend Bob Jones University—will again demand more politically risky and aware plays.

The young can already find a significant number of boldly provocative movies and cable TV shows, thus making many indifferent to the resuscitation of live theater ("it's not *our* generation's preferred outlet"). But not everyone under thirty feels that way, as some defiant, tough-minded offerings in small theaters and on campuses demonstrate. Should those voices gain a more spacious hearing, Emma Goldman waits in the wings, refusing to comb her hair, polishing yet again her inflammatory remarks.

Martin Duberman
April 2008

ACKNOWLEDGMENTS

I want to thank Ellen Adler for her belief in these plays and for her steadfastness in guiding them into print. Others at The New Press have contributed their time and talent and in this regard I especially want to thank Maury Botton, Jyothi Natarajan, and Anne Sullivan. As always, my partner Eli Zal gave me his unvarnished opinions, and his loving support.

RADICAL ACTS

In White America

ACT ONE

(On stage: three black and three white actors, two men and one woman in each case, and a guitarist. White Man comes forward, picks newspaper off table, and reads aloud from it the current date.)

WHITE MAN:

January 12, 1964
 If God had intended for the races to mix, he would have mixed them himself. He put each color in a different place.

BLACK MAN: The American white man has a conscience, and the non-violent method appeals to that conscience.

WHITE WOMAN: Negroes are demanding something that isn't so unreasonable—to get a cup of coffee at a lunch counter, to get a decent job.

BLACK WOMAN: What they really feel on the inside never changes. Eventually they'll wind up calling you a nigger.

WHITE MAN: Negro impatience can be readily understood, but defiance breeds doubt, and riots breed hatred.

BLACK MAN: Sure I love my white brother, but I watch him!

BLACK MAN: To integrate with evil is to be destroyed with evil. We want an area of this land we can call our own.

WHITE WOMAN: My children won't be taking sides—unless we idiots tell them there are sides to take.

BLACK MAN: After four hundred years of barbaric treatment, the American Negro is fed up with the unmitigated hypocrisy of the white man.

WHITE MAN *(Reading again from newspaper)*: If they got guts enough to come down here all they'll get is a load of buckshot. The white people have shown remarkable restraint in not killing niggers wholesale.

BLACK ACTRESS *(Sings):*
  Oh, freedom, Oh, freedom,
  Oh, freedom, over me!
  And before I'll be a slave,
  I'll be buried in my grave,
  And go home to my Lord
  And be free.

(Throughout the play the delivery of the narratives is alternated among the actors.)

NARRATOR: *The story of black people in the United States begins with the slave trade. A ship's doctor aboard a slave vessel in the mid-eighteenth century described his impressions.*

SHIP DOCTOR: The slave ships lie a mile below the town, in Bonny River, off the coast of Guinea. Sometimes fifteen sail meet here together. Scarce a day passes without some Negroes being purchased and carried on board. . . .

  The wretched Negroes are immediately fastened together, two and two, by handcuffs on their wrists and by irons rivetted on their legs. They are then sent down between the decks and placed in a space partitioned off for that purpose. They are frequently stowed so close as to admit of no other position than lying on their sides. Nor will the height between decks allow them to stand.

  The diet of the Negroes while on board consists chiefly of horse-beans boiled to the consistence of pulp.

  Upon the Negroes refusing to take food, I have seen coals of fire, glowing hot, put on a shovel and placed so near their lips as to scorch and burn them. I have also been credibly informed that a certain captain in the slave trade poured melted lead on such of his Negroes as obstinately refused their food.

  On board some ships the common sailors are allowed to have intercourse with such of the black women whose consent they can procure. The officers are permitted to indulge their passions among them at pleasure.

The hardships suffered by the Negroes during the passage are scarcely to be conceived. The exclusion of fresh air is the most intolerable. Whenever the sea is rough and the rain heavy it becomes necessary to shut every conveyance by which air is admitted. The Negroes' rooms very soon grow intolerably hot. The confined air produces fevers and fluxes which carry off great numbers of them. The floor of their rooms can be so covered with blood and mucus in consequence of the flux that it resembles a slaughterhouse. Last week by only continuing among them for about a quarter of an hour, I was so overcome with the heat, stench, and foul air that I nearly fainted; and it was only with assistance that I could get on deck. . . .

One evening while the ship lay in Bonny River, one of the Negroes forced his way through the network on the larboard side of the vessel, jumped overboard, and was devoured by the sharks. Circumstances of this kind are very frequent.

Very few of the Negroes can bear the loss of their liberty and the hardships they endure.

BLACK ACTRESS *(Sings)*:
And before I'll be a slave,
I'll be buried in my grave,
    And go home to my Lord
    And be free.

QUAKER WOMAN *(Reads aloud from parchment)*: February 11, 1790. To the Senate and House of Representatives of the United States: The Address of the people called Quakers, in their annual assembly convened.

Firmly believing that unfeigned righteousness in public as well as private stations, is the only sure ground of hope for the Divine blessing, we apprehend ourselves religiously bound to request your serious Christian attention to the gross national iniquity of trafficking in the persons of fellow-men.

Many are the enormities abhorrent to common humanity, and common honesty, which we judge it not needful to particularize to a body of men, chosen as eminently distinguished for wisdom as extensive information. But we find it indispensably incumbent on us to attempt to excite your attention to the affecting subject that a sincere and impartial inquiry may take place, whether it be not in reality within your power to exercise justice and mercy, which, if adhered to, we cannot doubt, must produce the abolition of the slave trade.

FIRST CONGRESSMAN: Mr. President, this petition prays that we should take measures for the abolition of the slave trade. This is desiring an unconstitutional act, because the Constitution secures that trade to the States, independent of Congressional restrictions, for a term of twenty-one years. Therefore, it ought to be rejected as an attempt upon the virtue and patriotism of the House.

SECOND CONGRESSMAN: I think it is incumbent upon every member of this House to sift the subject well, and ascertain what can be done to restrain a practice so nefarious. The Constitution has authorized us to levy a tax upon the importation of such persons. I would willingly go to that extent; and if anything further can be devised to discountenance the trade, consistent with the terms of the Constitution, I shall cheerfully give it my assent and support.

FIRST CONGRESSMAN: I fear that if Congress takes any measures indicative of an intention to interfere with the kind of property alluded to, it would sink in value very considerably, and might be injurious to a great number of citizens, particularly in the Southern states.

SECOND CONGRESSMAN: I think the gentleman carries his apprehensions too far. It appears to me that if the importation was crushed, the value of a slave would be increased instead of diminished.

FIRST CONGRESSMAN: I differ much in opinion. If through the interference of the General Government the slave trade was abolished, it would evince to the people a disposition towards a total emancipa-

tion, and they would hold their property in jeopardy. The petition-
ers may as well come forward and solicit Congress to interdict the
West India trade, because from thence we import rum, which has a
debasing influence upon the consumer. But, sir, is the whole morality of the United States confined to the Quakers? Do they understand the rights of mankind, and the disposition of Providence,
better than others? If they were to consult that Book, which claims
our regard, they will find that slavery is not only allowed but commended. And if they fully examine the subject, they will find that
slavery has been no novel doctrine since the days of Cain; but be
these things as they may, I hope the House will order the petition
to lie on the table, in order to prevent alarm to our Southern
brethren.

NARRATOR: *The Quaker petition on the slave trade was tabled. Yet the whole
question of the Negro's place in American life continued to disturb a few
thoughtful men. Among them was Thomas Jefferson.*

JEFFERSON: The love of justice and the love of country plead equally
the cause of these people, and it is a moral reproach to us that they
should have pleaded it so long in vain. Yet the hour of emancipation
is advancing. Nothing is more certainly written in the book of fate
than that these people are to be free; nor is it less certain that the
two races, equally free, cannot live in the same government. Nature, habit, opinion, have drawn indelible lines of distinction between them.
(Coming forward.)
The blacks are at least as brave, and more adventuresome. But
this may perhaps proceed from a want of fore-thought, which prevents their seeing a danger till it be present. They are more ardent
after their female; but love seems with them to be more an eager
desire, than a tender delicate mixture of sentiment and sensation.
Their griefs are transient. Those numberless afflictions, which ren-
der it doubtful whether heaven has given life to us in mercy or in
wrath, are less felt and sooner forgotten with them. In general,
their existence appears to participate more of sensation than re-

flection. It appears to me that in memory they are equal to the whites; in reason much inferior, as I think one could scarcely be found capable of tracing and comprehending the investigations of Euclid. It will be right to make great allowances for the difference of condition, of education, of conversation, of the sphere in which they move. Yet we know that among the Romans, the condition of their slaves was much more deplorable than that of the blacks on the continent of America. Notwithstanding, their slaves were often their rarest artists. They excelled too in science. . . . But they were of the race of whites.

To justify a general conclusion requires many observations. I advance it, therefore, as a suspicion only, that the blacks, whether originally a distinct race, or made distinct by time and circumstances, are inferior to the whites in the endowments both of body and mind.

BLACK ACTOR *(Sings)*:
My old missus promised me,
Hmm-mm-mm,
When she die, gonna set me free,
Hm-mm-mm.

Missus die nine years ago,
Hmm-mm-mm,
Here Ah is in the same old row,
Hm-mm-mm.

NARRATOR: *White men rarely heard the slaves themselves talk about their condition. One of the few exceptions was a conversation recorded by a Northern journalist, Frederick Law Olmsted, with a house servant named William.*

OLMSTED *(To audience)*: After leaving a plantation near New Orleans, I was driven about twenty miles in a buggy by one of the house servants. He was inclined to be talkative and as he expressed great affection and respect for his owner, I felt at liberty to question him on some points upon which I had always previously avoided conversing with slaves. *(Crossing to where the slave, William, is seated)* He first said that he came from Virginia. . . .

WILLIAM: I reckon there is no black folks anywhere so well made as those who was born in Virginny. Is you from New Orleans, massa?

OLMSTED: No, I live in the North.

WILLIAM: Da's great many brack folks dah, massa?

OLMSTED: No; very few.

WILLIAM: Da's a great many in Virginny.

OLMSTED: But I came from beyond Virginia—from New York.

WILLIAM: If I was free, I would go to Virginny, and see my old mudder. I don't well know, exactly, how old I is; but I rec'lect, de day I was taken away, my ole mudder she tell me I was tirteen years old. I felt dreadful bad, but now I like it here. De people is almost all French. Is dere any French in New York?

OLMSTED: Yes, but not as many as in Louisiana.

WILLIAM: I s'pose dah is more of French people in Lusiana den dah is anywhar else in all de world—a'nt dah, massa?

OLMSTED: Except in France.

WILLIAM: Wa's dat, sar?

OLMSTED: France is the country where all the Frenchmen came from, in the first place.

WILLIAM: Wa's dat France, massa?

OLMSTED: France is a country across the ocean, the big water, beyond Virginia, where all the Frenchmen first came from; just as the black people all came first from Africa, you know.

WILLIAM: *Is* de brack folks better off to be here, massa?

OLMSTED: I think so.

WILLIAM: *Why is it*, then, massa, when de brack people is free, dey wants to send 'em away out of dis country?

OLMSTED *(Taken aback)*: Some people think Africa is a better place for you. *(Changing the subject)* What would you do, if you were free?

WILLIAM: If I was free, massa; *if I was free* . . . I would—well, sar, de fus thing I would do, if I was free, I would go to work for a year, and get some money for myself—den-den-den, massa, dis is what I do—I buy me, fus place, a little house, and little lot land, and den—no; den-den I would go to old Virginny, and see my old mud-der. Yes, sar, I would like to do dat fus thing; den, when I com back, de fus thing I'd do, I'd get me a wife; den, I'd take her to my house, and I would live with her dar; and I would raise things in my gar-den, and take 'em to New Orleans, and sell 'em dar, in the market. Dat's de way I would live, if I was free.

OLMSTED: Well, now, wouldn't you rather live on a plantation with a kindly master like yours than to be free, William?

WILLIAM: Oh no, sir, I'd rather be free! Oh, yes, sir, I'd like it better to be free; I would dat, master.

OLMSTED: Why would you?

WILLIAM: Why, you see, master, if I was free—if I was *free*, I'd have all my time to myself. I'd rather work for myself. Yes. I'd like dat better.

OLMSTED: But then, you know, you'd have to take care of yourself, and you'd get poor.

WILLIAM: No, sir, I would not get poor, I would get rich; for you see, master, then I'd work all the time for myself.

OLMSTED: You don't suppose there would be much sugar raised, do you?

WILLIAM: Why, yes, master, I do. Why not, sir? What would de brack people do? Wouldn't dey hab to work for dar libben? And de wite people own all de land—war dey goin' to work? Dey hire demself right out again, and work harder dan dey do now to get more wages—a heap harder. I tink so, sir. I would do so, sir.

OLMSTED: The black people talk among themselves about this, do they; and they think so generally?

WILLIAM: Oh! yes, sir; dey talk so; dat's wat dey tink.

OLMSTED: Then they talk about being free a good deal, do they?

WILLIAM: Yes, sir. Dey—*(Suddenly on guard)*—dat is, dey say dey wish it was so; dat's all dey talk, master—dat's all, sir.

(The light fades.)

NARRATOR: *Some of William's fellow slaves were interviewed many years later about their recollections of slavery.*

MAN: I sets and 'members the times in the world. I 'members now clear as yesterday things I forgot for a long time. I 'members 'bout the days of slavery, and I don't 'lieve they ever gwine have slaves no more on this earth. I think God done took that burden offen his black children, and I'm aiming to praise Him for it to His face in the days of glory.

WOMAN: I's hear tell of them good slave days, but I ain't never seen no good times then. One time Aunt Cheyney was just out of bed with a suckling baby and she run away. Old Solomon gits the nigger hounds and takes her trail. They gits near her and she grabs a limb and tries to hist herself in a tree, but them dogs grap her and pull her down. The men hollers them onto her, and the dogs tore her naked and et the breasts plumb off her body. She got well and lived to be a old woman, but 'nother woman has to suck her baby, and she ain't got no sign of breasts no more.

MAN: Sometimes I wishes that I could be back to the old place, 'cause we did have plenty to eat, and at hog-killing time us had more'n a plenty. Old Master kill eight or ten set-down hogs at one time. . . . What a set-down hog? It's a hog what done et so much corn he got so fat that he feets can't hold him up, and he just set on he hind quarters and grunts and eats, and eats and grunts, till they knock him in the head.

MAN: Talking 'bout victuals, our eating was good. Can't say the same for all places. Some of the plantations half-starved their niggers till they wasn't fittin' for work. They had to slip about to other places to piece out their meals.

WOMAN: I recollects once when I was trying to clean the house like Ole Miss tell me, I finds a biscuit, and I's so hungry I et it, 'cause we never see such a thing as a biscuit . . . and she comes in and say, "Where that biscuit?" I say, "Miss, I et it 'cause I's so hungry." Then she grabs that broom and start to beating me over the head with it and calling me low-down nigger, and I guess I just clean lost my head 'cause I knowed better than to fight her if I knowed anything 't all, but I start to fight her, and the driver, he comes in and he grabs me and starts beating me with that cat-o'-nine-tails, and he beats me till I fall to the floor nearly dead. He cut my back all to pieces, then they rubs salt in the cuts for more punishment. Lord, Lord, honey! Them was awful days.

MAN: The niggers didn't go to the church building; the preacher came and preached to them in their quarters. He'd just say, "Serve your masters. Don't steal your master's turkey. Don't steal your master's chickens. Don't steal your master's hogs. Don't steal your master's meat. Do whatsomever your master tells you to do." Same old thing all the time.

MAN: My white folks didn't mind their niggers praying and singing hymns, but some places wouldn't 'low them to worship a-tall, and they had to put their heads in pots to sing or pray.

WOMAN: Once Massa goes to Baton Rouge and brung back a yaller gal dressed in fine style. She was a seamster nigger. He builds her a house 'way from the quarters. This yaller gal breeds fast and gits a mess of white young-uns. She larnt them fine manners and combs out they hair.

Once two of them goes down the hill to the dollhouse, where the Missy's children am playing. They wants to go in the dollhouse and one of the Missy's boys say, "That's for white children." They say, "We ain't no niggers, 'cause we got the same daddy as you has, and he comes to see us near every day." They is fussing, and Missy is listening out her chamber window. . . .

When Massa come home his wife hardly say nothing to him, and he asks her what the matter, and she tells him, "Since you asks me, I'm studying in my mind 'bout them white young-uns of that yaller nigger wench from Baton Rouge." He say, "Now, honey, I fotches that gal just for you, 'cause she a fine seamster." She say, "It look kind of funny they got the same kind of hair and eyes as my children, and they got a nose look like yours." He say, "Honey, you just paying 'tention to talk of little children that ain't got no mind to what they say." She say, "Over in Mississippi I got a home and plenty with my daddy, and I got that in my mind."

Well, she didn't never leave, and Massa bought her a fine, new span of surrey hosses. But she don't never have no more children, and she ain't so cordial with the Massa. That yaller gal has more white young-uns, but they don't never go down the hill no more.

MAN: One thing what make it tough on the niggers was them times when a man and he wife and their children had to be taken 'way from one another, sold off or taken 'way to some other state. They was heaps of nigger families that I know what was separated in the time of bondage that tried to find they folkses what was gone. But the mostest of 'em never git together again even after they sot free 'cause they don't know where one or the other is.

MAN: Slavery time was tough, boss. You just don't know how tough it was. I can't 'splain to you just how bad all the niggers want to get they freedom.

BLACK ACTRESS *(Sings)*:
Right foot, left foot,
Along the road,
Follow the drinking gourd.

Up to the North,
Drop your load,
Follow the drinking gourd.

NARRATOR: *Slaves constantly tried to flee the plantation and head North to freedom. Efforts by their masters to trace them led, in a few rare cases, to an exchange of letters.*

JOURDAN ANDERSON: To My Old Master, Colonel P. H. Anderson, Big Spring, Tennessee.

Sir: I got your letter, and was glad to find that you had not forgotten Jourdan, and that you wanted me to come back and live with you again. Although you shot at me twice before I left you, I am glad you are still living.

I want to know particularly what the good chance is you propose to give me. I am doing tolerably well here. I get twenty-five dollars a month, with victuals and clothing; have a comfortable home for Mandy,—the folks call her Mrs. Anderson—and the children—Milly, Jane, and Grundy—go to school and are learning well. The teacher says Grundy has a head for a preacher. They go to Sunday school, and Mandy and me attend church regularly. We are kindly treated.

Mandy says she would be afraid to go back without some proof that you were disposed to treat us justly and kindly; and we have concluded to test your sincerity by asking you to send us our wages for the time we served you. This will make us forget and forgive old scores, and rely on your justice and friendship in the future. I served you faithfully for thirty-two years, and Mandy for twenty years. At twenty-five dollars a month for me, and two dollars a week for Mandy, our earnings would amount to eleven thousand six hundred and eighty dollars. Add to this the interest for the time our wages have been kept back, and deduct what you paid for our clothing, and three doctor's visits to me, and pulling a tooth for Mandy, and the balance will show what we are in justice entitled to. Please send the money by Adam's Express, in care of V. Winters, Esq., Dayton, Ohio.

Say howdy to George Carter, and thank him for taking the pistol from you when you were shooting at me.

> From your old servant,
> Jourdan Anderson

MRS. SARAH LOGUE: To Jarm: . . . I write you these lines to let you know the situation we are in—partly in consequence of your running away and stealing Old Rock, our fine mare. Though we got the mare back, she never was worth much after you took her. If you will send me one thousand dollars, and pay for the old mare, I will give up all claim I have to you. In consequence of your running away, we had to sell Abe and Ann and twelve acres of land; and I want you to send me the money, that I may be able to redeem the land. If you do not comply with my request, I will sell you to someone else, and you may rest assured that the time is not far distant when things will be changed with you. A word to the wise is sufficient. . . . You know that we reared you as we reared our own children.

> Yours, etc.
>
> Mrs. Sarah Logue

JARM: Mrs. Sarah Logue: . . . Had you a woman's heart, you never could have sold my only remaining brother and sister, because I put myself beyond your power to convert me into money.

You sold my brother and sister, Abe and Ann, and twelve acres of land. . . . Now you ask me to send you $1,000 to enable you to redeem the *land*, but not to redeem my poor brother and sister! You say that you shall sell me if I do not send you $1,000, and in the same breath you say, "You know we raised you as we did our own children." Woman, did you raise your *own children* for the market? Did you raise them for the whipping post? Did you raise them to be driven off, bound to a coffle in chains? Where are my poor bleeding brothers and sisters? Can you tell? Who was it that sent them off into sugar and cotton fields, to be kicked and cuffed, and whipped, and to groan and die . . . ?

Did you think to terrify me by presenting the alternative to give my money to you, or give my body to slavery? Then let me say to you, that I meet the proposition with scorn and contempt. I will not budge one hair's breadth. I will not breathe a shorter breath. . . . I stand among free people.

NARRATOR: *Some blacks reacted to slavery not by fleeing, but by rising in rebellion. In 1831, the slave Nat Turner and his followers turned on their masters in Southampton County, Virginia.*

NAT TURNER: I was thirty-five years of age the second of October last, and born the property of Benjamin Turner. In my childhood a circumstance occurred which made an indelible impression on my mind. . . . Being at play with other children, when three or four years old, I was telling them something, which my mother, overhearing, said had happened before I was born. I stuck to my story, however, and related some other things which went, in her opinion, to confirm it. Others being called on, were greatly astonished, and caused them to say, in my hearing, I surely would be a prophet. . . .

I studiously avoided mixing in society, and wrapped myself in mystery, devoting my time to fasting and prayer. I obtained influence over the minds of my fellow servants—not by the means of conjuring and such-like tricks, for to them I always spoke of such things with contempt—but by the communion of the Spirit. . . . They believed and said my wisdom came from God.

About this time I had a vision—I saw white spirits and black spirits engaged in battle, and the sun was darkened—the thunder rolled in the heavens, and blood flowed in streams—and I heard a voice saying, "Such is your luck, such you are called to see; and let it come rough or smooth, you must surely hear it." I communicated the great work laid out for me to do. It was quickly agreed, neither age nor sex was to be spared.

It was my object to carry terror and devastation wherever we went. We killed Mrs. Waller and ten children. Then we started for Mr. William Williams. . . . Mrs. Williams fled, but she was pursued, overtaken, and after showing her the mangled body of her lifeless husband, she was told to get down and lay by his side, where she was shot dead. The white men pursued and fired on us several times. Five or six of my men were wounded, but none left on the field. . . . Finding myself defeated . . . I gave up all hope for the present. . . . I was taken, a fortnight afterwards in a little hole I had dug out with my sword. I am here loaded with chains, and willing to suffer the fate that awaits me.

BLACK ACTOR *(Sings)*:
For the old man is a-waitin'!
For to carry you to freedom
If you follow the drinking gourd.

NARRATOR: *In the North, although blacks were free, they were segregated and despised. The Rev. Samuel J. May described their treatment in Canterbury, Connecticut.*

MAY: In the summer or fall of 1832 I heard that Miss Prudence Crandall, an excellent, well-educated Quaker, had been induced by a
number of ladies and gentlemen of Canterbury, Connecticut, to
establish her boarding and day school there.

For a while the school answered the expectations of its patrons,
but early in the following year, trouble arose. Not far from Canterbury there lived a colored man named Harris. He had a daughter,
Sarah, a bright girl about seventeen years of age. She had passed,
with good repute as a scholar, through the school of the district and
was hungering for more education. Sarah applied for admission
into this new Canterbury school and Miss Crandall admitted her.

The pupils, I believe, made no objection. But in a few days the
parents of some of them called and remonstrated. "They would not
have it said that their daughters went to school with a nigger girl."
Miss Crandall was assured that, if she did not dismiss Sarah Harris,
her white pupils would be withdrawn from her.

She could not comply with such a demand. . . . Accordingly,
she gave notice that next term her school would be opened for
"young ladies and little misses of color." The whole town was in a
flame of indignation. Miss Crandall begged me to come to her as
soon as my engagements would permit. When I arrived I was informed that a town meeting was to be held. She requested that I
might be heard as her attorney.

The Hon. Andrew T. Judson was undoubtedly the chief of Miss
Crandall's persecutors. He was the great man of the town, much
talked of by the Democrats as soon to be governor, and a few years
afterwards was appointed judge of the United States District
Court.

JUDSON: Mr. May, we are not merely opposed to the establishment of
this school in Canterbury; we mean there shall not be such a school
set up anywhere in our state. The colored people never can rise
from their menial condition in our country; they ought not to be
permitted to rise here. They are an inferior race of beings, and
never can or ought to be recognized as the equals of the whites.
Africa is the place for them.

MAY: Mr. Judson, there never will be fewer colored people in this country than there are now. Of the vast majority of them this is the native land, as much as it is ours. The only question is whether we will recognize the rights which God gave them as men.

JUDSON: That nigger school shall never be allowed in Canterbury, nor in any town of this state.

MAY *(To audience)*: Undismayed by such opposition, Miss Crandall received early in April fifteen or twenty colored young ladies from Philadelphia, New York, Providence, and Boston. At once all accommodations at the stores in Canterbury were denied her. She and her pupils were insulted whenever they appeared in the streets. The doors and doorsteps of her house were besmeared; her well was filled with filth. Finally the house was assaulted by a number of persons with heavy clubs and iron bars; five window sashes were demolished and ninety panes of glass dashed to pieces.

For the first time Miss Crandall seemed to quail, and her pupils had become afraid to remain another night under her roof. The front rooms of the house were hardly tenantable; and it seemed foolish to repair them only to be destroyed again. After due consideration, therefore, it was determined that the school should be abandoned. The pupils were called together, and I was requested to announce to them our decision. Twenty harmless, well-behaved girls, whose only offense was that they had come together there to obtain useful knowledge, were to be told that they had better go away. The words almost blistered my lips. I felt ashamed of Canterbury, ashamed of Connecticut, ashamed of my country, ashamed of my color.

NARRATOR: *Many Northern blacks were active in the antislavery struggle, and some took part in other reform movements as well. One of the most famous was the illiterate ex-slave Sojourner Truth, who in 1851 unexpectedly rose at a Woman's Rights Convention.*

SOJOURNER TRUTH: Wall, chilern, whar dar is so much racket dar must be somethin' out o' kilter. I tink dat 'twixt de black folks of de Souf and de womin at de Norf, all talkin' 'bout rights, de white men will be in a fix pretty soon. But what's all dis here talkin' 'bout?

Dat man ober dar say day womin needs to be helped into carriages, and lifted ober ditches, and to hab de best place everywhar. Nobody eber helps me into carriages, or ober mud puddles, or gibs me any best place! And a'n't I a woman? Look at me! Look at my arm! I have ploughed, and planted, and gathered into barns and no man could head me! And a'n't I a woman? I have borne thirteen chilern, and seen 'em mos' sold off to slavery, and when I cried out with my mother's grief, none but Jesus heard me! And a'n't I a woman?

Den dey talks 'bout dis ting in de head; what dis dey call it? *(A voice whispering)* Intellect.

Dat's it, honey. What's dat got to do wid womin's rights? If my cup won't hold but a pint, and yourn holds a quart, wouldn't ye be mean not to let me have my little half-measure full?

Den dat little man in black dar, he say women can't have as much rights as men, 'cause Christ wan't a woman! Whar did your Christ come from? Whar did your Christ come from? From God and a woman! Man had nothin' to do wid Him!

If de fust woman God ever made was strong enough to turn de world upside down all alone, dese women togedder ought to be able to turn it back and get it right side up again! And now dey is asking to do it, de men better let 'em.

CAST *(Sings)*:
God's gonna set this world on fire,
God's gonna set this world on fire
One of these days, hallelujah!
God's gonna set this world on fire,
Gonna set this world on fire one of these days.

NARRATOR: *In 1859, John Brown, who has alternately been called a saint and a madman, made an unsuccessful attempt at Harpers Ferry, Virginia, to free the slaves. Brought to trial and sentenced to death, John Brown addressed the court.*

JOHN BROWN: I have, may it please the Court, a few words to say.

In the first place, I deny everything but what I have all along admitted—the design on my part to free the slaves. I never did intend murder, or treason. Had I interfered in behalf of the rich, the powerful, the intelligent, the so-called great, it would have been all right; and every man in this court would have deemed it an act worthy of reward rather than punishment.

This court acknowledges, as I suppose, the validity of the law of God. I see a book kissed here which I suppose to be the Bible. That teaches me that all things whatsoever I would that men should do to me, I should do even so to them. It teaches me, further, to "remember them that are in bonds, as bound with them." I endeavored to act up to that instruction. I say, I am yet too young to understand that God is any respecter of persons. I believe that to have interfered as I have done—as I have always freely admitted I have done—in behalf of His despised poor, was not wrong, but right. Now, if it is deemed necessary that I should forfeit my life for the furtherance of the ends of justice, and mingle my blood further with the blood of millions in this slave country—I submit; so let it be done!

NARRATOR: *Just before John Brown was led from his cell to the gallows, he handed a guard this last message.*

JOHN BROWN: "I, John Brown, am now quite *certain* that the crimes of this *guilty land* will never be purged away but with *blood*. I had, as I now think vainly, flattered myself that without very much bloodshed it might be done."
(Guitar chords of "John Brown's Body.")

NARRATOR: *Civil war broke out in April 1861. Mary Boykin Chesnut, wife of the senator from South Carolina, described in her diary the onset of war. April 8, 1861 . . .*

MRS. CHESNUT: Talbot and Chew have come to say that hostilities are to begin. The men went off almost immediately, and I crept silently to my room where I sat down to a good cry. . . . Mrs. Wigfall came

in and we had it out on the subject of civil war. We solaced ourselves with dwelling on all its known horrors, and then we added
some remarks about what we had a right to expect with Yankees in
front and Negroes in the rear. "The slave owners must expect a
servile insurrection, of course," said Mrs. Wigfall.

NARRATOR: *April 13, 1861 . . .*

MRS. CHESNUT: Fort Sumter has been on fire. . . . Not by one word or
look can we detect any change in the demeanor of these Negro servants. Lawrence sits at our door, as sleepy and as respectful and as
profoundly indifferent. So are they all. They carry it too far. You
could not tell they even hear the awful noise that is going on in the
bay, though it is dinning in their ears night and day. And people talk
before them as if they were chairs and tables, and they make no
sign. Are they stolidly stupid, or wiser than we are, silent and
strong, biding their time.

NARRATOR: *August 1863, Portland, Alabama . . .*

MRS. CHESNUT: Dick, the butler here, reminds me that when we were
children, I taught him to read as soon as I could read myself . . . but
he won't look at me now. He looks over my head, he scents freedom in the air. He always was very ambitious.

He is the first Negro that I have felt a change in. They go about in
their black masks, not a ripple or an emotion showing; and yet on
all other subjects except the War they are the most excitable of all
races. Now Dick might make a very respectable Egyptian Sphynx,
so inscrutably silent is he.
(Guitar effect of drum rolls.)

NARRATOR: *The first regiment of ex-slaves was mustered into the service of the
Union Army in 1862. It was under the command of a white officer from
Boston, Colonel Thomas Wentworth Higginson.*

HIGGINSON: November 24, 1862 . . . Reporting to General Saxton, I
had the luck to encounter a company of my destined command,
marched in to be mustered into the United States service. The first

to whom I spoke had been wounded in a small expedition after lumber, in which he had been under fire. *(Black Soldier steps forward and stands at attention. To Black Soldier)* Did you think that more than you bargained for, my man?

BLACK SOLDIER: I been a-tinking. Mas'r, *dat's jess what I went for.*

HIGGINSON *(To audience)*: I thought this did well enough for my very first interchange of dialogue with my recruits. *(Consulting his diary)* December 5, 1862. This evening, after working themselves up to the highest pitch, a party suddenly rushed off, got a barrel, and mounted some man upon it, who brought out one of the few really impressive appeals for the American flag that I have ever heard. . . .

(The lights dim on Higginson and come up on another Black Soldier.)

BLACK SOLDIER: Our mas'rs dey hab lib under de flag, dey got dere wealth under it, and ebryting beautiful for dere chilen. Under it dey hab grind us up, and put us in dere pocket for money. But de fus' minute dey tink dat ole flag mean freedom for we colored people, dey pull it right down, and run up de rag ob dere own. But we'll neber desert de ole flag, boys, neber; we hab lib under it for *eighteen hundred sixty-two years,* and we'll die for it now.

(Lights fade on the Soldier and come up on Higginson.)

HIGGINSON: Their religious spirit grows more beautiful to me in living longer with them. Imbued from childhood with the habit of submission, they can endure everything. Their religion also gives them zeal, energy, daring. They could easily be made fanatics, if I chose; but I do not choose. Their whole mood is essentially Mohammedan, perhaps, in its strength and its weakness. The white camps seem rough and secular, after this; and I hear our men talk about "a religious army," "a Gospel army," in their prayer meetings. They are certainly evangelizing the chaplain, who was rather a heretic at the beginning. . . .

FIRST BLACK SOLDIER *(Praying)*: Let me lib dat when I die I shall *hab manners,* dat I shall know what to say when I see my Heabenly Lord.

SECOND BLACK SOLDIER *(Praying)*: Let me lib wid de musket in one hand an' de Bible in de oder—dat if I die at de muzzle ob de musket, I may know I hab de bressed Jesus in my hand, an' hab no fear.

THIRD BLACK SOLDIER *(Praying)*: I hab lef' my wife in de land o' bondage; my little ones day say eb'ry night, Whar is my fader? But when I die, when I shall stan' in de glory, den, O Lord, I shall see my wife an' my little chil'en once more.

HIGGINSON: Expedition up the St. Mary's River: This morning, my surgeon sent me his report of killed and wounded: "One man killed instantly by a ball through the heart, and seven wounded, one of whom will die. Robert Sutton, with three wounds—one of which, being on the skull, may cost him his life—would not report himself till compelled to do so by his officers."

(He puts away the surgeon's report.)

And one of those who were carried to the vessel—a man wounded through the lungs—asked only if I were safe, the contrary having been reported. An officer may be pardoned some enthusiasm for such men as these. . . .

(He turns to another page in the diary.)

January 1, 1863. Today we celebrated the issuance of President Lincoln's Proclamation of Emancipation. It was read by Dr. W.H. Brisbane. Then the colors were presented to us by the Rev. Mr. French. All this was according to the program. Then, the very moment the speaker had ceased, and just as I took and waved the flag . . .

BLACK SINGERS *(Breaking in)*:

My country, 'tis of thee,
Sweet land of liberty,
Of thee I sing!

(The singing continues quietly under the rest of the speech.)

HIGGINSON: Firmly the quavering voices sang on, verse after verse; others of the colored people joined in; some whites on the platform began, but I motioned them to silence. I never saw anything so electric; it made all other words cheap; it seemed the choked voice of a race at last unloosed. Just think of it!—the first day they had ever had a country, the first flag they had ever seen which promised anything to their people! When they stopped, there was nothing to do for it but to speak, and I went on; but the life of the whole day was in those unknown people's song.

(The singing swells.)

SINGERS:

    . . . From every mountainside
    Let freedom ring!

ACT TWO

BLACK ACTOR *(Sings)*:
  No more auction block for me,
  No more, no more,
  No more auction block for me,
  Many thousand gone.

  No more pint of salt for me,
  No more, no more,
  No more pint of salt for me,
  Many thousand gone.

BLACK MAN: We was free. Just like that, we was free. Right off colored folks started on the move. They seemed to want to get closer to freedom, so they'd know what it was—like it was a place or a city. . . .

BLACK WOMAN: A heap of people say they going to name theirselves over. They name theirselves big names. Some of the names was Abraham, and some called theirselves Lincum. Any big name 'cepting their master's name.

BLACK MAN: The slaves don't know where to go. They's always 'pend on Old Marse to look after them. Three families went to get farms for theyselves, but the rest stay on for hands on the old place.

BLACK WOMAN: I remember someone asking—"You got to say 'Master'?" And somebody answered and said, "Naw." But they said it all the same. They said it for a long time.

BLACK MAN: They makes us git right off the place, just like you take a old hoss and turn it loose. That how us was. No money, no nothing.

BLACK MAN: What I likes best, to be slave or free? Well, it's this way. In slavery I owns nothing and never owns nothing. In freedom I's own the home and raise the family. All that cause me worriment, and in slavery I has no worriment, but I takes the freedom.

NARRATOR: *The whites reacted to the blacks' freedom in a variety of ways. A Northern woman, Elizabeth Bothume, went south to teach the ex-slaves.*

ELIZABETH BOTHUME: On October 25, 1864, I received the following communication: "You are hereby appointed by the New England Freedman's Aid Society a teacher of freed people at Beaufort, South Carolina." I found my location was to be at Old Fort Plantation. A large number of colored refugees had been brought here and I was impatient to begin. Each hour showed me that at the North we had but a faint conception of the work to be done.

While the zeal of these people for learning never flags, they have no possible conception of time. Men, women, and children hurry to the schoolhouse at all hours and at most unseasonable times, expecting "to catch a lesson." Reproof is unheeded, or not understood. "Us had something *particular* to do" is the invariable excuse.

I must confess, the ignorance of some of the visitors in regard to the condition of the freedman is positively astounding. Some officers belonging to the Tenth Army Corps of Sherman's army visited the school. I was expecting them, and had examined the children a little upon general subjects. Imagine my surprise, when they had sung and answered a few questions, to have one of the visitors get up and ask, "Children, who is Jesus Christ?" For a moment the whole school seemed paralyzed. Then an older boy sprang up, and exclaimed, "Him's Massa Linkum." . . .

Then General Howard made a short address, in which he gave them a motto, "To try hard." This all could understand. So when he asked what he should tell their friends at the North about them, they all answered, "Tell 'em we'se goin' to try hard."

At another school General Howard asked this question, and a little boy answered, "Massa, tell 'em we is rising."

NARRATOR: *The blacks' freedom disrupted the pattern of Southern life, as a Georgia woman, Eliza Andrews, noted in her diary.*

ELIZA ANDREWS: Washington, Georgia. No power on earth can raise an inferior, savage race above their civilized masters and keep them there. No matter how high a prop they build under him, the Negro is obliged, sooner or later, to find his level. The higher above his natural capacity they force the Negro in their rash experiments, the greater must be his fall in the end, and the more bitter our sufferings in the meantime.

The town is becoming more crowded with "freedmen" every day, and their insolence increases with their numbers. We have not even an errand boy now, for George, the only child left on the place, is going to school! . . . Everybody is doing housework. Father says this is what has made the Anglo-Saxon race great; they are not afraid of work. But it does seem to me a waste of time for people who are capable of doing something better to spend their time sweeping and dusting while scores of lazy Negroes that are fit for nothing else are lying around idle. Dr. Calhoun suggested that it would be a good idea to import some of those apes from Africa and teach them to take the place of the Negroes, but Henry said that just as soon as we had got them tamed, and taught them to be of some use, those crazy fanatics at the North would insist on coming down here to emancipate them and give them universal suffrage. A good many people seem to think that the Yankees are never going to be satisfied till they get the negroes to voting. Father says it is the worst thing we have to fear now.

(Guitar chords of "Dixie.")

NARRATOR: *By 1866, the voting question was paramount. On February 7, Frederick Douglass, the chief spokesman for his race, and George T. Downing, another prominent black leader, brought the issue to Andrew Johnson, President of the United States.*

GEORGE T. DOWNING: We present ourselves to Your Excellency in the name of the colored people of the United States. We are Americans, native born Americans. We are citizens. On this fact, and with confidence in the triumph of justice, we cherish the hope that we may be fully enfranchised.

PRESIDENT JOHNSON: I do not like to be arraigned by some who can get up handsomely founded periods and deal in rhetoric. While I say I am a friend of the colored man, I do not want to adopt a policy that I believe will end in a contest between the races, in the extermination of one or the other. God forbid that I should be engaged in such a work!

FREDERICK DOUGLASS: Mr. President, do you wish—

PRESIDENT JOHNSON: —I am not quite through yet. . . . The query comes up, whether these two races without time for passion and excitement to be appeased, and without time for the slightest improvement, are to be thrown together at the ballot box.

Will you say a majority of the people shall receive a state of things they are opposed to?

DOUGLASS: That was said before the war.

JOHNSON: I am now talking about a principle; not what somebody else said.

DOWNING: Apply what you have said, Mr. President, to South Carolina, where a majority of the inhabitants are colored.

JOHNSON: That doesn't change the principle at all. It is for the people to say who shall vote, and not for the Congress of the United States. It is a fundamental tenet in my creed that the will of the people must be obeyed. Is there anything wrong or unfair in that?

DOUGLASS (smiling): A great deal that is wrong, Mr. President, with all respect.

JOHNSON: It is the people of the States that must for themselves determine this thing.

God knows that anything I can do to elevate the races I will do, and to be able to do so is the sincere desire of my heart. (Abruptly) I am glad to have met you, and thank you for the compliments you have paid me.

DOUGLASS: I have to return to you our thanks, Mr. President, for so kindly granting us this interview. We did not come here expecting to argue this question with Your Excellency. . . . If you would grant us permission, of course we would endeavor to controvert some of the positions you have assumed.

JOHNSON: I thought you expected me to indicate what my views were on the subjects touched upon by your statement.

DOWNING: We are very happy, indeed, to have heard them.

DOUGLASS: If the President will allow me, I would like to say one or two words in reply. You enfranchise your enemies and disfranchise your friends.

JOHNSON: All I have done is to indicate what my views are, as I supposed you expected me to, from your address.

DOUGLASS: But if Your Excellency will be pleased to hear, I would like to say a word or two in regard to enfranchisement of the blacks as a means of *preventing* a conflict of races.

JOHNSON: I repeat, I merely wanted to indicate my views, and not to enter into any general controversy.

Your statement was a very frank one, and I thought it was due to you to meet it in the same spirit.

DOUGLASS: Thank you, sir.

JOHNSON: If you will all inculcate the idea that the colored people can live and advance to better advantage elsewhere than in the South, it would be better for them.

DOUGLASS: But we cannot get away from the plantation.

JOHNSON: What prevents you?

DOUGLASS: The Negro is divested of all power. He is absolutely in the hands of those men.

JOHNSON: If the master now controls him or his action, would he not control him in his vote?

DOUGLASS: Let the Negro once understand that he has an organic right to vote, and he will raise up a party in the Southern states among the poor, who will rally with him.

JOHNSON: I suggest emigration. If he cannot get employment in the South, he has it in his power to go where he can get it.

DOUGLASS (*To his fellow delegates*): The President sends us to the people. And we go to the people.

JOHNSON: Yes, sir; I have great faith in the people. I believe they will do what is right.

GUITARIST:

I am a good old Rebel,
And that's just what I am.
And for this land of liberty,
I do not give a damn.
I'm glad I fought against it—
I only wish we'd won,
And I ain't askin pardon,
For what I been or done.

(As the lights fade on the scene, they come up on the figure of a man wearing the hood of the Ku Klux Klan.)

NARRATOR: *In 1866, the Radical wing of the Republican party gained control of Congress and gave blacks the right to vote. At once, the Ku Klux Klan rose to power in the South. . . .*

THE HOODED FIGURE: Before the immaculate Judge of Heaven and Earth, and upon the Holy Evangelists of Almighty God, I do, of my own free will and accord, subscribe to the sacredly binding obligation: We are on the side of justice, humanity, and constitutional liberty, as bequeathed to us in its purity by our forefathers. We oppose and reject the principles of the Radical party.

GUITARIST:

I hate the Freedmen's Bureau
And the uniform of blue,
I hate the Declaration of Independence, too.
I hate the Constitution
With all its fume and fuss,
And them thievin', lyin' Yankees,
Well, I hate 'em wuss and wuss.

NARRATOR: *Acts of violence by the Klan were investigated by the federal government in a series of hearings and trials.*

PROSECUTOR: What was the purpose of the Ku Klux Klan? What were the raids for?

KLANSMAN: To put down Radicalism, the raids were for.

PROSECUTOR: In what way were they to put down Radicalism?

KLANSMAN: It was to whip them and make them change their politics.

PROSECUTOR: How many raids have you been on by order of the Chief?

KLANSMAN: Two, sir.

PROSECUTOR: Now, will you state to the jury what was done on those raids?

KLANSMAN: Yes, sir. We were ordered to meet at Howl's Ferry, and went and whipped five colored men. Presley Holmes was the first they whipped, and then went on and whipped Jerry Thompson; went then and whipped Charley Good, James Leach, and Amos Lowell.

PROSECUTOR: How many men were on these raids?

KLANSMAN: I think there was twenty in number.

PROSECUTOR: How were they armed and uniformed?

KLANSMAN: They had red gowns, and had white covers over their horses. Some had pistols and some had guns.

PROSECUTOR: What did they wear on their heads?

KLANSMAN: Something over their heads came down. Some of them had horns on.

PROSECUTOR: Disguises dropped down over their faces?

KLANSMAN: Yes, sir.

PROSECUTOR: What was the object in whipping those five men you have named?

KLANSMAN: The object, in whipping Presley Holmes, was about some threats he had made about him going to be buried in Salem grave-yard.

PROSECUTOR: What was the first to occur?

KLANSMAN: Well, sir, Webber—he was leading the Klan—ran into the yard and kicked down the door, and dragged him out, and led him off about two hundred yards, and whipped him.

PROSECUTOR: How many lashes did they give him?

KLANSMAN: I cannot tell you how many.

PROSECUTOR: Did they whip him severely or not?

KLANSMAN: His shirt was stuck to his back.

PROSECUTOR: What occurred at the next place?

KLANSMAN: They whipped Jerry Thompson at the next place; told him never to go to any more meetings; to stay at home and attend to his own business.

PROSECUTOR: What was done at the next place?

KLANSMAN: They went there and whipped Charley Good. They whipped him very severe; they beat him with a pole and kicked him down on the ground.

PROSECUTOR: What did they tell him?

KLANSMAN: To let Radicalism alone; if he didn't his doom would be fatal.

(The lights fade. They come up immediately on another examination. A black woman, Hannah Tutson, is being questioned.)

LAWYER: Are you the wife of Samuel Tutson?

MRS. TUTSON: Yes, sir.

LAWYER: Were you at home when he was whipped last spring?

MRS. TUTSON: Yes, sir; I was at home.

LAWYER: Tell us what took place then, what was done, and how it was done.

MRS. TUTSON: That night, just as I got into bed, five men bulged right against the door, and it fell in the middle of the floor. George McRae ran right to me. As I saw him coming I took up the child—the baby—and held to him. I started to scream, and George McRae catched me by the throat and choked me. And he catched the little child by the foot and slinged it out of my arms. They got me out of doors. The old man was ahead of me, and I saw Dave Donley stomp on him. They carried me to a pine, and then they tied my hands there. They pulled off all my linen, tore it up so that I did not have a piece of rag on me as big as my hand. I said, "Men, what are you going to do with me?" They said, "Goddamn you, we will show you; you are living on another man's premises." I said, "No; I am living on my own premises; I gave $150 for it and Captain Buddington and Mr. Mundy told me to stay here." They whipped me for a while. Then George McRae would say, "Come here, True-Klux." Then the True-Klux would step off about as far as *(Pointing to a member of the committee)* that gentleman and whisper; when they came back they would whip me again. Every time they would go off, George McRae would make me squat down by the pine, and he would get his knees between my legs and say, "Old lady, if you don't let me have to do with you, I will kill you." I said, "No"; they whipped me. There were four men whipping me at once.

LAWYER: How many lashes did they give you in all?

MRS. TUTSON: I cannot tell you, for they whipped me from the crown of my head to the soles of my feet. I was just raw. After I got away from them that night I ran to my house. My house was torn down. I went in and felt where my bed was. I could not feel my little children and I could not see them.

LAWYER: Did you find your children?

MRS. TUTSON: I did next day at 12 o'clock.

LAWYER: Where were they?

MRS. TUTSON: They went out into the field.

LAWYER: Did the baby get hurt—the one you had in your arms when they jerked it away?

MRS. TUTSON: Yes, sir; in one of its hips. When it began to walk one of its hips was very bad, and every time you would stand it up it would scream. But I rubbed it and rubbed it, and it looks like he is outgrowing it now.

GUITARIST:
You've got to cross that lonesome valley,
You've got to cross it by yourself.
There ain't nobody can do it for you,
You've got to cross it all alone.

NARRATOR: *The federal investigations were not followed by effective federal action. From 1878 to 1915 over 3,000 blacks were lynched in the South—a necessary protection, it was said, against rapists. Yet most lynch-*

ings were either for no offense or for such causes as "Insult,""Bad Reputa-
tion,""Running Quarantine,""Frightening Children by Shooting at Rab-
bits,"or "Mistaken Identity."

On January 21, 1907, United States Senator Ben Tillman, of South
Carolina, gave his views on the subject from the Senate floor.

SENATOR TILLMAN: Mr. President, a word about lynching and my attitude toward it. A great deal has been said in the newspapers, North
and South, about my responsibility in connection with this matter.

I have justified it for one crime, and one only. As governor of
South Carolina I proclaimed that, although I had taken the oath of
office to support law and enforce it, I would lead a mob to lynch
any man who had ravished a woman.

Mr. President . . . When stern and sad-faced white men put to
death a creature in human form who has deflowered a white
woman, they have avenged the greatest wrong, the blackest crime
in all the category of crimes.

The Senator from Wisconsin prates about the law. Look at our
environment in the South, surrounded and in a very large number
of counties outnumbered, by the Negroes—engulfed, as it were,
in a black flood of semi-barbarians. For forty years these Negroes
have been taught the damnable heresy of equality with the white
man. Their minds are those of children, while they have the passions and strength of men.

Let us carry the Senator from Wisconsin to the backwoods in
South Carolina, put him on a farm miles from a town or railroad,
and environed with Negroes. We will suppose he has a fair young
daughter just budding into womanhood; and recollect this, the
white women of the South are in a state of siege. . . .

That Senator's daughter undertakes to visit a neighbor or is left
home alone for a brief while. Some lurking demon who has
watched for the opportunity seizes her; she is choked or beaten
into insensibility and ravished, her body prostituted, her purity destroyed, her chastity taken from her, and a memory branded on her

brain as with a red-hot iron to haunt her night and day as long as she lives.

In other words, a death in life. This young girl thus blighted and brutalized drags herself to her father and tells him what has happened. Is there a man here with red blood in his veins who doubts what impulses the father would feel? Is it any wonder that the whole countryside rises as one man and with set, stern faces, seek the brute who has wrought this infamy? And shall such a creature, because he has the semblance of a man, appeal to the law? Shall men cold-bloodedly stand up and demand for him the right to have a fair trial and be punished in the regular course of justice? So far as I am concerned he has put himself outside the pale of the law, human and divine. He has sinned against the Holy Ghost. He has invaded the holy of holies. He has struck civilization a blow, the most deadly and cruel that the imagination can conceive. It is idle to reason about it; it is idle to preach about it. Our brains reel under the staggering blow and hot blood surges to the heart. Civilization peels off us, any and all of us who are men, and we revert to the original savage type whose impulses under such circumstances has always been to "Kill! Kill! Kill!"

NARRATOR: *The effect of white intimidation could be seen in the views of Mr. Booker T. Washington, the most prominent black leader at the turn of the century, when he addressed a predominantly white audience in Atlanta.*

WASHINGTON: The Negroes' greatest danger is that in the great leap from slavery to freedom we may overlook the fact that the masses of us are to live by the production of our hands. It is at the bottom of life we must begin, and not the top. You can be sure in the future, as you have been in the past, that you and your families will be surrounded by the most patient, faithful, law-abiding, and unresentful people that the world has seen.

In all things that are purely social we can be as separate as the fingers, yet one as the hand in all things essential to mutual progress.

The wisest among my race understand that the agitation of questions of social equality is the extremist folly. It is important and right that all privileges of the law be ours, but it is vastly more important that we be prepared for the exercise of those privileges. The opportunity to earn a dollar in a factory just now is worth infinitely more than the opportunity to spend a dollar in an opera house.

NARRATOR: *W.E.B. DuBois, later one of the founders of the NAACP, was not satisfied with Mr. Washington's leadership.*

DUBOIS: One hesitates to criticize a life which, beginning with so little, has done so much. And yet the time is come when one may speak in all sincerity and utter courtesy of the mistakes and shortcomings of Mr. Booker T. Washington. Mr. Washington represents in Negro thought the old attitude of adjustment and submission. He practically accepts the alleged inferiority of the Negro race and withdraws many of the high demands of Negroes as men and American citizens. Mr. Washington asks that black people concentrate all their energies on industrial education, the accumulation of wealth and the conciliation of the South.

We do not expect that the free right to vote, to enjoy civic rights, and to be educated, will come in a moment; we do not expect to see the bias and prejudices of years disappear at the blast of a trumpet. But we are absolutely certain that the way for a people to gain their reasonable rights is not by voluntarily throwing them away and insisting that they do not want them; that the way for a people to gain respect is not by continually belittling and ridiculing themselves; that, on the contrary, Negroes must insist, in season and out of season, that voting is necessary to modern manhood, that color discrimination is barbarism, and that black boys need education as well as white boys.

NARRATOR: *The segregation of federal employees became widespread for the first time during Woodrow Wilson's administration. To protest this policy, a delegation of black leaders, led by Monroe Trotter, called upon President Wilson in November 1914.*

MONROE TROTTER: Mr. President, one year ago we came before you and presented a national petition, signed by colored Americans in thirty-eight states, protesting against the segregation of employees of the National Government as instituted under your administration. We come to you, Mr. President, a year after to renew the protest and appeal.

PRESIDENT WILSON: After our last visit, I and my cabinet officers investigated as promised, and my cabinet officers told me the segregation was caused by friction between colored and white clerks, and not done to injure or humiliate the colored clerks, but to avoid friction. Members of the cabinet have assured me that the colored clerks would have comfortable conditions, though separated. The white people of the country, as well as I, wish to see the colored people progress, admire the progress they have already made, and want to see them continue along independent lines. There is, however, a great prejudice against colored people, and we must deal with it as practical men. Segregation is not humiliating but a benefit, and ought to be so regarded by you gentlemen. If your organization goes out and tells the colored people of the country that it is a humiliation, they will so regard it.

TROTTER (Angrily): Mr. President, it is not in accord with known facts to claim that segregation was started because of race friction of the white and colored clerks, for the simple reason that for fifty years white and colored clerks have been working together in peace and harmony and friendliness, doing so even through two Democratic administrations. Soon after your inauguration began, segregation was drastically introduced.

WILSON: If this organization is ever to have another hearing before me it must have another spokesman. Your manner offends me.

TROTTER: In what way?

WILSON: Your tone, with its background of passion.

TROTTER: But I have no passion in me, Mr. President, you are entirely mistaken; you misinterpret my earnestness for passion. We cannot control the minds of the colored people and would not if we could on the segregation question. Two years ago you were regarded as a second Abraham Lincoln—

WILSON: —I want no personal reference.

TROTTER: Sir, if you will allow me to continue you will see my intent.

WILSON: I am the one to do the interrupting, Mr. Trotter.

TROTTER: We colored leaders are denounced in the colored churches as traitors to our race.

WILSON: What do you mean by traitors?

TROTTER: Because we supported the Democratic ticket in 1912.

WILSON: Gentlemen, the interview is at an end.

NARRATOR: *During World War I the French, at the request of the American authorities, issued a directive concerning black American troops.*

FRENCH OFFICER: To the French Military Mission stationed with the American Army. August 7, 1918. Secret information concerning the black American troops.

It is important for French officers who have been called upon to exercise command over black American troops, or to live in close contact with them, to recognize that American opinion is unanimous on the "color question," and does not admit of any discussion.

The French public has become accustomed to treating the Negro with familiarity and indulgence.

These are matters of grievous concern to the Americans. They consider them an affront to their national policy. It is of the utmost importance that every effort be made to avoid profoundly estranging American opinion.

We must not eat with the blacks, must not shake hands or seek to talk or meet with them outside of the requirements of military service. Americans become greatly incensed at any public expression of intimacy between white women with black men.

Military authority cannot intervene directly in this question, but it can through the civil authorities exercise some influence on the population.

[Signed] Linard

(Guitar—"Mademoiselle from Armentières")

NARRATOR: *After World War I, black resentment became more vocal. Marcus Garvey's movement of Black Nationalism attracted hundreds of thousands of followers.*

MARCUS GARVEY: We are too large and great in numbers not to be a great people, a great race, and a great nation. We are the descendants of a suffering people. We are the descendants of a people determined to suffer no longer. The time has now come when we must seek our place in the sun. If Europe is for the Europeans, then Africa shall be for the black peoples of the world. We are not asking all the Negroes of the United States to leave for Africa. The majority of us may remain here, but we must send our scientists, our mechanics, and our artisans, and let them build railroads, let them build the great educational and other institutions necessary, and when they are constructed, the time will come for the command to be given, "Come home!"

The hour has come for the Negro to take his own initiative. No more fear, no more cringing, no more sycophantic begging and pleading. Destiny leads us to liberty, to freedom; that freedom that Victoria of England never gave; that liberty that Lincoln never meant; that freedom, that liberty, that will see us men among men, that will make us a great and powerful people.

BLACK ACTRESS *(Sings)*:
I'm on my way
To Canaan's land,
I'm on my way
To Canaan's land.

I'm on my way
To Canaan's land,
I'm on my way,
Good Lord, I'm on my way.

NARRATOR: *Out of the difficult years of the Depression emerged the colorful personality of Father Divine. His blend of religion, charity, and personal drama brought him thousands of both black and white followers.*

MISS BEAUTIFUL LOVE:

Peace, my dearest Father:

I thank You for allowing me to write as it is my deepest desire to try to please You more each minute. I thank You for Your world at large and Your beautiful, sweet Peace that You have given to all of the children.

I thank you to report some cases of retribution, Father.

There is one whose name is Yaddy, who used dirty words. He stated You were a little bigger sport than he was. His wife has given birth to a baby who has never closed its mouth. I saw the baby when it was about nine months old and its mouth hung open very wide.

There is one whose name is Mr. James Barr, who also thinks he is cursing You. He and his truck fell twenty feet below the level. . . . He was sent to the hospital . . . now he is going blind.

Father, I will try to please you each day. I will try to make You as happy as the rambling piano keys on Easter Sunday morning, or a happy angel when she does a holy dance.

Very truly yours,
Miss Beautiful Love

FATHER DIVINE:

My dear Miss Love:

You can see in every instance that those who tried to measure ME with the measure of a man received the reward meted out to finite man.

In the case of the man, who you say, classed ME with himself, retribution came to him. For it was retribution when his child was born its mouth wide open and cannot close it.

The man, who you say thought he could curse ME suffered retribution and is going blind. Things don't just happen, but they happen Just! What he intended for me came to him, heaped up, pressed down, and running over.

Thus, retribution rolls on, striking here and there at those who think they can criticize and slander ME, but none can reach ME. Hence, it does not pay to defy MY Name, for this leaves ME, as I AM, ever Well, Healthy, Joyful, Peaceful, Lively, Loving, Successful, Prosperous, and Happy in Spirit, Body, and Mind and in every organ, muscle, sinew, joint, limb, vein, and bone and even in every ATOM, fibre, and cell of MY BODILY FORM.

> Respectfully and Sincere, I AM
> REV. M.J. DIVINE, MsD., D.D.
> (Better known as FATHER DIVINE)

(Guitar—reprise of "I'm on My Way")

NARRATOR: *As the rest of the nation began to recover from the Depression, blacks continued to be economically exploited.*

LABORER: I was born in Elbert County, Georgia. I never went to school a day in my life. When I reached twenty-one I signed a contract—that is, I made my mark—to work on a farm for one year. My white employer was to give me $3.50 a week, and furnish me a little house on the plantation. All the people called him Senator. At the end of the first year, the Senator suggested that I sign up a contract for ten years; then, he said, we wouldn't have to fix up papers every year. I asked my wife about it; she consented; and so I made a ten-year contract.

It was then made plain to us that in the contracts, we had agreed to be locked up in a stockade at any time the Senator saw fit. And if we got mad and ran away, we could be run down by bloodhounds, and the Senator might administer any punishment he thought proper. What could we do about it? We shut our mouths, and went to work.

But at the close of the ten-year period, to a man, we all wanted to quit. We refused to sign new contracts—even for one year. But two or three years before, the Senator had started a large store, which was called the commissary. All of us laborers were forced to buy our supplies—food, clothing, and so on—from that store. We were charged all sorts of high prices.

Well, at the close of the tenth year, when we meant to leave, the Senator said to some of us with a smile—and I never will forget that smile—I can see it now. . . .

(Lights up on two white men, the Senator and his storekeeper. The store-keeper is holding an account book.)

SENATOR: Boys, I'm sorry you're going to leave me. I hope you will do well in your new places—so well that you will be able to pay the little balances which most of you owe me.

(He turns to the storekeeper, who steps forward and reads from the account book.)

STOREKEEPER: Frank Raines: One hundred and seventy-three dollars. Joe Simpson: One hundred and forty-six dollars. Cato Brown: One hundred and ninety-eight dollars . . .

(The lights fade on the two white men.)

LABORER: According to the books there was no man who owed less than $100. I owed $165, according to the bookkeeper. No one of us would have dared to dispute a white man's word. We were told we might go, if we signed acknowledgments. We would have signed anything, just to get away. So we stepped up and made our marks. The next morning it was explained to us that in the papers we had signed we had not only made acknowledgments of our debt, but had also agreed to work for our employer until the debts were paid by hard labor. And from that day forward we were treated just like convicts. Really we had made ourselves slaves, or peons, as the laws called us.

The working day on a peon farm begins with sunrise and ends when the sun goes down. Hot or cold, sun or rain, this is the rule. It was a hard school that peon camp was. A favorite way of whipping a man was to strap him down to a log and spank him fifty or sixty times on his bare feet with a piece of plank. I could tell more, but I've said enough. . . .

But I didn't tell you how I got out. When I had served for nearly three years—and you remember I owed them only $165—one of the bosses came up to me and said that my time was up. He was the one who was said to be living with my wife. He took me in a buggy into South Carolina, set me down and told me to "git." I been here in the Birmingham district since and I reckon I'll die either in a coal mine or an iron furnace. It don't make much difference which. Either is better than a Georgia peon camp.

(Guitar—a few bars of "Sometimes I Feel Like a Motherless Child")

NARRATOR: *When the Second World War began, segregation was still the official policy of the United States armed forces. It remained so throughout the war. Persistent rumors of conflict between black and white troops reached Walter White, Secretary of the NAACP, who went overseas to investigate. Among the places he visited was Guam.*

WALTER WHITE: There were no Negro combat troops in Guam, only service units. Negro resentment at this would probably never have been translated into action had not a long series of unchecked and unpunished insults and attacks been made upon these Negroes. Stones, empty beer bottles, and other missiles were thrown from trucks into the Negro camp accompanied by such epithets as "niggers," "night-fighters," and "black sons-of-bitches." Twice hand grenades were hurled into the Negro camp. Small gangs of Marines began to run Negroes out of Agana, the largest town on Guam.

On the afternoon of Christmas Day, 1944, two intoxicated Marines shot and killed a Negro sailor. Neither of them was even arrested. . . .

Around nightfall, a jeep with a machine gun mounted on it drove past firing into the Negro camp. By this time the camp was in a state of almost hysterical apprehension. Negroes climbed aboard two trucks and set out for Agana. A road block was thrown up and all of the Negro men—forty-four in number—were arrested. . . .

Among the crimes charged against them were unlawful assemblage, rioting, theft of government property, and attempted murder. The recommendations of the Board of Inquiry, despite the evidence, resulted in courts-martial and the sentencing of all forty-four men to prison terms. Happily these were later reversed when we appealed the convictions. But we had to take the cases all the way to the Secretary of the Navy and the White House to achieve this.

It was this pattern which was responsible for the cynical remark I heard so often from Negro troops—"We know that our battle for democracy will begin when we reach San Francisco on our way home!"

NARRATOR: *There was no major breakthrough until 1954, when the Supreme Court declared segregation in public schools unconstitutional. Southern resistance to the court's decision came to a head three years later at Little Rock, Arkansas, when a fifteen-year-old girl tried to go to school at Central High.*

GIRL: The night before I was so excited I couldn't sleep. The next morning I was about the first one up. While I was pressing my black and white dress—I had made it to wear on the first day of school—my little brother turned on the TV set. They started telling about a large crowd gathered at the school. The man on TV said he wondered if we were going to show up that morning. Mother called from the kitchen, where she was fixing breakfast, "Turn that TV off!" She was so upset and worried. I wanted to comfort her, so I said, "Mother, don't worry!"

Dad was walking back and forth, from room to room, with a sad expression. He was chewing on his pipe and he had a cigar in his hand, but he didn't light either one. It would have been funny, only he was so nervous.

Before I left home Mother called us into the living room. She said we should have a word of prayer. Then I caught the bus and got off a block from the school. I saw a large crowd of people standing across the street from the soldiers guarding Central. As I walked on, the crowd suddenly got very quiet. For a moment all I could hear was the shuffling of their feet. Then someone shouted, "Here she comes, get ready!" The crowd moved in closer and then began to follow me, calling me names. I still wasn't afraid. Just a little bit nervous. Then my knees started to shake all of a sudden and I wondered whether I could make it to the center entrance a block away. It was the longest block I ever walked in my whole life.

Even so, I still wasn't too scared because all the time I kept thinking that the guards would protect me.

When I got right in front of the school, I went up to a guard. He just looked straight ahead and didn't move to let me pass him. I stood looking at the school—it looked so big! Just then the guards let some white students go through.

The crowd was quiet. I guess they were waiting to see what was going to happen. When I was able to steady my knees, I walked up to the guard who had let the white students in. He, too, didn't move. When I tried to squeeze past him, he raised his bayonet and then the other guards closed in and they raised their bayonets.

They glared at me with a mean look and I was very frightened and didn't know what to do. I turned around and the crowd came toward me.

They moved closer and closer. Somebody started yelling, "Lynch her!" "Lynch her!"

I tried to see a friendly face somewhere in the mob—someone who maybe would help. I looked into the face of an old woman and it seemed a kind face, but when I looked at her again, she spat on me.

They came closer, shouting, "No nigger bitch is going to get in our school. Get out of here!" Then I looked down the block and saw a bench at the bus stop. I thought, "If I can only get there I will be safe." I don't know why the bench seemed a safe place to me, but I started walking toward it. I tried to close my mind to what they were shouting, and kept saying to myself, "If I can only make it to the bench I will be safe."

When I finally got there, I don't think I could have gone another step. I sat down and the mob crowded up and began shouting all over again. Someone hollered, "Drag her over to this tree! Let's take care of the nigger." Just then a white man sat down beside me, put his arm around me and patted my shoulder.

(During the last part of speech, a white actor sits beside her on bench.)

WHITE MAN: She just sat there, her head down. Tears were streaming down her cheeks. I don't know what made me put my arm around

her, saying, "Don't let them see you cry." Maybe she reminded me
of my fifteen-year-old daughter.

Just then the city bus came and she got on. She must have been
in a state of shock. She never uttered a word.

GIRL: I can't remember much about the bus ride, but the next thing I
remember I was standing in front of the School for the Blind,
where Mother works. I ran upstairs and I kept running until I
reached Mother's classroom.

Mother was standing at the window with her head bowed, but
she must have sensed I was there because she turned around. She
looked as if she had been crying, and I wanted to tell her I was all
right. But I couldn't speak. She put her arms around me and I
cried.

WHITE ACTOR *(Sings)*:
They say down in Hines County
No neutrals can be met,
You'll be a Freedom Rider,
Or a thug for Ross Barnett.
(Whole cast, looking at each other, not the audience, quietly sings four lines
of "Which Side Are You On.")

NARRATOR: *After 1957, the black protest exploded—bus boycotts, sit-ins,*
Freedom Rides, drives for voter registration, job protests.

BLACK MAN: After four hundred years of barbaric treatment, the
American Negro is fed up with the unmitigated hypocrisy of the
white man.

WHITE MAN: The Negroes are demanding something that isn't so unreasonable.

BLACK MAN: To have a cup of coffee at a lunch counter.

WHITE MAN: To get a decent job.

BLACK WOMAN: Negro Americans has been waiting upon voluntary
action since 1876.

WHITE MAN: If the thirteen colonies had waited for voluntary action
this land today would be part of the British Commonwealth.

WHITE WOMAN: The demonstrations will go on for the same reason the thirteen colonies took up arms against George III.

BLACK MAN: For like the colonies we have beseeched.

BLACK WOMAN: We have implored.

BLACK MAN: We have supplicated.

BLACK MAN: We have entreated.

BLACK WOMAN: We are writing our declaration of independence in shoe leather instead of ink.

WHITE MAN: We're through with tokenism and gradualism and see-how-far-you've-comeism.

WHITE MAN: We're through with we've-done-more-for-your-people-than-anyone-elseism.

BLACK WOMAN: We can't wait any longer.

BLACK MAN: *Now* is the time.

WHITE ACTOR *(Stepping forward, reads from document)*: We the people of the United States, in Order to form a more perfect Union . . .

WHITE ACTOR *(Cont'd)*: . . . establish Justice, insure domestic Tranquility, provide for the common defense, promote the general Welfare, and secure the Blessings of Liberty to ourselves and our Posterity, do ordain and establish this Constitution for the United States of America . . .

BLACK ACTRESS *(Sings under "We the people . . . ," slowly building in volume)*:
Oh freedom—
Oh, freedom—
Oh, freedom over me!
And before I'll be a slave,
I'll be buried in my grave,

WHOLE CAST:
. . . And go home to my Lord
And be free!

END OF PLAY

ALTERNATE ENDING

The decision to make "Little Rock" the last major scene came about only after considerable experimentation. At various times later selections from Martin Luther King, James Baldwin, Malcolm X, and President Kennedy were added on, but I finally decided not to develop the post-1957 story; it was difficult to "top" the Little Rock scene dramatically, and, at any rate, I felt [in 1964] events since then were sufficiently familiar.

For the actual close of the play, I originally used a speech of Lincoln's instead of the Preamble to the Constitution. But this did not "play" as well as it read, and so the Preamble was substituted. As this is a reading version of the script, however, I thought it would be well to include the "Lincoln ending." Perhaps some future production might again wish to experiment with it as an alternate.

This speech would follow "*Now* is the time," and would be read instead of "We the people . . ." and without the singing of "Oh freedom. . . ."

BLACK ACTOR: Fellow-citizens, *we* cannot escape history. We will be remembered in spite of ourselves. No personal significance, or insignificance, can spare one or another of us. The fiery trial through which we pass will light us down, in honor or dishonor, to the latest generation. We shall nobly save, or meanly lose, the last best hope of earth. The way is plain, peaceful, generous, just—a way which, if followed, the world will forever applaud, and God must forever bless. *(He closes book)*

Abraham Lincoln's second annual message to Congress. December 1, 1862.

Good night.

Mother Earth

ACT ONE

(Gangplank of the Buford tied up in port awaiting debarkation, 1919. Men and women, a forlorn lot, are making their way up the gangplank. A commotion at the foot of the gangplank as Emma Goldman and Alexander Berkman arrive and are immediately surrounded by a group of reporters.)

FIRST REPORTER: Is there any last statement you'd like to make, Miss Goldman? Or you, Mr. Berkman?

BERKMAN: We made our statements at the trial.

EMMA *(Glancing up the gangplank)*: You wouldn't want them to leave without us, would you?

FIRST REPORTER: You haven't lost your sense of humor.

EMMA: It comes and goes.

SECOND REPORTER: Are you bitter about President Wilson's deporting order?

BERKMAN: We're only two of some three hundred.

(Man on a stretcher is carried past them up the gangplank. Emma bends down to hug him and whisper a few words.)

EMMA *(To reporters)*: The doctor says that if the journey is not longer than a month, he has a good chance of surviving. Though as you may have heard *(Gesturing toward the ship)*, the "good ship *Buford*" was condemned by the United States government as unseaworthy.

THIRD REPORTER: Do you know your destination?

EMMA: No one will tell us. If you could enlighten us, we would be grateful.

THIRD REPORTER: They've told you nothing?

EMMA: They've told us a great deal. They've told us that we're "dangerous enemies" of the country, that we're lawless anarchists who have blasphemously denounced the tyrannies of church and state. To hold such opinions, they say, is madness, to *express* them, treason. But our destination? No, of that they have told us nothing.

THIRD REPORTER: The speculation is that it will be Russia.

BERKMAN: We hope it is Russia.

SECOND REPORTER: Your allegiance *is* with the Bolsheviks, isn't it, Miss Goldman?

EMMA: My allegiance is with people. I don't recognize the swollen pride of any nation.

SECOND REPORTER: Why do you hate America?

EMMA: Pardon me, sir, but you sound like a fool.

SECOND REPORTER: For twenty-five years you've railed against our government.

EMMA: For *thirty-five* years. Against *all* governments.

SECOND REPORTER: Then you do hate America.

EMMA: Sir, you *are* a fool. I'll never stop loving this country. Longing for its possibilities.

FIRST REPORTER: Mr. Berkman, do you find any irony in the fact that Henry Clay Frick—the man you tried to assassinate thirty years ago—has died this very week?

BERKMAN: Thousands of people have died this week.

FIRST REPORTER: Oh, come now, Mr. Berkman.

EMMA: Alexander Berkman has paid his debt in full: twenty-two years in your prisons. Henry Clay Frick has died with *his* debts unpaid.

SECOND REPORTER: Is that all you have to say about Frick?

BERKMAN: You can add: Mr. Frick has been deported by God.

(Emma and Berkman start up the gangplank.)

THIRD REPORTER *(Calling after them):* This is the end of the line, Emma Goldman, isn't it?

EMMA: Oh, no. Only another beginning. . . .

(The deportees, crowding the rails, start singing "The International." The ship's whistle sounds. Emma and Berkman have their arms tightly interlocked.)

EMMA *(Almost to herself)*: It was almost thirty-five years ago. . . . It's hard to believe . . .

BERKMAN: What is, dear?

EMMA: It's thirty-five years ago, nearly to the day, that I landed here in New York. . . . It could have been this very gangplank I walked down. . . . *(Laughs)* And what did I do? I headed straight for Sachs's café! Do you remember, old comrade?

(Emma—a second actress—and Helena as young women gradually emerge from the background during the ensuing dialogue. Both are dragging cardboard suitcases; and Emma a sewing machine as well.)

BERKMAN: Lugging that ridiculous sewing machine! Who could ever forget?

(A guard grabs Berkman.)

GUARD: Male prisoners in steerage. Down below! *Fast!*

THE YOUNG EMMA: There! Number thirty-one! We're *here*, Helena!

HELENA: Oh, thank God! I'm exhausted . . .

(The older Emma and Berkman embrace. Emma clings to him.)

EMMA: Sasha . . . Sashenka . . .

BERKMAN: Now, now, old girl. It's only for a few weeks. We've endured years.

(The guard roughly removes Berkman from the deck, as scene shifts to a crowded tenement street in New York City, 1886.)

EMMA: I told you we'd find it, silly. New York is no crazier than Saint Petersburg.

HELENA: I've been hearing Papa's warning in my ears all day: The police will arrest you as "loose women."

EMMA: Papa! Papa! He thinks women are born to make *gefüllte* fish! And the *smartest* get to cut noodles.

(They are at the door to Number 31. Emma searches the nameplates.)

EMMA: Aha—Tante Rosenzweig! We're here, Helena!

(They grab and hug each other. Emma pushes the apartment buzzer.)

EMMA: Tell Tante I'll be back by nightfall.

HELENA *(Flabbergasted)*: You *what?*

EMMA *(Beaming)*: I've sworn to myself that the first door I'd enter in the New World would be—Sachs's café.

(Excited noises from the top of the stairs.)

EMMA: They're coming. *(Kisses Helena)* Two hours, dear sister . . .

HELENA: *Meshugana!* Just like Papa. *Meshugana!*

(Emma starts to leave, then hurries back and picks up the sewing machine to take with her.)

HELENA: What are you doing?

EMMA: It must never be out of my sight.

HELENA: It weighs two stone! You don't even know where Sachs's café is!

EMMA *(Holding up the machine)*: Independence: light as a feather!

(She hurries off. Scene shifts to Sachs's café. Emma is talking to the bartender. No one else is in the place, except for two men seated at one of the tables.)

EMMA: But I thought he came here to Sachs's café *all* the time.

BARTENDER: Johann Most is a busy man, young lady.

EMMA: Emma Goldman is my name.

BARTENDER: Well, Miss Goldman, newspapers don't edit themselves.

EMMA: *Die Freiheit* has been my Bible. In Russia it passes from hand to hand. Johann Most is a hero in Russia. . . .

BARTENDER: Yes, so some say.

EMMA: *Some?*

BARTENDER: It's a small movement, but we wouldn't be anarchists if each was not his own leader, eh?

EMMA: Ah—so you're a comrade!

BARTENDER: This is Sachs's café, Miss Goldman.

(They laugh.)

BARTENDER: And when did you get here from Russia?

EMMA: Today.

BARTENDER: *Today?* You've been here one day?!

EMMA: Not all of it. We left Ellis Island this morning.

BARTENDER: Good God! *(Calling out to the two men at the table)* Sasha! Fedya!

(The two look up.)

BARTENDER: Come meet a new comrade. *(To Emma)* Do you know anyone in New York?

EMMA: An aunt. My sister came with me.

(Berkman and Fedya are at the bar.)

BARTENDER: Miss Goldman, this is Alexander Berkman, called by everyone Sasha.

(Emma extends her hand forcefully.)

EMMA: How do you do, Sasha?

BERKMAN *(Cold)*: How do you do, Miss Goldman.

BARTENDER: And this is Fedya Meyerman.

(Fedya makes a sweeping bow.)

FEDYA: I am deeply honored, Miss Goldman.

BERKMAN *(Scornful)*: Clown.

FEDYA *(Mocking)*: A clown and a "spendthrift." You may as well know the worst at once, Miss Goldman.

(Emma flushes with pleasure.)

BARTENDER: Miss Goldman just arrived this morning. She's looking for Johann Most.

EMMA: Please, you must call me Emma. I am not formal.

(Fedya extends his arm.)

FEDYA: Well, Emma, come to our table.

BERKMAN *(Stern)*: Why are you looking for Johann Most?

EMMA: Because I'm an anarchist. I want to work for the Cause.

FEDYA: Please, first some wine, then the Cause. *(Leans down to take her sewing machine)* Here, let me take that.

EMMA: Why?

FEDYA *(Surprised)*: Why?

EMMA: I'm strong. *(Picks up the sewing machine)*

FEDYA *(Joking)*: Aha—an émancipée. A *radicalke!* Sasha may like you yet.

EMMA: It's a sewing machine. It's how I made my living in Saint Petersburg.

BERKMAN: I, too, am from Saint Petersburg. It has given many brave sons to the revolution. Even a few daughters.

EMMA: My uncle Yegor was imprisoned in the Petro-Pavlovsky Fortress. For being an anarchist.

BERKMAN *(Decisively)*: Come to the table.

(As they move to the table, they continue to talk.)

EMMA: My sister also sews. We hope to start a cooperative dress shop. Like Vera in Chernyshevsky's *What Is To Be Done*. Meantime, I'll get a job in a factory.

BERKMAN *(Surprised)*: You've read Chernyshevsky? Impossible. His books are banned in Russia.

EMMA *(Angry)*: I've read all the forbidden books: Chernyshevsky, Turgenev, Goncharov. Yes, and I was accepted at the gymnasium—a girl, a Jewish girl, accepted at the gymnasium! It's where I learned to speak English . . .

FEDYA: That's amazing, Emma!

EMMA *(Reproachfully, at Berkman)*: My father didn't think girls should go to school.

FEDYA: Did you go?

EMMA: I told him I'd throw myself into the Neva river if he refused to let me. He said, "The pig woman cheated me. You should have been a boy."

(They laugh, Berkman grudgingly.)

EMMA: I used to hope I'd come down with a terrible disease. I thought it might make father kind—like when he drinks wine on Sukkoth.

BERKMAN: I'm sorry if I hurt your feelings—Emma.

FEDYA *(Yelling to the bartender)*: Wine, wine! To Sukkoth and pig women, to Chernyshevsky and Vera!

BERKMAN: There's no money for wine.

EMMA: I have money. Five dollars! Can you buy food at Sachs's? I haven't eaten all day.

FEDYA: The best steak in New York, Emma—for *forty* cents!

EMMA: Aren't you hungry, Sasha?

BERKMAN: Give Fedya my forty cents. He'll buy flowers with it.

FEDYA: Sasha thinks I squander money on useless things: flowers, wine, oils, and brushes for my painting.

EMMA: You're a painter! How marvelous, Fedya.

BERKMAN: An anarchist can't enjoy luxuries when the people are starving.

EMMA: Beautiful things are necessities, not luxuries.

FEDYA *(Smiling)*: Ah! A "bourgeois" ally!

BERKMAN: There is only one necessity, and that is the Cause. It requires sacrifice. Fedya sacrifices *when convenient*.

EMMA: You sound like Rakhmetov in Chernyshevsky's novel. So single-minded.

BERKMAN: I thank you for the compliment.

FEDYA: Sasha is a true disciple of Johann Most—a man of "the deed," of planned assassination.

BERKMAN: All means are justified in the war of humanity against its enemies.

FEDYA *(Animated and serious)*: Violence will destroy anarchism. Anarchists are the champions of life. Most's philosophy of "the deed" is contempt for life.

BERKMAN: To commit the deed is to toss the stone which will start the avalanche. To remove a tyrant through assassination is to take one life in order to give life to the many.

EMMA: But even Johann Most says the deed should be the last resort— when there is no other way.

BERKMAN: Most is German.

FEDYA *(To Emma)*: Have you ever seen him?

EMMA: No.

FEDYA: He isn't exactly Romeo.

EMMA: Fedya!

FEDYA: Old. No jaw. His face all twisted. You said you liked beautiful things.

EMMA: Beauty isn't a physical property. I don't think like a shopgirl, Fedya.

BERKMAN *(To Emma)*: You see what I mean. Do you want to meet Most? When he debates the socialist Schleier at Ukrainian Hall, I will take you. Afterwards I'll introduce you. Most will make you understand the deed.

EMMA: I will meet Most? I don't believe it! *(Starts to get up)* I must tell my sister!

FEDYA: There's plenty of time. First have your steak.

(Berkman snorts in disgust.)

EMMA: Yes, we must all have steak—to celebrate. *(Calls out to the bartender)* Steak for three!

FEDYA: And wine.

EMMA: And wine!

BERKMAN: I told you I'm not hungry.

EMMA: A strong man like you not hungry? Impossible. Please, Sasha. To help me celebrate!

FEDYA *(Coaxing)*: Eh, Sasha, come . . .

EMMA: Comrades are supposed to share, no? *Please*, Sasha.

(As Berkman scowls, scene shifts back to the Buford, *1919. Emma and other woman are emptying out their suitcases.)*

GUARD: All right. Hurry it up. Hurry it up, ladies. If you want those clothes sent down to the men, I need them now. I'm late for my watch.

WOMAN ONE: Underwear, too, Emma?

EMMA: *Everything*! Sweaters, socks, underwear—*everything*. . . . The men in steerage are freezing. And we must save what we can from our meals. Their food is so bad, the sick ones can't hold it down.

WOMAN TWO: We're lucky by comparison.

EMMA: Always, dear Dora. *(Laughs)* That's because women are thought to be the "delicate" ones. *(Snorts derisively)* But not too delicate to work twelve to fourteen hours in a factory!

GUARD: I'm waiting, ladies, but not for much longer.

WOMAN ONE: Nobody in this country puts in such hours any more.

EMMA: And do you know why? Because we fought it, we refused to be slaves. But when I first came here in 1886—mind you, that was thirty-five years ago!—one of my first jobs *(Her voice fades as scene begins to shift)* was in a factory owned by a man named Garson . . . a big man . . . a nasty man . . .

(We are now in Garson's factory, 1886. Lunch break. Emma and other young women are eating noodle pudding from their paper bags. Emma is excitedly waving a newspaper at them.)

EMMA: But they're innocent men, *innocent*! Doesn't that matter to you?

FIRST WOMAN: So *you* say. Who knows.

EMMA *(Slaps newspaper)*: Look! The *Chicago Tribune*, May 4, 1886: "Anarchists Throw Bomb in Haymarket Square. Workers Inaugurate Reign of Terror." Those workers met in Haymarket to protest police brutality. The *police* are violent, not the anarchists.

SECOND WOMAN *(Sympathetic)*: But *someone* threw a bomb, Emma. Five men *are* dead.

FIRST WOMAN: The police in Haymarket Square didn't kill themselves. Someone murdered them. And murderers should be hung.

EMMA: And what of the workers killed, eh? The papers barely mention *them*! I tell you they've arrested Parsons and Spies because they're leading anarchists. It's an excuse to break the movement! The state will hang them all—mark my words.

FIRST WOMAN: You're so sure of everything.

SECOND WOMAN: My Fred says women shouldn't mix in politics.

FIRST WOMAN: Especially women new to the country. America isn't Russia, you know.

EMMA: It's worse than Russia! Twelve hours a day sewing overcoat belts. Two fifty a week in pay. In Russia we could at least talk and sing. *And* go to the toilet without permission.

SECOND WOMAN: Tell your complaints to Mr. Garson. He owns this factory. My noodle pudding's cold, with all the talk.

EMMA: Yes, why not Garson?

(She strides off angrily.)

FIRST WOMAN *(Calling after her)*: If the government hangs them all, it will be a service to decent people!

(Scene shifts to Garson's office. Emma is explaining to his secretary why she must see him.)

EMMA: Tell Mr. Garson it is urgent. It has to do with factory production. With a possible slowdown.

SECRETARY: Do you have permission to leave your machine?

EMMA: Never mind—*I'll* tell him!

(She strides past the protesting secretary into Garson's inner office. He's seated at his desk, which has a vase of American Beauty roses on it.)

GARSON: Yes?

EMMA: What beautiful roses. *(He looks up, surprised)* I once tried to buy one in a flower shop. It cost a dollar—almost half my weekly salary.

GARSON: What is it you want?

EMMA: Yesterday Tanya Rosenbluth, who works the machine next to mine, fainted and fell to the floor.

GARSON: What is your name?

EMMA: Emma Goldman.

GARSON: I thought so. You're the one who insisted the foreman stop the machines.

EMMA: Tanya was very ill. I had to squeeze the juice of an orange from my lunch basket into her mouth.

GARSON: I've already had a full report of the episode. The girl was shamming. And you encouraged the sham, so the two of you could take the day off and idle in the park.

EMMA: I told the foreman to deduct from my pay. Tanya needed fresh air.

GARSON: And is he deducting for your time now?

EMMA: I didn't *ask* him to, if that's what you mean.

GARSON: I assumed as much.

EMMA *(Getting angry)*: Am I not even allowed to voice a complaint, a *legitimate* complaint, without having my pay docked?

GARSON: I am the one who decides what is legitimate! This is *my* factory, Miss Goldman. You apparently need to be reminded of that.

EMMA *(Trying to control her mounting fury)*: And *you* apparently need to be reminded that the people who work for you are *human beings* who can barely afford to put food on the table! After room, board, and carfare, Mr. Garson, I have *forty cents* a week left over!

GARSON: None of my other girls complain.

EMMA: I can never afford to buy a book, to hear a concert. . . .

GARSON: My other girls, of course, are German. Russians are known for extravagance. You have fancy tastes for an immigrant girl. Perhaps if you learned the importance of hard work, of—

(Emma picks up the vase of roses on Garson's desk and throws it at him.)

(Scene shifts to Ukrainian Hall. Johann Most and Ari Schleier are in the midst of a debate. Most is in his mid-forties, autocratic and cold, yet charismatic—and a brilliant speaker: caustic, fluent, incisive. Emma, Berkman, Fedya, and Helena are in the audience.)

MOST: —It is true that anarchists differ in the tactics they employ for achieving the good society. But what makes us all anarchists is our agreement as to what the good society *is*. It is a society free of dictation. Anarchists scorn to rule, and refuse to be ruled. Why are we against imposed authority? Because we are *for* life—in all its splendid diversity, not stifled by false piety. Socialism is wrong-headed because it puts faith in political action and in the state as the vehicle for social transformation. . . . Surely we have learned by now that parliaments are mere Houses of Marionettes. And surely we have learned, too, that means become ends. If you use the state to obtain your goal, the state becomes your goal . . . an end unto itself.

(A section of the audience cheers and waves the black flag of anarchism. Emma, in her excitement, leans over and impulsively hugs Berkman. He is startled, annoyed. Schleier is now on the speaker's platform.)

SCHLEIER: —You talk of means becoming ends. A commendable warning. Yet it seems a curious one coming from Johann Most, the man who wrote *Science of Revolutionary Warfare*—a manual for preparing nitroglycerin bombs.

(Some in the audience start booing, shouting for Schleier to sit down.)

SCHLEIER: The "propaganda of the deed," as you call it. In other words, Dr. Most, you advocate the use of violence to bring about a nonviolent society. Are anarchists a separate breed of men, able to use any means without becoming contaminated by them?

(Most strides angrily to the podium.)

MOST: I will take exactly one minute to clarify. Though with a mind as muddled as yours, sir, I doubt it will be time well spent. I have advocated "propaganda by the deed" *only* when other avenues to change have been foreclosed. Even the Nazarene, who came to preach peace, resorted to violence to drive the money changers from the temple.

(Fedya shakes his head in disapproval. Berkman applauds wildly. Emma uncertainly starts applauding too.)

MOST: No group in power has ever surrendered it voluntarily. In every case the use of force—or the threat of it—is required. How can socialists claim that they abhor violence when they defend government—for the state is the chief promoter of violence. Or have you not heard of something called war? If you kill the state's enemies, you are a hero. But if you use violence *against* the state, you are a murderer. Anarchists do not believe that there is "good" violence and "bad" violence. We despise *all* violence, all coercion. But before we can create a society free of coercion, those in control of the state—the state itself—must be dislodged. And sometimes by violence.

(A man jumps to his feet.)

MAN *(Shouting at Most)*: You speak like a fool! Man is by nature an aggressive animal. Remove the restraints of government, and you will have chaos, not harmony.

VOICE: Bourgeois ideology!

MAN: Socialism is based on the hard facts of life. Socialism is realism. Anarchism is utopianism.

(Emma, rising almost involuntarily from her seat, suddenly begins to speak.)

EMMA: To a conservative mind, a "practical" scheme means one already in existence! But the *height* of "realism" is to recognize that what does not yet exist, what has never been tried, is nonetheless possible! The *true* realist is he who rejects so-called "historical necessity" in the name of what is not yet known.

(Tremendous applause. Emma dazed, as if awakening from a trance. She suddenly becomes self-conscious, fumbling. Berkman helps her to her seat.)

(As the meeting breaks up, a crowd gathers around Emma to congratulate her. Most comes up.)

MOST: And who is this remarkable young lady?

EMMA: Dr. Most, I apologize. I didn't mean to . . .

MOST: Apologize? You spoke eloquently. Don't you agree, Berkman?

BERKMAN: Louise Michel come to life.

EMMA: Who?

MOST: Who? The heroine of the Paris Commune! Apparently your gifts are natural, not studied.

EMMA: I haven't read as much as I should.

FEDYA: Except for Chernyshevsky.

MOST: You must read more. The Germans. The revolutionary poets: Freiligrath, Schiller, Heine. I will prepare a list for you. But I still do not know your name.

EMMA: Emma Goldman. And this is my sister, Helena.

MOST: There are few women in our ranks. They come to meetings to find men. Then both vanish, like the fishermen at the lure of the Lorelei. The revolutionary zeal of womanhood has never impressed me.

BERKMAN: Emma is from Russia.

MOST *(Sardonic)*: Ah yes, passionate Russia. We shall see. *(To Emma)* You have talent as a speaker. Notable talent. It must be put to use.

EMMA: But I've never spoken in public before. I didn't know what I was doing.

BERKMAN: No false modesty, Emma. With comrades, it only wastes time.

MOST: Tomorrow we'll talk more. I must go to the newspaper. No one else, it seems, can write a line of copy. Where are you staying, Miss Goldman?

EMMA: Well, Helena and I are—

FEDYA: —She's staying with us.

(Emma astonished.)

FEDYA: Why not? Comrades share, remember? We have a whole loft, and no one but me and Sasha in it . . .

BERKMAN *(Scornfully)*: Plus your in-and-out girlfriends.

MOST: Come for me at *Die Freiheit* tomorrow night, Miss Goldman. I'll take you to Terrace Garden, and we will talk more of Louise Michel.

EMMA: Thank you, Dr. Most.

MOST: Let us say nine o'clock. Good evening, everyone. *(Most exits)*

HELENA: Emma, how marvelous!

EMMA: I can't believe it!

BERKMAN: You must be careful, Emma. Most is attracted to you.

EMMA: Sasha—he could be my father! And what could he see in me, a factory girl, uneducated.

BERKMAN: Revolutionaries have no right to a personal life. *(Gruff)* It's time to go home.

FEDYA: Come along, Emma. You too, Helena.

HELENA: No, no. I'll stay with Aunt. I'm the family conservative.

EMMA: I don't know, Fedya, do you think—

FEDYA: Think? Think what? Are you going to give us another speech— this one on bourgeois morality?

EMMA: Sasha: do *you* invite me?

BERKMAN: You've been invited.

FEDYA: Be a little more cordial, dear comrade.

BERKMAN *(Suppressed fury)*: I warn you, Fedya, don't toy with me. I'm not, like you, a part-time revolutionist. My life is for the Cause. Yes, Emma can stay with us. Because she cares about our principles.

FEDYA *(Sarcastic)*: It's the Cause I was thinking of. Offering a haven in this hard city to Dr. Most's promising lecturer.

BERKMAN: And there will be no more talk of Most.

(Berkman storms ahead. As Emma and Helena embrace, scene shifts back to the Buford, 1919. Emma is being shaken awake by a guard.)

GUARD: Hey! Hey!!

EMMA: What . . . what is it?

GUARD: Are you alive or dead?

EMMA: Is something wrong? Where am I? What's happened?

GUARD: You're in the middle of the ocean, that's where.

EMMA *(She's now awake)*: Oh yes . . . I seem to have spent most of my life in transit . . . *(Trying to put him at ease)* Never mind, young man . . . Now tell me—since they seem to have neglected formal introductions—just who are the hell are *you*?

GUARD: A private in the United States Army. I have my orders about you.

EMMA: Is one of them to prevent me from sleeping?

GUARD: You've been asleep twelve hours.

EMMA: *What?* I've never slept that long in my life.

GUARD: It must be your bad conscience.

EMMA: It must be because the United States Army kept us awake for three days.

GUARD: They gave us a full briefing on you. You're a terrorist. *And* an ex-convict.

EMMA: Well, it's at least true that I was in jail last week.

GUARD: —for helping the Bolshies . . .

EMMA: —for publishing an article in *Mother Earth* against drafting young men like you to kill other young men.

GUARD: Is that your nickname—"Mother Earth"?

EMMA *(Laughing)*: It's the title of a magazine I ran for many years. Until President Wilson suppressed it as treasonable.

(Emma gets out of bed and heads toward the cabin door.)

GUARD: Where do you think you're going?

EMMA: To the toilet. Any objection?

GUARD: You don't go without me.

EMMA: Fine. I'm always glad for new experiences.

(Blackout. Lights up on Terrace Garden, 1886. Most and Emma are seated at a table in animated conversation.)

EMMA *(Reading the label on the wine bottle)*: "Liebfraumilch. What a lovely name—"milk of woman's love."

MOST: For wine, yes. For woman's love, no. The one is poetry. The other, finally, prose.

EMMA: I've never tasted wine. Father wouldn't allow it.

MOST: And have you tasted love? Or did Father forbid that, too?

EMMA: I learned not to listen to Father.

(Most laughs, then raises his wine glass in a toast.)

MOST: *Prosit*, my young, naive lady!

EMMA *(Bristling)*: We mature early in my family.

MOST *(Laughing)*: Very well! To my mature, ardent comrade! *(They drink)* There is great need in our ranks for ardent ones. And I have great need for ardent friendship.

EMMA: You're idolized by thousands.

MOST: Yes, *mein Kind*, idolized, but not loved. One can be very lonely among thousands. Did you know that?

EMMA: I often long to be alone.

MOST: Where did you get silky blond hair and blue eyes? You said you were Jewish.

EMMA: At the pigs' market, my father would say.

(Most laughs again.)

MOST: I haven't had such a happy evening in years. You have a ready tongue, my little girl.

EMMA: Please don't call me that. I'm a young woman, not a child.

MOST: Indeed you are a woman, Emma. May I call you that?

EMMA: Yes, I'd like you to.

MOST: Good. And you are to call me Johann. Now, Emma. Do you know what I have in mind for you?

EMMA *(Downcast)*: Lecturing.

MOST: Yes, lecturing—but later, later. After you've read more and I've explained the social struggle to you, the mistakes of Marx, the glories of Bakunin. But now, Emma, what I have in mind for you *now*—is music and theater. *Carmen* at the Metropolitan, the plays of Schiller at the Yiddish Art!

(Emma almost jumps with excitement.)

EMMA: Oh, Johann, I once saw an opera. When I was ten in Königsberg, my teacher took me to *Trovatore*. How I cried! *(Gestures in flamboyant self-parody)* "O, teuere Mütter, o teuere Mütter." *(They both break into gales of laughter)*

MOST: You're born for the stage, my little *Blondkopf*. You must see *all* of Schiller: *Wilhelm Tell, Die Räuber,* and *Fiesco*—all *(Whispering confidentially)* Did anyone ever tell you that Johann Most, the dangerous anarchist, wanted more than anything in this world to be an actor? It was my passion as a young man, my obsession. I saved every *pfennig* to buy tickets. And always for Schiller. Above all, I longed to perform Schiller. Aah . . .

EMMA: Then you should have, Johann. Everyone should do what he wants to do.

MOST: I did try once. The theater manager told me I might make a

clown, but never an actor . . . well, you know . . . my face. . . .
Not exactly a matinee idol.

(Emma, touched, puts her hand comfortingly on Most's sleeve.)

MOST *(Animated):* You may not believe it, Emma, but I was a handsome
youth. *(He touches his cheek)* Then some strange poisoning here. And
a bad surgeon. *(Laughs)*

(In the background the band starts to play Strauss.)

MOST: Ah—*Der Zigeunerbaron!*

EMMA: Oh, let's dance, Johann! Can we dance?

MOST: I think I can remember how.

*(They move to the dance floor. As they pass one table, Most acknowledges two
young men. Most and Emma start to dance. He is awkward, stiff; Emma, un-
embarrassed, reckless. The two young men rise and angrily separate Most
and Emma.)*

YOUNG MAN: Dr. Most, it's undignified, frivolous. It hurts the Cause.

EMMA: I do what I want—that *is* the Cause!

MOST: Be calm, Emma.

YOUNG MAN: People are watching.

EMMA: They're watching because you interfered. Anarchists are supposed to mind their own business—and only their own.

YOUNG MAN: We can discuss it another time.

EMMA *(Raising her voice):* I haven't joined the movement to become
a nun.

YOUNG MAN: Dancing in public places is unseemly.

(The band stops playing.)

EMMA: If I can't dance, it isn't my revolution!

MOST *(Embarrassed):* Come, Emma. This is getting out of hand.

(He starts to lead her away. She yells back at the young man.)

EMMA: Anarchism is freedom from convention!

YOUNG MAN: Theatrics! Egotism!

*(Emma takes off her shoe and throws it at the young man. Blackout. Emma's
yelling continues, under. Lights up on the loft apartment. Emma is screaming at Berkman.)*

EMMA: I will not be told what I must do and when I must do it! Not by
you, not by anyone!

BERKMAN: Most has no right to squander money. We'd all like to eat and drink at Terrace Garden. You have to decide what you care about.

EMMA: I care about many things.

BERKMAN *(Acidly)*: Precisely. You lack priorities. For you pleasure and revolution are coequal.

EMMA: I became an anarchist to assert my humanity, not to deny it.

BERKMAN: Sentimentality. You're a child. You understand nothing.

EMMA: I understand the difference between sentiment and emotion.

BERKMAN *(Almost to himself)*: Which is precisely what I said about Edelstadt.

EMMA: I can't hear you!

BERKMAN: *Edelstadt*! An anarchist. A poet. I shared a room with him. He died two years ago of tuberculosis.

EMMA: What does that have to do with—

BERKMAN *(Interrupting, furious)*: —They wanted to take money from the treasury to send him to Denver. I refused to agree. *(He starts to crumble)* No funds belonging to the movement should ever be spent for private, sentimental reasons. Most must be held to account. Revolutionary ethics demand that . . . *(Starts to sob)* He died— Edelstadt *died*! I shared a room with him . . .

(Emma rushes to comfort him.)

EMMA: Oh, Sasha. How terrible! Sasha . . . Sasha . . .

(She tries to embrace him, but he moves away—gently.)

BERKMAN *(Quietly)*: I don't matter. No individual matters.

EMMA: Sasha, you're either a knave or a hero.

BERKMAN: I'm an instrument. Nothing more.

EMMA: Instruments don't have feelings.

BERKMAN: I've learned to control my feelings.

EMMA: Have you ever been in love, Sasha?

BERKMAN: Yes.

EMMA: What happened?

BERKMAN: She wanted to marry.

EMMA: How foolish of her.

(Berkman is surprised.)

EMMA: I've been married.

BERKMAN: That can't be.

EMMA *(Amused)*: It's very easy to get married, Sasha. Many people manage it.

BERKMAN: But you're so young.

EMMA: He worked the machine next to mine in the factory. He talked well and read a lot. Father had always said *(Laughs)*, "You have too much energy, you'll become a whore." So I married. It lasted less than a year. He was impotent. I made the mistake of being sympathetic. That drove him to gambling. So I left.

BERKMAN: Did you mind he couldn't be your lover?

EMMA: Of course I minded. Wouldn't you?

BERKMAN: Have you ever been with a man?

EMMA: A boy I knew in Saint Petersburg worked in one of the great hotels. He took me one day to see the rooms. In one of them, he seized me and tore open my waist dress.

BERKMAN: How awful.

EMMA: I was as eager as he. The only shock was to find out how wild contact can be between a man and a woman.

BERKMAN: Shameful.

EMMA *(Laughs)*: It was a beautiful room. And he was handsome. But marriage?—never again. If I love a man, I'll give myself to him without rabbis and laws. And when the love passes, I'll leave without permission. *(Pause)* Sasha . . . are you attracted to me?

BERKMAN: Of course.

EMMA: I'm glad. I feel the same.

(She moves toward him and affectionately puts her arms around him. He moves away.)

BERKMAN: Emma, I beg you. I cannot risk personal attachments.

EMMA: I want no *attachment*. I give freely and take freely. Different people call out different qualities in me.

BERKMAN: You mean you'd let several men share you?

EMMA *(Angry)*: What a stupid word!

BERKMAN *(Abstractedly)*: Everyone is free to do what they want.

EMMA: How would you feel if I gave myself to Johann?

BERKMAN *(Trying to conceal his upset)*: I just said, everyone is a free agent. If you're attracted to him, sleep with him.

EMMA: I'm not physically attracted. But he needs affection. He gives so much to others.

BERKMAN *(Sardonic)*: Duty calls, eh?

EMMA: I respond to Johann. To his sadness, his tenderness.

BERKMAN: That's not what I call love.

EMMA: I didn't call it anything.

BERKMAN: You can't sleep with a man who doesn't arouse you.

EMMA: I just told you he *did*.

BERKMAN: I mean physically.

EMMA: That's *your* idea of love.

BERKMAN *(Angry)*: You talk gibberish. The physical is everything to you, it's nothing to you! You sleep with a young boy because you want him, with an old man because he wants you!

EMMA *(Cool)*: You care too much about logic.

BERKMAN: Yes, I like to make sense out of life!

EMMA: You like to put sense into it.

(Berkman starts pacing, increasingly upset.)

BERKMAN: Do you intend to sleep with Most? Answer me directly!

EMMA: I don't plan my feelings.

BERKMAN: You'd better plan! You can be sure Most has plans. He's out to seduce you—you fool!

EMMA: He doesn't have to seduce me. All he has to do is tell me his honest feelings, so I can respond to them. And he does. He doesn't disguise his feelings behind theories.

(Berkman explodes. He jumps on Emma and starts tearing at her clothes. They grapple on the couch. He rips her dress, then starts kissing her passionately.)

BERKMAN: *Dorogaya . . . dorogaya . . .*

(Blackout. Lights up on Most's office at Die Freiheit. *He and Emma are consulting a large map of New York State).*

MOST: Binghamton will be the best place for you to try your wings. There's an active group of comrades in the city. You'll have a friendly audience. After that, Plattsburgh, Oswego, Syracuse, Utica—

EMMA: Johann, do you *really* think I can? I'm frightened to death. I don't even know what to talk about.

MOST: Stop being foolish. We've been over it many times. Above all, you're to argue against the movement for an eight-hour day, to say that it will dilute the workers' discontent. They must be made to see that our aim is to destroy capitalism, not reform it.

EMMA: But will they listen to a woman?

MOST: They will listen to Emma Goldman. If I can't resist her, how can they? *(Embraces her)* You have reawakened me to life, Emma. I thought . . . all "this" was over for me. But my *Blondkopf* has made me young again. You will be my helpmate, my voice. I want you for my own.

EMMA: Be careful, Johann. I am no one's property.

(She turns away. Lights shift. When they come back up, Emma is posing for Fedya, naked from the waist up. Her tension has dissolved into laughter.)

EMMA: Fedya, my back is killing me. I agreed to pose, but not for the entire day.

FEDYA: I can't concentrate.

EMMA: You should paint roses. They're less erotic.

FEDYA: You're a shameless woman.

EMMA: I'm a tired woman. *(Starts to get up)* And I still have to pack. The train is in two hours.

(Emma starts to get dressed.)

EMMA: Fedya, I'm so excited. I can't believe this is happening to me.

FEDYA: You have a marvelous body, Emma. It's of the earth.

EMMA: It's a peasant's body. Artists are supposed to like delicate things.

FEDYA: Then maybe I'm not an artist.

(He retreats to the sofa. Emma continues to dress.)

EMMA: Helena will come with me as far as Rochester. She'll probably remain there with our other sister, Lena. They say work is easier to get in Rochester and—

(She stops in mid-sentence as she catches sight of Fedya, his head buried in the pillow, sobbing.)

EMMA: Fedya—for God's sake, what's wrong!

(She rushes over and puts her arms around him.)

EMMA: Fedya, what is it, what is it?

FEDYA: I've tried to fight it, Emma, because of Sasha. I know how much he loves you.

EMMA: And I love Sasha. Fiercely—as Sasha is fierce. But what is that to do with us? Do you think my emotions are so puny that they're drained by a single expression? *(Laughs)* Only the bourgeois think you must love one person at a time.

FEDYA *(Confused)*: But . . . but the physical part . . . the . . .

EMMA: If feeling is there, the rest follows. There are many kinds of feeling, and there are many ways of expressing it. There is no conflict, only wider fulfillment.

FEDYA: Sasha would be wild. He would never share you.

(Emma's face clouds with anger.)

EMMA: You, Sasha, Johann—you all use the same words! No one "shares" me. I respond to what someone calls out. And if you try to restrict my response, then you'll call out nothing. Besides, you're wrong about Sasha. He believes in freedom. In any case, there'll be no deception.

FEDYA *(Quietly)*: Emma, you're a marvel.

(As she leans down to embrace him, blackout. Lights come back up on Emma and Berkman in same spot.)

BERKMAN: I do believe in your freedom to love. Yes, I'm jealous. It's part of my background. I hate it. And I'll conquer it. The jealousy would be worse if Fedya wasn't my friend and comrade. And if I thought of you merely as a woman. But you're more than that to me. You're a fighter and a revolutionary.

EMMA: Sasha, you're more beautiful than I even knew. We're two sane romantics in a crazy world. *(They embrace)*

BERKMAN: Now hurry! Or Binghamton will never see our new Perovskaya! Oh—I almost forgot. *(Hands her an American Beauty rose)* As a token of my love, Dushenka. And a harbinger of luck!

EMMA *(Warmly teasing)*: Such extravagance!

(Scene shifts to Emma on the lecture platform. The audience has only a few people in it. One of them is Helena.)

EMMA: Anarchism is the philosophy of the sovereign individual. But it is also a theory of social harmony. There is a mistaken notion that anarchism means destruction and chaos.

(The audience is bored. Helena is upset that Emma's abstractions are losing the audience's attention.)

EMMA: Yet there is no conflict between the individual and the social instinct, any more than there is between the heart and the lungs. Anarchism asserts the possibility of *voluntary* association to fulfill the *actual* needs of the multitude—rather than the imposed needs of the powerful few. It means a new kind of social organism.

(Tepid applause from audience. Emma retreats in confusion from the stage. Scene shifts to Emma and Helena.)

HELENA: I know it's all true and important. But I kept thinking: "Where's Emma in what she's saying?"

EMMA: I'm not separate from my ideas.

HELENA: But you're more than your ideas. Talk about *your* life, about being a woman. The way you did to Papa.

EMMA: You used to beg me *not* to speak my mind to Papa.

HELENA: Then I was frightened for you. *(Laughs)* Now I'm frightened for them!

EMMA: Johann wants me to concentrate on the eight-hour-day question.

HELENA: One papa is enough in every woman's life.

EMMA: Helena, you're becoming an émancipée!

HELENA: It's how I summon up courage to say goodbye. *(They embrace)*

EMMA: It won't be long, dear sister.

HELENA: Remember: *your own life.* You're one of the few capable of *living.* Now *tell* of it!

(Blackout. Emma's lecture voice begins while stage is dark. Then lights come up. She is on the platform.)

EMMA: . . . For women, the home is prison and marriage a curse. I talk to you from my own experience. I have been a body slave in marriage, and a wage slave in capitalism. *(Murmurs and boos from the audience.)* The two institutions are alike: paternal and parasitic. Capitalism robs man of his birthright, poisons his body, keeps him in ignorance and poverty. Marriage robs woman of independence, annihilates her social consciousness, paralyzes her imagination. *(Louder boos.)* Women are now calling for the vote. And the vote they must have. But true emancipation goes far beyond the vote. The most vital right is the right to love and be loved. And love is not compatible with subordination. It knows of but one great thing: to give of one's self boundlessly, in order to find one's self richer, deeper, better . . .

(Catcalls. Some of the audience stomp out in indignation.)

EMMA: Don't bellow like calves, speak up like men!

(A man jumps to his feet.)

MAN: We came here, madam, to hear a discussion of the Social Question, not a panegyric to free love.

EMMA: My point, sir, is that women are part of society—or should be. We're tired of being treated as angels or whores. We want to be treated as human beings, to be placed on *earth*. When woman has learned to be as self-centered and as determined as man is, to delve into life as he does and pay the price for it, she will achieve her liberation. *And,* incidentally, will also help *him* become free.

(A second man rises in the audience.)

SECOND MAN: Your ideas would result in houses of prostitution at every street corner.

EMMA: Love given freely empties the houses of prostitution. Besides, sir, if the men of the future look like you, the houses will be emptier still.

(Laughter from the audience.)

THIRD MAN: I, too, advocate the same standards for women and for men. But *un*like you, madam, I call for self-control, not self-indulgence. I am forty years old, and I am proud to say publicly that I have remained pure.

EMMA: Sir, I would advise a medical examination.

(Uproar in the audience.)

FOURTH MAN: Do you provide those? I'm free tonight.

EMMA: Sir, if you have a wife I pity her. If you have daughters, I urge
you to put them up for adoption . . .

*(Scene shifts to Emma on another lecture platform, in midspeech. The audi-
ence is larger than before.)*

EMMA: . . . We have as much liberty as we are willing to take. The
wealthy few will go on robbing you unless you become daring
enough to resist. *Demonstrate* before the palaces of the rich! *Demand*
work! If they do not give you work, demand bread! If they deny
you both, *take* bread. It is your sacred right!

*(Uproarious applause. Furious booing. An old man rises in the audience. He
is haggard and lean.)*

OLD MAN *(Kindly)*: If I may say a word or two, my dear young lady.

EMMA: Of course. This is an open forum.

OLD MAN: I like your new world, young lady. I think the anarchist
dream—no rulers, voluntary harmonious association—is the best
dream. But what are we old ones to do? We won't live to see such a
world. Is it so wrong for us to want a few reforms *now*? To long for
an eight-hour day, for a few extra hours for reading, maybe, or to
walk in a park? Am I so wrong to want a little release?

(Applause from the audience.)

EMMA *(Fumbling, upset)*: I . . . I meant only that . . . that the movement for an eight-hour day must not sidetrack our revolutionary
energies. *(Scene begins to shift)* But I . . . I do understand what you
say . . . I sympathize with what you say . . . with the very human
need to walk and read, to . . .

*(Her voice is now inaudible. We are in Most's office. He's glaring at the
headlines of various newspapers lying on his desk He slaps them angrily,
then turns to Emma.)*

MOST: This is not my voice!

EMMA: I discovered one of my own. And I must speak with it if I am to
be heard.

MOST: Yes, yes, I know all about the poor old worker who brought you
to tears. It's fine to feel sorry for old men—but their needs can't
displace the needs of the future.

EMMA: Why can we not work on both fronts: for a long-range anarchist society and for the short-term amelioration of the workers' condition?

MOST *(Laughs sardonically)*: Mmm—so said the Social Democrats in Germany. Remember, my dear, that I once sat in the Reichstag. I know all about "legislation to help the workers." It *doesn't* help them. It buys them off. It loosens one shackle so that the rest of the chain can grip them more firmly. And in the process the masses come to believe that their rulers *care*. Make no mistake: it's the average man's faith in the existing order that constitutes the greatest obstacle to change. And *that* is what you are encouraging.

EMMA *(Upset)*: I can't be a parrot. I have to say what I feel.

MOST: Like most of the young, you confuse feeling with thought. If you knew more, you would *feel* differently. *(Slaps the newspapers again)* This is not your voice. It's Berkman's! That arrogant Russian Jew—what does he know of life?

EMMA *(Furious)*: *I* am a Russian Jew! Is that a crime?!

MOST *(Shifting to a conciliatory tone)*: *Liebschen, Liebschen,* you have the opportunity to be a great woman, a leader. If only you would allow yourself to be guided. You know how much I need you, how much I care about you. I must get you to see that you cannot serve two causes at once. Or two men.

EMMA *(Wrenching away from him; angry)*: Or three men. Or four men. Or as many men as *I* choose! And without "*serving*" any of them!

MOST: You sound like a child, a petulant child who has too many wants.

EMMA: What you mean is: I have as many wants as men do!

(She exits abruptly. Scene shifts to loft. Emma is sewing a coat. Berkman enters, dejected.)

EMMA: No luck, eh?

BERKMAN: Nothing. They're even laying off the day laborers.

(Emma holds up the coat she's sewing.)

EMMA: We're all right, Sashenka. Mrs. Korngold's promised me ten dollars for it. And I'll—

(Fedya comes bursting into the room.)

FEDYA: Emma! Sasha! Have you heard the news?!

EMMA: What?—what news?

FEDYA: There's been a pitched battle at the Homestead factory between the strikers at U.S. Steel and the Pinkerton detectives! Half a dozen workers have been killed! A little boy among them. Dozens more wounded. Martial law has been declared.

EMMA: Fedya—*what*? When did it happen! How many killed?

FEDYA: Last night. Henry Clay Frick, head of U.S. Steel—

EMMA: —Fedya, we *know* that! Go on, go on!

FEDYA: Frick hired Pinkerton detectives to break the strike. They attacked last night. But the workers had been tipped off. They fought off the Pinkertons twice, then set fire to the oil slick all around the river. The Pinkertons threw down their arms—they *surrendered*!

(Emma gasps in amazement. She and Fedya dance a jig around the room. Berkman is deathly quiet.)

EMMA: The workers are awake! Awake!

FEDYA: At last! At last!

BERKMAN *(Fiercely)*: The waiting is over. *Finally*—the waiting is over.

(Emma and Fedya stop dancing.)

FEDYA: What do you mean? Frick still refuses to negotiate. He says he's dealing with a riot, not a strike. He vows to crush it. It's a declaration of war.

BERKMAN: Precisely.

(He grabs his jacket and starts to leave.)

EMMA: Sasha—where are you going?

BERKMAN: I must see Most.

EMMA: *Most?* Why Most?

BERKMAN: The moment has come. The right moment has finally come.

FEDYA: What are you talking about?

BERKMAN: I wouldn't expect you to understand. The deed, of course. Frick's death will echo around the world. It will strike terror into the hearts of exploiters everywhere.

EMMA: What?—the deed?

BERKMAN: It will prove the working class has its avengers.

FEDYA: Sasha, listen to me. Most would like nothing better than to have you out of the way for good.

BERKMAN: The deed will give us possession of ourselves. It will make us men.

EMMA: Let Most do it!

BERKMAN: No one will take that honor from me.

EMMA: Sasha, *please*—there are better ways to help the Homestead workers. We can raise money for the families of those killed. And—

BERKMAN *(Ice cold)*: —And we could send you on another speaking tour about the eight-hour day. I'm tired of words.
(Pause.)

EMMA: Then let me go with you.

BERKMAN *(Disconcerted)*: Nonsense! We can't expend two lives on one man.

EMMA: If I'm along, escape will be easier. A woman can—

BERKMAN: —I'm not interested in escape, can't you understand that? The court will condemn me to death. But *you* must stay alive. You must plead the meaning of my deed to the world, make it see that my act was not directed against Frick the man, but Frick the symbol of injustice. We must each serve the Cause in the way we are best equipped. My job is to commit the deed. Yours is to explain it.

EMMA: No one decides what my "job" is.

BERKMAN: If you really want to help . . . it costs fourteen dollars to get to Pittsburgh. I need a new suit to get into Frick's office. And a revolver. Help me think how to raise the money . . .

FEDYA: *This is madness!* There are avenues to change in this country besides assassination.

BERKMAN: Oh yes—those token reforms that blunt the workers' discontent, make them indifferent to their own misery.

FEDYA: If they're indifferent, why shouldn't you be?

BERKMAN: Progress depends on a few. Only a few can see what is needed. They open the eyes of the others.

FEDYA: Now you think you're the Savior!

BERKMAN: If you won't help, say so.

FEDYA: The workers in America *crucify* their Christs!

EMMA: No, Fedya, no. The workers *will* understand. They know Frick and U.S. Steel are the enemy—and that's all they need to know.

FEDYA: Rubbish! You heard the telegram the strikers sent Andrew Carnegie in Scotland: "Kind master, tell us what you wish us to do and we shall do it for you." Ugh! I tell you the workers will be the first to call you a murderer. Not a savior, a murderer. All your "deed" will do is convince them that anarchism means violence— which is what our enemies have been telling them for years. You may kill Frick, but you'll kill anarchism along with him. *(To Emma)* Can't you stop him? Or do you approve?

EMMA: I don't know. *(To Berkman)* Let me go with you.

FEDYA *(Aghast)*: Emma, Emma!—this is not some schoolgirl adventure!

EMMA *(Furious)*: How dare you?! How dare you treat me like some silly female—you, Fedya, you who I thought understood . . . My political decisions are not a function of my glands.

BERKMAN *(Quietly)*: The matter has been decided for us. There simply isn't enough money for two people to get to Pittsburgh.

EMMA: I will get enough money.

(Emma moves to the door.)

BERKMAN: Where are you going at this time of night?

EMMA: I'll tell you about it later.

FEDYA: I'm sorry, Emma . . . I'm so sorry . . .

(Blackout. Lights up on the street. Emma stands nervously in a doorway. She has on cheap black stockings and high heels. She starts walking slowly down the street, then turns into another doorway. To calm down she massages her temples. A man's voice booms out at her.)

MAN: Hey, lady, you in business or not?

(Emma looks up, startled, into the face of a fat, drunken man.)

EMMA: No . . . no . . .

(She darts out of the doorway, almost running down the street. At the corner she gets hold of herself, and retraces her steps back to the doorway. A man of about sixty, white-haired, tall, distinguished, enters and watches her from a

distance. Then he moves toward her. Seeing him approach, Emma steels her-
self not to run.)

MAN *(Gently)*: Would you care to have a drink with me, miss?

(Emma mutely nods yes. He offers his arm and they move down the street.
Scene shifts to them sitting at a table in a saloon. Emma is trying to adjust
her corset without being obvious.)

MAN: Looks like you're having a little trouble.

EMMA: I'm all right.

MAN: Have you ever worn a corset before?

EMMA: Of course. It's stuffy in here.

MAN: We can leave any time.

EMMA: I'd like another beer. My throat's parched.

(The man signals for more beer.)

MAN: You did a lot of walking. I watched you go back and forth. You've
got an interesting technique. Most of the girls slow down when a
man approaches. You double your pace.

(Emma seems torn between laughter and tears. The man puts his hand un-
derstandingly on her arm.)

MAN: It's your first time, isn't it.

EMMA: Not . . . really.

MAN: You're not much of a liar, either.

EMMA: You have to go with me.

MAN *(Amused)*: Do I? How much are you offering?

EMMA: I *must* have fifteen dollars.

MAN: I'll tell you what. *(Reaches in his billfold)* Here's ten, and we'll call
it a night.

EMMA: You mean, you're going to just *give* me ten dollars?

MAN: Why not? That corset must have cost a pretty penny.

EMMA: I borrowed it.

MAN: I may be quite mistaken, but I've a feeling you're not cut out to
be a streetwalker.

EMMA: No one is "cut out" to be a streetwalker. Thousands of
young girls are driven by economic necessity, by the horrors of
capitalist—

MAN: —now, now, none of that. Serious discussion bores me. You're an awfully nice kid, you know.

EMMA: I was twenty-three last month.

MAN: Mmm. Well, yes, there *is* something of the old lady about you. But even old folks can be silly. Look at me: I'm sixty-one and constantly doing foolish things. Now take your ten dollars and scoot home.

(As Emma kisses him on the forehead, scene shifts back to the loft.)

FEDYA *(Laughing)*: Well, who can blame him? Sex and a lecture on capitalism don't mix. Most is right: you were born for the platform.

BERKMAN *(Angrily)*: You're cheapening Emma's gesture. You're a shallow man, Fedya.

FEDYA *(Chagrined)*: Forgive me, Emma . . . I'm not understanding . . . not understanding . . . any of this . . . I'll go to the corner and get us something to eat . . . perhaps I can be useful that way . . .

(Fedya exits. Emma starts to cry. Berkman puts his arms around her. They sit on the sofa. Lights dim.)

EMMA: But you're part of my flesh and blood. I can't just . . . go on . . .

BERKMAN: You'll have to. What if I never have a trial? There'd be no one to tell the world of my purpose.

EMMA: Sasha, you can't be so hard.

BERKMAN: The task is hard. We must be.

EMMA: I'll never see you again.

BERKMAN: You'll be with me to the last. We must think of humanity.

EMMA: But isn't humanity . . . us?

(Berkman is silent.)

EMMA: What are you thinking about, dearest?

BERKMAN: In Saint Petersburg, when I was ten, I heard the rabbinical saying that "with one instant of righteousness, the Messiah would come to earth." It seemed such a beautiful promise, so easy to fulfill.

EMMA: The rabbis used to warn us that "no man has the power to hasten the steps of the Deliverer." They always counseled submission. Which is why nothing ever changed . . .

(Berkman is pleased. He hugs her.)

BERKMAN: You do understand, dearest. We need a new hope. *(He kisses her gently and rises to go; lights dim)* It's time.

EMMA: Oh no, Sasha . . . Sashenka . . . !

BERKMAN *(Gently)*: Shush . . . be still . . . *(He kisses her again, then moves away. Emma sits alone crying)*

EMMA: Sashenka . . . Sashenka . . .

(Blackout. Lights up on Frick's office. A carpenter is working on a bookshelf on one side of the room. A receptionist enters.)

RECEPTIONIST: Excuse me, sir. There's a man outside from a New York detective agency. He was here yesterday but you were engaged.

FRICK: What does he want?

RECEPTIONIST: He says he has information about a threat on your life.

FRICK: I'm not interested in such nonsense. Send him away.

RECEPTIONIST: Sir, don't you think you'd better see him? Those rumors reported by the *Times* may have been—

FRICK: —people who pay attention to rumors spend their lives chasing shadows. Send him away.

RECEPTIONIST: Yes, sir.

(Receptionist returns to outer office.)

RECEPTIONIST *(To Berkman)*: Mr. Frick will not see you.

BERKMAN: Won't see me?

RECEPTIONIST: That's right.

BERKMAN: You mean he can't see me now?

RECEPTIONIST: He won't see you at all. He's not interested in your information. Good day, Mr. Berkman.

(The receptionist sits at her desk Berkman hesitates for a moment, then rushes past her into Frick's inner office.)

FRICK: What's the meaning of this? Who are you?

BERKMAN: Are you Henry Clay Frick?

FRICK: I am. And who are you, sir?

(Berkman draws a revolver.)

BERKMAN: I am Alexander Berkman. And I'm here to revenge the workers you murdered at Homestead.

(He fires. Frick, wounded, lets out a sharp cry and falls against the arm of his chair. Berkman raises the revolver to fire again, but the receptionist bursts into the office.)

FRICK: Murder! Help! Murder!

RECEPTIONIST *(To carpenter)*: Grab him! Grab him! Hit him with the hammer! Hit him!

(The carpenter tries to pinion Berkman, while the receptionist rushes to Frick. With a great effort, Berkman struggles free, dashes to Frick, pushes the receptionist aside, draws a knife, and plunges it into Frick's thigh. Berkman is raising his arm for a second strike when the carpenter hits him from behind with the hammer. Berkman crumples to the floor. At this moment, two other men, the one another workman in overalls, the other a police officer, rush into the office. Frick, moaning, raises his hand and with great effort speaks.)

FRICK: Don't kill him. Don't kill him . . . Leave him to the law . . . Don't kill him.

(Frick falls back against his chair. The receptionist and the second workman carry Frick to a couch. The officer and the carpenter stand over Berkman.)

BERKMAN: My glasses . . . I've lost my glasses . . .

OFFICER: You'll be lucky if you don't lose your head.

CARPENTER: Murderer!

BERKMAN *(To carpenter)*: But . . . you're . . . you're a working man . . .

OFFICER: Who are you? What is your name?

RECEPTIONIST: His name is Berkman. Alexander Berkman. He said he was a detective from New York.

OFFICER: What is your real name?

RECEPTIONIST: I'm going for a doctor. *(Exits)*

BERKMAN: My name is Alexander Berkman.

OFFICER: We'll soon find out about that.

FRICK *(weakly)*: Raise his head . . . Raise the man's head . . . I wish to see his face . . .

BERKMAN: If I have failed, Frick, there will be others to take my place.

OFFICER: Do you identify this man as your assailant, Mr. Frick?

(Frick nods weakly.)

OFFICER *(To the two workmen)*: Give me a hand with him.

(The officer and the two workmen start to drag Berkman off. Lights fade.)

FRICK: The law . . . you must leave him to the law . . .

(Blackout. Lights up on Berkman in his cell. He extracts a capsule hidden in his shoe, puts it next to his cot, then lies back and begins to write a note.)

BERKMAN: "My darling Emma. Comrade, you were with me at the last. Tell them I gave up what was dearest to me for an ideal. Tell them that I'm—"

(Noise at his door. Berkman grabs the capsule and tries to swallow it. But the guards rush in, pry his jaw open, and extract the capsule from his mouth.)

GUARD *(Examining the capsule)*: A dynamite cartridge.

(Shoves Berkman against the wall.)

GUARD: Thought you'd cheat the state, huh? *(Shoves him again)* We got other plans for you. Terrorists don't get off that easy.

BERKMAN: Unless they head up a government, or a corporation.

(Guard hits Berkman so hard, he falls to the floor. Blackout. Lights up on Sachs's café. A meeting is in progress. The crowd is large and boisterous. Emma and Fedya are seated in the middle of it. Most is speaking.)

MOST: . . . as I've said repeatedly, I've needed time to think over the implications of Berkman's act before making any statement about it. It's now become clear that the attempt on Frick's life has brought an outpouring of public sympathy to him. He is using it to maximum advantage, firing all workers associated with the strike and refusing to hire anyone belonging to a union. . . . Frick has seized on this as an opportunity to completely crush the union movement. . . . I've chosen today, the day of Berkman's trial, to give my views on this unhappy state of affairs. Indeed, before our meeting ends we should have news of the trial verdict. The staff at *Die Freiheit* is standing by the telegraph and will bring us word as soon as it arrives . . .

(Emma tries to rise from her seat, but Fedya restrains her.)

MOST: I note that the people closest to Berkman are with us today. Indeed, one of them, Miss Emma Goldman, has been implicated by several newspapers as an accomplice.

EMMA *(Jumping up)*: I cannot claim that honor for myself alone. The papers have also named you, Johann Most, as the one person, above all others, who has long urged the necessity of "the deed."

(Most tries to appear unperturbed, urbane.)

MOST: Quite right, Miss Goldman. The papers have mentioned my name; often. And for that reason, too, it is necessary that I clarify my position today. That is, if Miss Goldman will allow me to continue.

(Emma is about to reply, but Fedya gently pulls her back to her seat.)

MOST: . . . As you know, when living in exile in London I publicly applauded the assassination of Czar Alexander II. For doing so, I was sentenced to eighteen months at hard labor. My friends advised me to flee. I refused. I served the sentence gladly.

(Emma looks relieved at Most's last words. Several people sitting near her give her reassuring pats.)

MOST: Each "deed" must be judged individually on its merits. *(Pause)* In regard to Alexander Berkman . . . *(Pause)* Rumors have abounded that he was one of Frick's own agents.

(Shouts from the crowd.)

FIRST VOICE: Shame!

SECOND VOICE: Slander!

(Most raises his hands for silence.)

MOST: I, for one, have never given the slightest credence to such reports—though it does seem strange that at such close range Berkman failed to kill Frick.

(Angry shouts from the crowd.)

MOST: I have since learned, however, that Berkman had little practice with a gun—other than target shooting at Russian picnics.

(Some in the crowd laugh, others boo. Emma jumps up again.)

EMMA: I warn you, Johann Most! I am here to defend Sasha's honor— even if that means destroying yours!

MOST: Miss Goldman is hysterical. There's no point proceeding if she's to be allowed these outbursts.

(Most sits down abruptly. Contradictory shouts from the crowd.)

VOICE: Throw her out!

SECOND VOICE: Bring her to the front!

THIRD VOICE: Let her speak!

FOURTH VOICE: Get rid of her!

(A man rushes into the room and makes his way toward Most. When he reaches him, he whispers in his ear. Most raises his hands for quiet.)

MOST: Your attention! Your attention!

(The crowd quiets.)

MOST: We have word from Berkman's trial! Quiet, please! Word has arrived from the trial!

(Emma looks terror-stricken. Fedya grabs her, and they move to the front of the crowd.)

MOST: Word has just come over the telegraph. The trial is over. The judge refused to let Berkman deliver his statement.

VOICE: The sentence! What was the sentence?!

MOST: Felonious assault is ordinarily punished by seven years in prison. Berkman has been sentenced to twenty-two years.

(Pandemonium in the crowd. Emma, near hysteria, violently pushes Fedya away and starts toward Most. Tears pour down her cheeks. Her words are barely audible.)

EMMA: . . . A tomb . . . a tomb. . . . Are you satisfied, Johann Most? Are you satisfied, little father? He's twenty-one years old. Twenty-one years old. My Sasha sent to a tomb, while Frick lives. And you live. *(She reaches Most.)* You, our teacher, our father. You, who taught us of the deed. The noble deed to free the people. You—a traitor, a traitor to everything, to everyone. . . .

(Emma's hand comes out from under her coat. A horse whip is in it. Before anyone can stop her, Emma lashes Most across the face and neck with the whip, all the while screaming "Traitor!" at him. The whip breaks. Emma throws the pieces at Most, who lies crouched on the floor trying to protect his head. Fedya reaches Emma and forcibly restrains her. She collapses in his arms.)

(Blackout. Lights up on Emma and Fedya sitting on a park bench.)

FEDYA: I'll take you to friends. They can hide you for a few days. With your name in the papers, the police will be looking for you.

EMMA: No. I can't endanger anyone else. I'll be all right. I'll find a room.

FEDYA: You should leave New York for a while.

EMMA: I'll see.

FEDYA: At least Sasha is alive. We can work for his release. You must lead the protest. You can travel the country explaining Sasha's motives.

EMMA (*Kissing him on the cheek*): You say all this even though you're against what he did.

FEDYA: Sasha isn't responsible.

EMMA (*Startled*): Sasha knew exactly what he was doing! Don't take that from him. If he wasn't responsible, then who?

FEDYA: No one . . . things . . .

EMMA: I don't care for that.

FEDYA: No one does.

EMMA: And I don't believe it. I wish to be held responsible for what I do.

FEDYA: For attacking Most?

EMMA: I did attack him.

FEDYA: Did you know what you were doing?

EMMA: I knew I was hitting him. I could have stopped . . . I think . . .

FEDYA: Then why didn't you?

EMMA: He deserved it. He betrayed us—and himself.

FEDYA: You used to pity his twisted jaw.

EMMA: He shouldn't have fallen in love with me.

FEDYA: And you shouldn't have been young and appealing. You should not have been Emma.

EMMA: I'm so tired. You're confusing me.

(*Fedya rises, puts his arm around her.*)

FEDYA: Come, we'll go home. And tomorrow we'll start the fight for Sasha's freedom.

EMMA: His deed was not in vain, even though Frick lives. Sasha has called the whole world's attention to the people's suffering.

FEDYA: There. You are no longer confused.

(*Emma shakes her head in disagreement.*)

EMMA: Nothing will ever be simple again.

FEDYA: Nothing ever was. Come, Emma. Tomorrow you'll have much to do.

EMMA: Fedya, do you really think Sasha can survive? A strong young tree, robbed of sun and light. How can it live?

(*She starts to cry. Fedya puts her head on his shoulder.*)

(*Blackout.*)

END OF ACT ONE

ACT TWO

(The Buford, *1919. Emma's cabin. Lights dim. In silhouette, a guard walks back and forth in front of her cabin. Periodically, he sits down wearily on the railing and closes his eyes. Emma lies motionless on her cot.)*

BERKMAN *(Voice-over)*: October 19, 1892. Dearest Girl: It's just a month since they locked me away here. You were wise not to return to the loft. They'll be searching for you as an accomplice. . . . I don't know what will happen to me. I hardly care. . . . Write often. I clutch desperately at the thread that still binds me to the living, yet it seems to unravel in my hands. . . . what good can my continued survival do? Why impose upon myself the duty of existence?

EMMA *(Voice-over)*: There is a strain in your being, call it pride, stubbornness, or hardness even, that will see you through. *Count* on it. *I* do . . . After sleeping on streetcars and hiding with friends, I finally found a room—in a brothel! Well, I'm not proud if they aren't. I've become a confidante for them. They compete with one another in being kind to me, in giving me their sewing to do and thus I'm able to earn a living. . . .

(Lights up as Emma raises her head from the cot. Seeing her, the guard jumps up and enters the cabin.)

EMMA: You must be very tired with all that walking back and forth.

GUARD: I know my duty.

EMMA: Yes, you seem very conscientious. But why don't you sit for a while? I promise not to jump overboard.

(She gets a camp chair from the cabin and puts it in front of him.)

EMMA: I made my living as a nurse for many years, and I know nervous exhaustion when I see it. Sit. I'll keep watch for you.

GUARD: The sergeant might come along.

EMMA: I'll stand at the rail and be lookout. And if I see Berkman blowing anything up, you'll be the first to know.

(The guard sits.)

EMMA: We're heading into German waters, aren't we.

GUARD: How did you know that?

EMMA: The captain's had the lifeboats ready for days. First they give us an unseaworthy boat, then they head us into minefields. I can understand the willingness to see a few hundred anarchists blown up, but you'd think the American government would have a little more regard for its own soldiers.

GUARD *(Grudgingly)*: Some of the men are grumbling.

EMMA: Yes, I know.

GUARD: You do?

EMMA: Several soldiers have talked to us about mutiny.

GUARD: I don't believe you!

EMMA: That's your privilege. Gossip is a good way to spend time on shipboard, don't you think? The days are so long. *(She smiles at him)*

GUARD: Everywhere you go, there seems to be treason.

EMMA: What a nice compliment, young man. Thank you. But you mustn't confuse unpopular ideas with treason. The notion of freeing the slaves was once highly unpopular—among Northern as well as Southern whites. *(Pause; the guard looks dumfounded)* Eh? Well, never mind. I'll spare you one of my lectures. You seem like a nice young man.

GUARD: Is prison as bad as this?

(Lights begin to dim.)

EMMA: Prison is terrible. This is, too. *(She smiles warmly at him)* But there are human possibilities everywhere. When I was in hiding from the police—the first time, that is—I finally had the opportunity to read modern drama.

GUARD: What's that?

EMMA: The modern drama? Theater, the stage. *(Lights are now out. Emma*

is voice-over) Modern drama is associated with the name of Henrik
Ibsen. Nora says it all in Ibsen's *The Doll's House* when she tells her
husband, "I lived by performing tricks for you."

(Lights up on Emma, in the middle of a lecture.)

EMMA: When Nora walks out of her gilded cage, she proves that
women need not keep their mouths shut, and their wombs
open . . .

(Police burst onto the lecture platform and start to handcuff Emma.)

POLICEMAN: You're under arrest, Emma Goldman.

*(A man, Ed Brady, jumps up from the audience and tries to intervene. He's
about forty, attractive, intelligent-looking.)*

BRADY: What's she done, for God's sakes? You can't break up a meeting
for no reason!

POLICEMAN: Stay out of this, mister, or you'll go along with her.

BRADY: What you're doing is against the law.

POLICEMAN: It ain't against common sense. Red Emma shoulda been
in jail long ago.

(As they hustle Emma off, she calls back to Brady.)

EMMA: Thank you, comrade. What is your name?

BRADY: Ed Brady. I'll come see you. It was a great speech!

*(Blackout. Lights up on office of the chief of police. Emma is being ques-
tioned.)*

CHIEF: We've been expecting you for a long time, Miss Goldman.
Frankly, I thought you'd arrive on a stretcher.

EMMA: Sorry to disappoint you.

CHIEF: If you don't behave, there's a good chance you'll leave on one.

EMMA: What are the charges against me?

CHIEF: Incitement to riot.

EMMA: For talking about *Ibsen*?!

CHIEF: For being an anarchist fanatic. I don't doubt this "Ibsen" is one,
too. Of course, I might manage to have the charges against you
dropped if—

EMMA: —I want no charges dropped. I want them *specified*.

CHIEF: Let us not argue the point, Miss Goldman. I'm interested in a
more positive exchange.

EMMA: Should I bother to guess why? You'll go easy on me if I keep you informed of the activities of my comrades—

CHIEF: —nothing elaborate, mind. No formal reports would be expected, no—

EMMA: —you do amaze me, Captain O'Neil. How can you understand me so little even while knowing so much about me?

CHIEF: Your reports would be held in the strictest confidence. No one would ever know that it was you who had—

EMMA: —how *dare* you make such a suggestion?! I'd go to prison for life before I'd act Judas for you and your kind!

CHIEF: Perhaps we can arrange exactly that—since it seems to be your dearest wish!

(Guards grab Emma. As she struggles and lights fade, we hear Berkman, voice-over.)

BERKMAN *(Voice-over)*: In the mess hall, the patriotic warden reads us news about the war with Spain as we try to eat the slop they put in front of us. On and on he drones about our noble victories, as a thousand men pick at the worm-infested food. . . . The memory of the life I had outside these walls intensifies my misery. . . . At night I wake with a passionate desire for the sight of your face, the touch of your hand . . .

(Lights up on Emma in her prison cell, being interrogated by the matron.)

MATRON: If you behave decently, the parole board might cut the year sentence to eleven months. It's up to you.

EMMA: How generous! Only eleven months for the crime of speaking my mind.

MATRON *(Abruptly)*: Any disease?

EMMA: I could use a bath, if that's what you mean.

MATRON: Don't pretend you don't know what I mean. Most of the women who arrive here have venereal disease.

EMMA: As do many "respectable" people. I don't happen to have it, which is due more to luck than virtue.

MATRON: What religion?

EMMA: Atheist.

MATRON: Atheism is prohibited. Attendance at some religious service is required.

EMMA: I'll do nothing of the kind! You'll have to drag me!

(The matron starts to walk away.)

EMMA: Just a minute! I have certain rights, and I know them. I want my mail. And I want reading material.

(The matron picks up a book lying on the table and hands it to Emma.)

MATRON: This Bible will keep you profitably occupied.

(Emma throws the Bible at the matron's feet.)

EMMA: I want a *human* book.

MATRON (Exploding): You desecrate God's word! You'll burn in hell!

EMMA: I burn wherever I go, madam. It's a matter of principle.

(Matron exits. Exhausted, Emma collapses on her cot. Lights dim.)

EMMA *(Voice-over)*: Well, dear Sasha, I've joined you as a jailbird, but not for long, I think. They lack the evidence to hold me. Being locked up gives me some small taste of the horror you've been living, and your brave endurance of it . . .

BERKMAN *(Voice-over)*: Welcome, dear pal, to the society of the living dead. . . . May your stay be brief! As for me, the warden refuses all visitors . . . and I get little mail these days, except from you, old faithful. Fedya seldom writes. I suppose his growing success as a magazine illustrator takes all his time. . . . I try to understand . . .

EMMA *(Voice-over)*: There's something I need to tell you, dearest Sasha. You should know that an Austrian comrade, a man named Ed Brady, has been visiting me here in jail, and we've formed an attachment of sorts. It won't last—I somehow know that—but there will be other men, and I want to be aboveboard about that. You know that I believe sex is a life-giving force and to deny its expression would dry up my creativity. Can you understand? Can you give me your blessing?

BERKMAN *(Voice-over)*: Thank you for telling me the truth about you and this man Ed Brady. You do right to rejoin the world in *every* way. I not only understand, I thoroughly approve . . .

EMMA: I'm going to be released day after tomorrow, and will leave at once on a lecture tour. As an ex-con, I'm now much in demand. People don't seem to care whether I talk about anarchism, the modern drama, or my life as a wanton woman. They simply want to gaze in horror at me. Fine, so long as they pay the admission fee. The movement needs every penny . . .

BERKMAN: How wonderful to hear of your release, dear! I can't imagine how it must feel to be on the outside again, to move about at will. . . . I send you all wishes for some happiness . . .

(Lights up on Emma and Ed Brady walking excitedly through a vacant apartment.)

EMMA: Four whole rooms! I could make this small one mine, Ed. I could do most of my sewing right here.

BRADY: Your work room.

EMMA: Work and sleeping. I must have a room to myself, Ed. Try to understand.

BRADY: I don't understand.

EMMA: I need privacy. In prison I hadn't a moment to myself.

BRADY: Emma, I want to make a home for you. For us.

EMMA: So do I, Ed. You know that.

BRADY: But I want you *in* it. Lectures for the Cause, protest meetings to get Sasha paroled. . . . The more your fame grows, the less I seem to see of you. . . . It's . . . It's your mania for meetings . . .

EMMA: Is that what my work means to you—a "mania for meetings?" What are you saying, Ed? That you'd be happy if I stayed home all the time?

BRADY: Don't be angry with me, but dearest, you're meant to be a mother, by build, by feelings.

EMMA *(Angry)*: Men can consecrate themselves to an ideal *and* be fathers. Women must *choose*! Well, I've chosen. I *want* a child; desperately sometimes. But I won't give up all of humanity to become absorbed in a single human being.

BRADY: Not even in me? I hate sharing you with anything or anybody.

EMMA: What a familiar sound that has.

BRADY: Every man feels the same.

EMMA: Almost every man. But not Sasha.

BRADY: Sasha's always stood between us! Always I'm measured against Sasha! Sasha's suffering, Sasha's imprisonment, Sasha's sacrifice, Sasha's—Sasha is your *obsession!*

EMMA *(Cold fury):* —Sasha is not an obsession. He is a *fact.*

BRADY: Your precious Sasha!

EMMA *(Blazing):* Sasha's locked in prison—but understands our love. You're free—and want to make our home a prison.

BRADY: I need you, Emma. I need our home.

EMMA: Then be big enough to accept what I freely offer.

BRADY: I love Emma Goldman, the woman.

EMMA: The woman and her ideas are one.

BRADY: You *know* I believe in the importance of your work. It's only when it monopolizes every aspect of—

EMMA: —you want a *wife!* I want someone who believes in what I do.

BRADY: Applause! Glory! The limelight! *That's* what you care about!

EMMA *(Calmly):* It's a mistake to move in together.

BRADY: You don't mean that.

EMMA: Oh, but I do . . . profoundly. . . . Let's part while we're friends, Ed. I'm going on tour anyway. . . . It's the easiest time to make a break . . .

BRADY: You're making a terrible mistake, Emma, terrible . . .

EMMA: You're rooted in the old. Well, stay there. But don't think you can hold me there with you. I'll tear you out of my heart!

(She storms out. Blackout. Lights up on Emma on a lecture platform, which swivels and turns to suggest a variety of venues.)

EMMA: . . . America's declaration of war against Spain is not inspired by humanitarian feelings for the Cuban people, but by a desire to expand our sugar market. *(Noises of protest from the audience)* War itself is barbarism, but to clothe it in protestations of humanity is sickening.

(Louder protests from the audience. Emma stops her prepared lecture and confronts the crowd directly.)

EMMA: Don't bellow like calves! Talk like men! If you want a contest, we'll have it. Let the noise be *your* effort. Then, when you've stopped, I'll give you mine.

(An elderly man, elegantly dressed, steps up to the platform and bangs his cane fiercely on the ground.)

ELDERLY MAN: Silence! Silence! Stop this hooliganism! I wish to hear what this woman has to say. If you *don't*, then leave the hall like the civilized creatures you *think* you are.

(The crowd quiets down somewhat. Emma gives the man a sweeping bow.)

EMMA: I thank you, sir. . . . What I was trying to say is that patriotism is a superstition—and a more brutal one than religion. Religion at least originates in man's inability to explain the natural world. Patriotism, on the other hand, is an artificial creation that—

MAN IN AUDIENCE: —that's wrong, wrong! Love of country is rooted in human nature itself!

EMMA: "Human nature?" Now what, pray tell, is that?

MAN: Study your history and you'll find out! People have always loved their countries!

EMMA: I *have* studied history, sir. It's the story of false boundary lines as opposed to genuine human connection. Besides, sir, to deduce human nature from human history is like discussing the "nature" of lions after studying those caged up in zoos. . . . All we learn is how deformed we become when confined to a narrow space and whipped into conformity. To know what human beings are really like, we must throw open the cages, let the beasts freely play and roam—they'll soon enough draw you a true map of their nature.

(As Emma moves to another lecture platform, a newsboy suddenly races across the stage.)

NEWSBOY: Extra! Extra! President McKinley shot! Extra! Extra! Read all about it! President McKinley shot twice at Exposition grounds in Buffalo!

(Blackout.)

(Lights up on police headquarters. Leon Czolgosz is being grilled. He shows

signs of having been badly beaten. He's frightened and cowed. He speaks in broken English.)

OFFICER: You took an oath to kill the president, didn't you? Hey — *you!* Look up! You swore to kill the president, didn't you?

CZOLGOSZ: No, sir.

OFFICER: Louder!

CZOLGOSZ: I done my duty. I knew I would be catched.

OFFICER: Did you hear Emma Goldman speak in Los Angeles?

CZOLGOSZ: Yes, sir.

OFFICER: You heard her say it would be a good thing if all rulers were wiped off the face of the earth, didn't you?

CZOLGOSZ: She no say that.

(A second officer grabs him by the collar.)

OFFICER: Listen, Czolgosz, her speech is on record. You know what happens when you lie?

CZOLGOSZ: She no say president. She say government bad. No belief in government.

OFFICER: And the head of the government should be killed, right?

CZOLGOSZ: She no say that.

OFFICER: When did she put the idea in your head to kill the president? Was it in Los Angeles?

CZOLGOSZ: My idea. *My* idea. No one tell me.

OFFICER: Why are you shielding her, Czolgosz?! It's you who'll go to the electric chair. She's already denounced you as a loafer and a nut.

CZOLGOSZ *(Hurt)*: It no matter. She not do my act. *My* idea. *My* act. I did for American people.

(Blackout. Lights up on Emma's apartment. Fedya, prosperously dressed, is with her.)

FEDYA: You *must* leave the city, Emma. They're bound to try to implicate you. I can arrange for accommodations wherever you like. Money's no longer a problem . . .

EMMA: But Fedya, *why*, for heaven's sake? I wasn't *in* Buffalo. I've never heard of the poor boy—Choogosh, Chowgosh—I can't even pronounce his name.

FEDYA: Czolgosz. Leon Czolgosz. Emma, they'd like nothing better than to lock you up again.

EMMA: But the charges are nonsense. It's well known that I've changed my mind about violence. I've said over and over, in public, that if revolutionaries cannot solve the need for terror, then I am against revolution.

FEDYA: The authorities don't believe you.

EMMA: Probably because what *they* believed at age twenty, they go on believing for the rest of their lives.

FEDYA: They've rounded up dozens of our comrades already.

EMMA: I've even said that I regret horsewhipping poor Johann Most. The man was, after all, my teacher.

FEDYA: Czolgosz admitted hearing you speak in Los Angeles. The papers have converted that into your having inspired him. It could be enough to hang you.

EMMA: You exaggerate. As always.

FEDYA: Emma, Emma, *stop* being so stubborn! For *once* allow yourself to be guided! I beg of you. Friends can hide you tonight. Tomorrow we can make arrangements for Canada.

EMMA: If I escape, what do you think will happen to Czolgosz?

FEDYA: Czolgosz will be all right, if McKinley lives.

EMMA: "All right?" Ah, Fedya, think of those words in terms of Sasha. Nine long years in prison.

FEDYA: *You're reliving Sasha through Czolgosz!* That's the whole trouble! But Czolgosz is *insane!*

EMMA: That's always the comfortable explanation. A mass meeting must be organized.

FEDYA: What?! The city's in a panic. No hall could conceivably be hired. You're an impossible woman! If you persist in your defiance, you'll have only yourself to blame.

EMMA: How profoundly I wish that were true. For tonight I'll go to the Norrises. We'll see from there.

(Blackout. Lights up on the Norris home. Emma is running water in the sink. She stops for a second as if she hears a sound coming from the next

room, but then dismisses it. Suddenly there's a loud crash. Several policemen burst into the room. One of them grabs Emma.)

POLICEMAN: Are you Mrs. Robert Norris?

(Emma shakes her head from side to side, as if not understanding.)

POLICEMAN: Are you deaf, lady? What the hell's the matter with you?

CAPTAIN: Who are you?

EMMA: I not speak English. Swedish servant-girl. Maid.

CAPTAIN *(Releasing her; to his men)*: Search everywhere. The closets, the basement, the garden, everywhere. We know she was here. *(To Emma)* Where are the Norrises?

EMMA: Miss go shop. Mister go newspaper; type-type.

(The captain takes out a picture of Emma Goldman and shoves it in front of her face.)

CAPTAIN: See this?

EMMA: Yes, yes. Pretty woman.

CAPTAIN: It's a picture of a lady name of Emma Goldman. Has she been here, in this house?

EMMA: No, never see such woman. Look like big woman. *(Gesturing to men going through cartons)* No find in small box.

CAPTAIN: Oh, shut up!

(He pushes her out of the way. One of the policemen calls out.)

POLICEMAN: Hey, Captain Schuettler, come here and look at this! *(Holds up a foundation pen)* The initials E.G.

CAPTAIN: Then she *was* here! And she'll be back. Miller, Richardson, hide in the upstairs rooms. Hagerty, into the basement. Malone, station yourself behind the—

EMMA *(Interrupting)*: —Captain Schuettler—

CAPTAIN: —I told you to stay out of the way!

EMMA: I am Emma Goldman.

CAPTAIN *(Startled)*: Well, I'll be damned! That was quite a performance.

EMMA: Mmm. They say I have a flair for the stage. But there's no point carrying this charade to the point where you destroy the Norrises' home and reputation.

CAPTAIN: Grab her! Quick!

(As the policemen seize Emma, blackout. Lights up on Chief O'Neil's office. Emma is led in, handcuffed.)

O'NEIL: Welcome back, Miss Goldman!

(A policeman roughly positions Emma in a chair in front of O'Neil's desk.)

EMMA: And what is the charge this time?

O'NEIL: You stand accused of being an accomplice in the attempt on President McKinley's life.

EMMA: I have neither met nor ever laid eyes on the poor lad they call Czolgosz.

O'NEIL: We have witnesses who have seen you with Czolgosz! Do you hear me?! Seen you with their own eyes!

EMMA: They must be remarkable for distance, Mr. O'Neil, since at the time of the attempt on McKinley's life, I was in St. Louis.

O'NEIL: Your lover, Czolgosz, has already confessed that it was under *your* influence that he shot the president.

EMMA *(Amused)*: My *lover*? Oh, come, Mr. O'Neil! Do you really think *(She opens her arms wide to reveal her full, earthy body)* that that poor, frail boy——? Never mind. The police, I should know by now, are quite capable of "believing" whatever serves their purposes.

O'NEIL: The entire country is convinced you are a murderess.

EMMA: Truth has never been established by majority vote.

O'NEIL *(Exasperated)*: If harm does come to you, you'll have only yourself to blame. And your life *is* in danger.

EMMA: That is what lives are for. I thank you for the warning.

(As O'Neil signals for Emma to be taken away, blackout.)

BERKMAN *(Voice-over)*: Dearest Girl: The Pardon Board again refused to hear my case. I must serve out the whole of my remaining five-year term. As well, my dear companion, Russell, has died of spinal meningitis. The doctor insisted he was shamming. Russell begged to see me, to have me nurse him, but the warden denied me even one visit. . . . Losing him, I feel in terror of going mad . . . I am trying to hang on . . . five more years . . .

(Lights up outside the police building. Emma is surrounded by reporters.)

EMMA: Gentlemen, gentlemen, please! I finally get to breathe the fresh air, only to have you suffocate me!

FIRST REPORTER: You're news, Miss Goldman! And our job is to report it. . . . How long do you think you'll stay out of prison?

EMMA: That's not up to me.

SECOND REPORTER: Will you continue to defend Czolgosz?

EMMA: I've never defended his act. I've tried to explain it.

FIRST REPORTER: It's simple: the lad's insane.

EMMA: The boy's been beaten and tortured enough to drive anyone insane.

FIRST REPORTER: Do you approve of assassination?

(Upstage, the image of Czolgosz appears on the stand. He's pale and emaciated, his head bandaged, his face swollen. His large, wistful eyes roam the courtroom, searching for a friendly face. Finding none, he drops his gaze.)

EMMA: Cruelty begets cruelty. . . . As long as our rulers employ violence, violence will be employed against them. Yet here is the difference: McKinley, murdering thousands in his war to annex the Philippines, is garlanded with honor; Czolgosz, murdering McKinley, will be burned to death in the electric chair.

(Another reporter dashes in, shouting.)

THIRD REPORTER: It's just come over the wire! McKinley is dead!

SECOND REPORTER: Your reaction, Miss Goldman?

EMMA: Many have died today, most in poverty and misery. Why should I feel more regret over McKinley's death than over the others?

(The reporters start to dash out. One calls back.)

FOURTH REPORTER: I think you're nuts, Miss Goldman. But you're damned good copy!

(Spot out on Emma. Spot up on Czolgosz, being strapped to the electric chair. A mask is placed over his face.)

YOUNG CHILD *(Voice-over)*:

I am oh so sorry
That our President is dead
And everybody's sorry
So my father said

And the horrid man who killed him
Is a-sitting in his cell
And I'm glad that Emma Goldman
Doesn't board at this hotel
(The executioner stands with his hand on the switch, awaiting the signal.
The warden steps forward to Czolgosz.)

WARDEN: Do you have any final words?

(Mumbled sounds from under the mask.)

CZOLGOSZ: . . . My act . . . Mine alone . . . I did for American people.

(The warden steps back and signals the executioner, who throws the switch.
Czolgosz's body twitches. Blackout.)

BERKMAN *(Voice-over; enraged)*: What a fool you were to defend Czolgosz! Can't you understand that the United States is now devoid of proletarian consciousness? Acts of political violence are now *futile*. My deed against Frick took place in a world alive to injustice. My deed *mattered*! It illuminated the struggle!

EMMA *(Voice-over; calm)*: Mere theories no longer move me, Sasha. Not yours or anyone's. I defended not an act of violence, but a poor boy who the world had forsaken, a doomed human being. That doesn't affect the fact that *your* deed, and *your* subsequent Calvary, remain at the center of my being, and ever shall. . . . Of *that*, never be in doubt.

(Lights up on the Buford.)

GUARD *(Shy)*: Do you mind if I ask you a personal question?

EMMA *(Charmed)*: Don't be embarrassed. After all, I don't have to answer.

GUARD: Well, it's like, you sound so busy all the time, what with going to prison and making all those speeches. . . . I mean, didn't you ever do anything else?

(Emma laughs appreciatively.)

EMMA: A very sensible question, young man. It sounds like I never had fun, doesn't it? Well, the truth is, I had lots of good times. I *insisted* on good times! We anarchists believe in joy, in *living*. This old lady always knew she had a body as well as a head!

GUARD: Oh, wow, Miss Goldman—I wasn't asking you about *that*!

EMMA: Oh, my, now I've embarrassed you. I was *only* going to say that when I speak of "good times," I don't mean knitting shawls or cooking kasha. Do you have a girlfriend, young man? What *is* your name?—I'm tired of "young man."

GUARD: Paul L. McBride.

EMMA: May I call you Paul?

GUARD: Okay . . . but don't tell anyone . . .

EMMA: It's our secret. So, Paul, do you have a girlfriend?

GUARD: I guess so.

EMMA: Come, come, Paul, you mustn't be vague on important matters.

GUARD: Her name's Annie. I like her a lot.

EMMA: Do you have sex together?

GUARD: Oh, no!!

EMMA: No, you don't? Or no, you're shocked that I asked?

GUARD: Both.

EMMA: Sex is a wonderful gift, Paul. It's nothing to be ashamed of.

GUARD: Oh, wow, Miss Goldman, no more—please!

EMMA: Modesty's a silly thing, Paul. It stands in the way of honest exchange. You want to please your girlfriend, don't you?

GUARD: I guess so . . . sure . . .

EMMA: You're being vague again. *If* you want to please Annie, you must know certain facts. Foremost, is that women enjoy sex, when encouraged to, at least as much as men. In fact, the sex embrace creates a greater storm in women, is more intense. By "sex," I mean affection, love, and passion all rolled together.

GUARD: It all sounds the same to me.

EMMA: To most men. But they're not the same. Passion is a wild thing, affection much quieter.

GUARD: And love, Miss Goldman? Did you ever find *that*? Pardon me for asking . . .

EMMA *(Somewhat thrown)*: Well, you see, my dear young man—

GUARD: —You did urge me to be frank. And the name is Paul.

EMMA: Yes, Paul . . . you're quite right. . . . But you see . . . those of us who commit our lives to political work pay a terrible price. We find stretches of personal happiness, but the work keeps tearing us away . . .

(Lights begin to fade on the Buford, and Emma, by the end of her speech, is speaking voice-over.)

EMMA: But yes, I've found love at times. And once, with Mr. Berkman, a love that has lasted forever . . . a deep, companionable love. . . . When he was finally released from jail in 1906, I was no longer a young woman. . . . Oh, far from the young woman he'd last seen so many years before . . .

(Her voice fades out, as Berkman's voice becomes more distinct.)

BERKMAN *(Voice-over)*: Can you believe it, dearest girl? In three days I will see you once again. . . . It is your devotion that has kept me alive, made me stick it out. Is it any wonder I call you the Immutable? And now at last the day is here . . .

(Lights up on a railroad platform. Emma is waiting for the train bearing Berkman to come to a stop. She has a bouquet of roses in one hand. Her other hand is around a pillar, holding on to it for dear life. The train stops. Several people get off. Then, Berkman. He has on an ill-fitting suit and an incongruous summer straw hat. He looks bewildered, almost paralyzed. As the crowd clears away, the line of vision to Emma is open. Berkman starts toward her. Emma doesn't move. Her face is terror-stricken. Berkman throws his arms around her. They stand in an embrace, barely moving, saying nothing. Emma brushes the tears from her eyes and silently hands Berkman the roses.)

(Sounds of footsteps, running toward them. A young woman, Alice, appears, her face flushed with excitement.)

ALICE: Oh, thank heaven! I was so afraid I'd missed you.

EMMA *(To Alice)*: Be calm, dear, be calm. . . . Sasha, this is Alice. She works with us on our magazine, *Mother Earth.*

(Berkman mumbles an inaudible greeting.)

ALICE: They're frantic at the reception! They thought maybe something went wrong at the last minute.

BERKMAN *(Frightened)*: Reception?

EMMA *(Soothingly)*: Only a few friends, dear. At my apartment. They insisted they had to welcome you.

ALICE: Oh, Mr. Berkman. It's such an honor. . . . You and Johann Most have always been—

EMMA *(Interrupting)*: —Alice dear, please, be calm . . .

BERKMAN *(Almost somnambulant)*: Most is dead. Most is dead.

EMMA: You know, then?

BERKMAN: They told me you spoke at the memorial meeting.

EMMA: Yes, dear. I felt I owed it to the early years.

BERKMAN *(Quietly)*: Yes, the early years . . . the early years . . . *(To Alice)* Why are you staring at me?

ALICE: It's only that it's early in the season for a boater, Mr. Berkman. Oh, they're very fashionable, they really are. But in February a derby, a nice dark derby, might be better. Can I take your hat?

BERKMAN: No!

EMMA: It might be more comfortable, dear.

BERKMAN: My head. They shaved my head. At the last minute, they shaved my head.

(He looks as if he might break down, but manages to control himself.)

BERKMAN: Two hundred prisoners asked the warden if I could pass along the cell block to say goodbye. He said no. Then they shaved my head.

(Again he looks as if he might cry. Emma puts her arm around him and the two of them walk into Emma's apartment. Berkman rubs his hands along the wallpaper, caressing it.)

BERKMAN: So soft . . . so soft . . .

EMMA: Come sit down, dear.

(Berkman slowly goes over to her on the couch.)

BERKMAN: All those others, I hardly knew a face. And Fedya? Where is Fedya?

EMMA: He'll be here, dear. Fedya illustrates for a big magazine now. He never turned his back, dear. But his life is different now . . .

BERKMAN: The new ones talk so much.

EMMA: They were excited. They worked so hard raising the five hundred dollars for you. They said they *had* to present it on your first day.

BERKMAN: . . . I can't talk . . . yet. All those left behind in prison . . . they wouldn't let me say goodbye, Emma . . . no goodbyes . . . no goodbyes.

(He breaks down in fierce sobs, burying his head in Emma's lap. Blackout. Lights back up on Emma's apartment several days later. She, Alice, and one or two other helpers are working on the magazine. Various layouts are on the floor. Berkman is slumped on the couch, taking no part.)

EMMA *(To Berkman, holding a mock-up of the cover)*: The new issue of *Mother Earth*—what do you think, Sasha? Does the cover catch the eye?

BERKMAN *(Perfunctory)*: Yes. Are there more blintzes? The meat ones, the ones with meat?

EMMA: Dearest, you ate two dozen at breakfast!

BERKMAN: They're to eat! If you didn't want me to eat them, why did you cook them?

(Emma quickly puts down her work.)

EMMA: I'll cook more. I've got batter for a hundred.

BERKMAN *(Jumping up)*: Don't mother me. I'm not a sick child. *(Pause)* This is absurd. You have important work to do. Or so you seem to believe. *(Starts to leave)*

EMMA: Sasha, you know how much the magazine means to—

BERKMAN: —words, words! What have they to do with revolution? Another little essay on Ibsen maybe? Soon the society ladies will give teas for you, and you can shock them with your "advanced ideas."

EMMA *(Blowing up)*: Sasha, you're being impossible! And I'm sick of it! No one's good enough, perfect enough, pure enough! Ever since your release, all I've heard is what's *wrong*: with me, with our comrades, with the movement . . . *(Suddenly contrite, she moves toward Berkman)* Oh, please, Sasha dear, don't let's quarrel. No one knows any more what to do. We do what we can.

(Berkman roughly pushes her away and starts towards the door.)

BERKMAN: Do nothing. For *you* that would be a desirable change!

(Berkman exits and stage revolves to another area, representing a bar. Two prostitutes, one middle-aged, one young, are at Berkman's table. All three are drunk.)

OLDER PROSTITUTE *(As she pokes Berkman)*: Now listen, you, she wrote them poems herself. Let's have a little respect, eh? *(To younger prostitute)* Read 'im the other one, dear. *(Pokes Berkman again)* Ah, here's the one; brings tears to me eyes every time.

YOUNGER PROSTITUTE *(To Berkman, timidly)*: You sure you like poetry?

BERKMAN: I don't *care!* Just leave me, leave me alone.

OLDER PROSTITUTE: *I* like poetry! *Read!*

YOUNGER PROSTITUTE:

Mother dear, the days were young
When posies in our garden hung.
Upon your lap my golden head I laid,
With pure and happy heart I prayed.

(Berkman staggers away. As stage revolves, he collapses on a cot in a filthy hotel room. Repeated knocking at the door.)

VOICE: Mister? Hey—mister?!

BERKMAN *(Weakly)*: Yes.

VOICE: You all right in there?

BERKMAN: Yes.

VOICE: You ain't been out of the room in three days.

BERKMAN: . . . Twenty-two years . . .

VOICE: What say?

(Berkman doesn't answer.)

VOICE *(Receding)*: Well, you got to Wednesday to rot. Rent's due noon Wednesday.

(As lights fade on Berkman, they come up in Emma's apartment. She's arguing with Alice.)

EMMA: I know I promised to speak two weeks ago! Get someone else. Get anyone.

ALICE: It's you they want to hear.

EMMA: Well, they can't! I'm tired of all the words, tired of them!

ALICE *(Comforting her)*: He'll come back, Emma. I know he will.

EMMA *(Quietly)*: Why would he? Why stand by the wreckage of a life?

ALICE: But he's still a young man! Barely in his forties.

EMMA: I meant *my* life.

(Berkman, haggard, suddenly appears in doorway. Emma rushes over to him and holds him in an embrace. She starts to cry.)

EMMA *(Over and over)*: Oh, my dear . . . oh, my dear . . .

(Blackout. Lights back up on Emma's apartment. Berkman is in bed. He opens his eyes. Emma's figure appears over him.)

EMMA: Awake, dearest?

BERKMAN: Yes. When did I come here?

EMMA: Two days ago. You've been very ill.

BERKMAN: Where was I before?

EMMA *(Stammering)*: You . . . you were . . . absent. *(Turning toward door)* One minute, dear, the soup is here.

(At the door Alice hands Emma a large bowl of soup. Emma suddenly stops her. Alice looks at her quizzically.)

ALICE: Is something wrong?

EMMA: *You* take the soup to him. You take it. Yes, yes—you.

ALICE: I don't understand, Emma.

EMMA *(Almost to herself)*: The years between—he's never had them. He needs . . . he needs to be twenty-one again.

ALICE: I love you, Emma . . .

(Alice disappears through the bedroom door with the soup. The lights isolate Emma outside the door.)

EMMA *(Barely audible)*: Sachs's cafe. I wonder what has happened to Sachs's cafe . . .

(She puts her head in her hands and starts to cry.)

END OF ACT TWO

ACT THREE

(Emma's apartment, Berkman's bedside. He's talking to Fedya.)

FEDYA: . . . We can only try for a little more harmony, a few more possibilities . . .

BERKMAN: But everything is so different from what I remembered, Fedya. Our comrades, the movement—it's not as it was.

FEDYA: I know what you miss, dear Sasha: the old sense that we were living on the very threshold of revolution. That *tomorrow* the world would be new. I miss it too.

BERKMAN: Everything is strange. Everyone talks so much.

FEDYA: Be patient. You'll see that only the form has changed. Our entry into the war has reawakened radicals everywhere. *(Laughing)* Even *I* am getting active again!

(Emma enters the room.)

EMMA: Well, look at you two—it's like old times.

BERKMAN: Would that it were.

FEDYA: It's getting late. Emma and I must be off to the meeting.

BERKMAN: What meeting?

FEDYA: About the Criminal Anarchy Law. Anyone opposing the "patriotic struggle" against Germany will be deported.

EMMA: President Wilson equates dissent with communism.

BERKMAN: I think I'd—I'd like to come along.

(Emma moves toward him eagerly.)

EMMA: Oh, Sasha, how wonderful—!

BERKMAN: Ask Alice if she can find my boater, will you? *(Feels the top of his head)* Maybe I won't need it. My hair's grown in a little.

(Stage revolves. Emma is on a lecture platform, concluding her remarks. Berkman and Alice are sitting in the front row of the auditorium, holding hands. Fedya is also there.)

EMMA: . . . For those among you who reject the business of killing they call war, let me say that I will plead your cause and stand by you anywhere. *(Applause)* Yes, in refusing the draft, you'll be breaking the law. But that is often the only way to bring about change. George Washington broke the law to set this country free. William Lloyd Garrison broke the law to challenge the crime of slavery. *(Loud applause)* But today you need to hear not from me, but from a man who's paid in full for his rejection of the state and its authority, a man who now joins us in the No-Conscription League. I give you one of anarchism's true heroes: Alexander Berkman.

(Berkman rises and comes up on the platform to loud applause. Emma immediately steps down.)

BERKMAN *(Hesitantly)*: As you know, I am only recently out of prison. . . . I have not yet talked in public. . . . This is the first time . . .

(Encouraging applause from the audience.)

BERKMAN: Prison is like the army. Both are designed to destroy human feeling . . . but somehow feeling survives . . .

(He suddenly stops, looks panicky. He turns to Emma. She rushes up to stand by him on the platform. Berkman continues.)

BERKMAN: . . . Many of our socialist comrades say we must join the Allies. But what are they allied for? To preserve the old world, a world that serves the few at the expense of the many. In this the Allies are no different from the Prussians they oppose. The international workers' movement will be destroyed if the workers of any country put nationalistic fervor above the interests of their class. *(Suddenly stops)* I think . . . I think that's all I have to say for now.

(Cheers from the audience. Emma embraces Berkman. They move down to another area representing the office of Mother Earth. Alice and several friends are busy with the magazine—typing, preparing layouts, etc. Emma and Berkman join them. Suddenly there's the sound of heavy stomping of feet on the stairway. Four men burst into the office, led by a federal marshal.)

MARSHAL: Emma Goldman! Alexander Berkman! You're under arrest.

EMMA: And who are you?

MARSHAL: United States Marshal Thomas D. McFadden.

EMMA: I'd like to see your warrant.

(McFadden holds out a copy of Mother Earth.*)*

MARSHAL: Are you the author of the no-conscription article published in this magazine?

EMMA: Obviously, since my name is signed to it. Now where is your warrant!

MARSHAL: I represent the United States government.

(He signals to his men to seize Emma and Berkman. Others start ransacking the desks and overturning the press.)

MARSHAL: Get everything: subscription lists, files, manuscripts— everything.

EMMA *(Pointing to books on shelves)*: You'll find the most treasonable matter, Mr. McFadden, on those shelves. The volumes by Tolstoy, Thoreau, and George Bernard Shaw.

MARSHAL: Are they employees of your press?

EMMA *(Amused)*: Inspirers, perhaps. Not employees.

MARSHAL *(To policemen)*: Seize those books!

EMMA: I do hope you'll put us all on trial together. I've always wanted to meet Mr. Shaw.

MARSHAL: You're remanded to the Tombs. Your trial will be in five days.

(As Emma and Berkman are taken off in handcuffs, the lights change and the stage becomes a courtroom, Judge Mayer presiding. Emma and Berkman stand before the bench.)

BERKMAN: As it is the evident intention of the government to turn this proceeding into a persecution, we will take no part in it.

JUDGE MAYER: The court will appoint counsel to defend you.

EMMA: We want no counsel. We each wish to deliver a brief statement. Beyond that, we are indifferent. There is no possibility of justice from these proceedings.

JUDGE MAYER: You may deliver *brief* statements.

BERKMAN *(Reading)*: This is not a hearing. It is an inquisition into our ideas, and a denial of our right to express them. It is an invasion of private conscience. I emphatically refuse to participate in it.

JUDGE MAYER: Miss Goldman.

EMMA: I will be *almost* as brief, your honor.

JUDGE MAYER: I will give you no other choice, Miss Goldman.

EMMA *(She speaks extemporaneously)*: The real and terrible menace of these proceedings is that they're designed to exile those of us who dare to question things as they are. With all the intensity of my being, I—

JUDGE MAYER *(Interrupting)*: —You are being neither brief nor cogent, Miss Goldman. Your time is up.

(Lights change and fade as Judge Mayer pronounces sentence.)

JUDGE MAYER: The jury has found you guilty. Do the defendants have anything to say as to why sentence should not be imposed?

EMMA: We stand convicted of one crime only: that we are anarchists, that we have a dream of universal brotherhood, that we refuse to become reconciled to the amount of wretchedness in the world.

(Lights are out.)

JUDGE MAYER *(Voice-over)*: There is no place in our country for those who would nullify our laws. You are to be immediately deported from the country. The court stands adjourned.

(Berkman and Emma put on coats and hats, grab suitcases, and cross to a ramp representing the gangplank of the Buford, *tied up in port awaiting debarkation. Alice approaches, and Berkman and Alice embrace.)*

ALICE: Somehow, dear . . . I'll join you somehow . . .

BERKMAN: . . . Precious Alice . . . it won't be long, dear. . . . It can't be long . . .

(Helena rushes up to embrace Emma.)

EMMA: Oh, my dearest, dearest sister . . . the moment has finally come . . .

HELENA: I can't bear to say goodbye. . . . When will I ever see you again?

EMMA: Hush, now, hush. We're the same flesh and blood. We will always be together. And who knows?—President Wilson may beg us to return. He can't play the patriot if he has no traitors underfoot. Dearest Helena, I'm sorry to have brought so much trouble to you and your family over the years . . .

HELENA: What?! You're our greatest treasure, our pride and joy. We boast of you to everyone . . . *(She starts to cry)* Oh, how I'll miss you, dear sister. . . . Please, please return to us soon . . . *(She hurries off)*

EMMA *(Calling after her)*: . . . Goodbye, dear Helena . . . it won't be long . . . it won't be long . . .

(A commotion at the foot of the gangplank as a group of reporters surround Emma and Berkman.)

FIRST REPORTER: Your allegiance *is* with the Bolsheviks, isn't it, Miss Goldman?

EMMA: I don't recognize the swollen pride of *any* nation.

SECOND REPORTER: Why do you hate America?

EMMA: You sound like a fool, sir. I'll never stop loving America. Or longing for its possibilities.

FIRST REPORTER: You've railed against the United States for twenty-five years!

EMMA: No, against the American government. The American *people* have a daring and inventive spirit. For the moment, it's harnessed to an immature brain, devoid of class consciousness. Yet one day the compassionate American soul will fulfill itself.

SECOND REPORTER: And you, Mr. Berkman? If the rumors are true, you're headed for Russia. Is it going to be any better there?

BERKMAN: We're being deported from America as felons. We'll be welcomed in Russia as comrades. How can that *not* be better?

(Blackout.)

EMMA *(Voice-over)*: January 20, 1919. Dearest Helena: At last—our final night on board the *Buford*! We debark tomorrow at a Finnish port, where we'll be given three days' rations and speeded in locked trains to the Russian border. So after all these years, I'm to behold again *Matushka Russiya*, and my heart starts to pound. Once more home; once more an émigré without a home. . . . Sasha says we will behold Russia freed at last from her ancient master—the *dubinushka,* the wretched peasants of the earth, raised from the dust, the worker in a world of his own creating. Ah, how I hope, my dear Helena, how I hope. . . .

(Lights up on the gangplank as the prisoners start to debark. The guard calls out to Emma as she descends.)

GUARD: Miss Goldman! Miss Goldman!

(Emma turns her head and sees him.)

EMMA: Ah, my dear comrade!

GUARD *(Laughing)*: Shush!—lower your voice!

EMMA: You're a very nice lad, Paul, and I thank you for all the good company during the trip!

GUARD: Can I ask you one last question?

EMMA: Of course you can!

GUARD: Were you ever tempted to steal my gun?

EMMA: What would I have done with it? Oh, I know—shoot myself!

GUARD: Not you. Never. Nor anybody else I think . . .

EMMA: Please get out of the army soon, Paul—and stay out!

GUARD: You're a very nice lady!

EMMA: Try to persuade President Wilson of that.

GUARD: I *will*!

EMMA: Say hello to Annie for me. Good luck, my boy!

(Emma turns back and descends platform.)

GUARD *(Calling after her)*: And good luck to you . . .

(Cross-fade as Emma and Berkman arrive in Moscow and drop their bags. Bill Shatov is already in their apartment.)

EMMA: The receptions, Bill, we've been overwhelmed with receptions! How good to see you, my old friend—it's a breath of America!

SHATOV: Now, now, no looking back!

BERKMAN: It's been inspiring beyond words, Bill! We're eager to see more, to learn more.

EMMA: The border, though, was a nightmare, Bill. Every three seconds soldiers were shining flashlights in our faces, demanding pass cards. Oh, and some of the people along the road, Bill! So pale-faced and sad! Why? Why should that be? The people *made* the revolution, the people should surely be joyful that—

SHATOV *(Interrupting; affectionate)*: —Emma, *Emma*! I see you haven't changed a bit. Still the same old persistent pest!

BERKMAN *(To Shatov)*: Save your breath. We've been through it a dozen times. Emma is unable to grasp that revolution in theory is not the same as revolution in practice.

SHATOV: Emma, you've just arrived! Be patient. For *once* in your life, be patient. Russia is ringed with enemies. You have no idea of conditions: the Allied blockade, the intervention, the counterrevolutionary plotters. You can't create a new world in a day.

EMMA: But you can destroy one. I've even heard of a secret police, the Cheka—that *can't* be true, Bill, can it?

SHATOV *(Less affectionate)*: —Emma, I'm going to be stern with you. You anarchists have always been the romantics of revolution. You've never understood the fearful cost it would entail, the fierce determination of its enemies to destroy it. You cannot fight fire and sword with an ideal.

EMMA: My dear Bill, you cannot fight it any other way—not, that is, without losing the ideal.

BERKMAN *(Furious)*: I won't listen to another word! You've been on Russian soil a matter of days, and already, in your imperious way, you've mapped the continent! Our job is to make ourselves useful, not to throw up petty objections at every turn! I won't hear any more of it—is that clear?

SHATOV: Sasha's right, Emma. The baby you've labored all your life to bring to birth has at last been born. Don't berate it for not yet speaking perfect sentences.

EMMA *(Quietly)*: You must be right. So many good people are saying the same . . . I must work. I must work hard. And wait . . .
(Scene shifts as Emma crosses to the office of the Commissioner of Education, Lunacharsky.)

LUNACHARSKY: You can be an invaluable help, coming as you do from the United States. We are introducing the American system of education throughout Soviet Russia.

EMMA *(Astonished)*: If I may, Comrade Lunacharsky, that system is considered outmoded. John Dewey, the finest pedagogical mind in America, has put it under indictment as far too rigid and authoritarian. Surely a discredited system should not serve as a model for revolutionary Russia!

LUNACHARSKY: Many of Russia's children are defectives, illiterate and depraved—thanks to centuries of mistreatment. The only hope of educating them is through the strictest discipline.

EMMA *(Dismayed)*: But, comrade, the newest educational models clearly show that—

LUNACHARSKY *(Interrupting; dismissive)*: —Yes, of course, we must hear the new ideas, too. A conference, perhaps. A special conference. We will notify you.

(He abruptly exits. Cross-fade as Emma is joined by a Soviet doctor.)

DOCTOR: . . . The wretched conditions here—in all the hospitals—is overwhelming. . . . The dearth of medical supplies, widespread disease and malnutrition, the lack of trained staff . . . The task is colossal.

EMMA: I'm a trained nurse, Dr. Karsky. I'm sure I can be of help. I'll certainly do my utmost.

DOCTOR: I expect nothing less from a comrade. I know of your great work in the communist movement in America.

EMMA: The anarchist movement.

DOCTOR: Oh, yes. But there's really no difference.

EMMA: There's every difference. State coercion under communism has no relationship to the voluntary cooperation we anarchists employ. But none of that will affect my usefulness as a nurse.

DOCTOR *(Coldly)*: In Soviet Russia everyone who wants to work is welcome. So long as he is a true revolutionist.

EMMA: We anarchists defend the revolution. What we don't defend is the dictatorship of the state.

DOCTOR: The state, my dear Miss Goldman, is all that stands between us and utter chaos. *(He turns to leave)* Your application will have to go through channels. It may take several months.

EMMA: But you just said the need was urgent!

DOCTOR: We will contact you. *(He exits)*

(Cross-fade as Emma crosses to the office of Zinoviev, head of the Third International.)

EMMA: . . . But why, Comrade Zinoviev, must so many starve?

ZINOVIEV: Hunger is due to the Allied blockade.

EMMA: Must the city freeze, too? We're surrounded by woodland. If allowed, people could simply go out with ax and rope and haul enough wood home to keep warm.

ZINOVIEV: Which would destroy revolutionary discipline. Priorities, Miss Goodman! Yours seem decidedly out of order.

EMMA: But, comrade!—thousands are dying. The city's population has fallen drastically.

ZINOVIEV: You seem to think that's our fault! Take your complaints to the Allies who blockade our ports, and to the enemies trying to destroy us from within.

(He exits angrily. Cross-fade as Emma joins Berkman in their room.)

EMMA: . . . The persecution and suffering are everywhere! And the cure they offer is *more* bureaucracy and centralization, more suppression of dissent! The dungeons of Taganka prison filled with our anarchist comrades! The revolution's been betrayed, Sasha! Why won't you see it?!

BERKMAN: Your standard is the fate of individuals. You can't measure a gigantic upheaval by a few specks of dust.

EMMA: Abstract rubbish! To say that individual lives don't matter is to betray anarchist ethics!

BERKMAN: Revolution in a primitive country with an ignorant populace cannot survive without drastic measures.

EMMA: *Against* the people?

BERKMAN: You must distinguish between the Revolution and the regime. Currently they're worlds apart, but in time, they—

EMMA: —the regime is *killing* the Revolution. If there's any chance of saving it, we must denounce those who have captured and misdirected it.

BERKMAN: We cannot give fuel to the Revolution's enemies by denouncing the regime.

EMMA: What are you saying, Sasha?! That I should keep silent about the horrors I see everywhere?

BERKMAN: *Yes*, that's what I'm saying. In speaking out you'll succeed in calling attention to yourself—which you've never minded—but at the expense of giving ammunition to reactionaries everywhere.

EMMA: If I worried how reactionaries might use my words, I'd *always* be silent. . . . I'll never hold my tongue. Sew up your own, if you like.

BERKMAN: The older you get, the more impossible you are!

EMMA: *Your* character hasn't exactly improved with age! Everything you do is premeditated, narrow, unforgiving. You've become a *prig*. You worry only about what the comrades might say about you! *(They glare in fury at each other. Emma relents first)* Oh, Sasha! . . . The times are so terrible . . . our nerves are shattered. . . . We must try and be kinder to each other . . .

BERKMAN: Yes . . . the Revolution will find its way back . . . and we will work for it together . . .

EMMA *(Suddenly struck with an idea)*: Balabanoff! *She* will tell us the truth! We must see Balabanoff. Will you come with me?

BERKMAN *(Nervously)*: Balabanoff is out of favor. . . . She's been removed from her position as—

EMMA: —*Exactly*! She's seen the regime from the inside—and has cleared her skirts!

BERKMAN: Nonsense—she was booted! Go see her if you like. She'll give you more ammunition for your prejudices.

(He turns to leave, as Emma crosses over to another apartment where a frail, middle-aged woman with large, sad eyes enters, carrying a tea tray.)

EMMA: Please, Miss Balabanoff, let me help.

BALABANOFF: You must call me Angelica. I'm sorry to be unwell for your visit. Why did you wait so long before coming? You should have let me know at once.

EMMA: We know how busy you are.

BALABANOFF: Was. Now that I'm no longer secretary of the International, I have considerable time on my hands. *(Sighs; sadly)* There's nothing like living in behalf of a great cause, eh? Without it, life seems empty . . .

EMMA: I've tried to find useful work, Angelica. I've gone everywhere. The interviews seem to start well, but then end badly. I'm at my wit's end . . .

BALABANOFF: Have some tea, dear. . . . Eat something. . . . Food is hard to come by these days . . .

EMMA: We've been in Russia two months and I understand less of what's going on than when I arrived. Sasha says I'm a malcontent by nature . . .

BALABANOFF: And so you should be. How else does the world get changed? . . . This little orange cake is especially delicious. Friends bring me these delicacies. I feel so guilty when people have no bread, but nothing else stays in my stomach.

EMMA: We've heard it was your opposition to centralization that led to your removal.

BALABANOFF: Even a rumor is occasionally true.

EMMA: Then you agree with me, Angelica! The revolution *has* been betrayed!

BALABANOFF: Now, now, dear! *(Evasive)* Aren't you being a bit hasty? *(Emma suddenly starts to weep)*

BALABANOFF: My dearest Emma, what did I say? Are you ill, dear? Is it something I said? *(She embraces Emma)*

EMMA: No, no. . . . It's just that . . . we've had so many shocks, Angelica . . . I find everything so hard to understand, so different from what I—

BALABANOFF *(Gently chiding)*: —oh, Emma, Emma . . . what is there to understand? You're an *anarchist*, and Lenin has declared anarchism "infantile leftism." People are afraid to be associated with you!

EMMA: Is it true that many anarchists are in prison?

BALABANOFF: Yes. I'm afraid it is. You must understand, dear Emma, that I am not an anarchist. Your brave new world free of rulers is admirable. But it can't come into being without an intermediate stage—the dictatorship of the proletariat—just as Marx said. And to elevate the proletariat to power, the Party and the State are essential instruments.

EMMA: But a state controlled by workers would also turn into a tyranny. It's the *nature* of the state, regardless of who controls it.

BALABANOFF: Emma, Emma, in a time of turmoil, we must curb our dogmatism, must try to bend a little.

EMMA: A little?! I've twisted myself into knots accommodating the horrors I see around me.

BALABANOFF: Perhaps you have too much faith, my dear, in the innate goodness of people. Most Americans do. But such faith—you'll pardon me—is naive, and you must wean yourself from it. Otherwise your perspective will be ruled—and ruined—by sentimentality. Am I speaking too frankly?

EMMA: Of course not . . .

BALABANOFF: The late war, my dear, was for me the great disillusion. I expected working people everywhere would refuse to fight. But the workers rushed to enlist, rushed to put the interests of their nation above the interest of their class. It made me less sure of everything.

EMMA *(Hesitant)*: Are you . . . are you personally safe, Angelica? Is it all right to ask?

BALABANOFF: Dear Emma, you must not fear for me. I'm not in personal danger. Lenin knows that I remain loyal to the revolution. No, it's your anarchist comrades we must fear for . . .

EMMA: Who can believe it?—anarchists imprisoned by a *revolutionary government*!

BALABANOFF: Their fate rests in the hands of one man—Lenin.

EMMA: Lenin! He's become the Revolution's chief enemy! Think of it—the Revolution destroyed by the man who's been seen as its prophet and embodiment.

BALABANOFF *(Quiet; sad)*: Perhaps the Revolution's chief enemy is life itself—the rock that breaks the finest spirits, the best intentions.

EMMA *(Agitated)*: "Life"? What is "life" other than the energy people im-part to it? I cannot believe, I *will* not believe, that some mysterious power can turn all effort to naught!

(Pause.)

BALABANOFF *(Quietly)*: You must meet with Lenin himself. *He* knows how to meet life's demands in full. I am still able to arrange an interview.

EMMA: What?—meet with Lenin?! Angelica, am I up to it? Will my courage hold?

BALABANOFF: Lenin won't consider you a personal threat. He won't grant you that importance. Under those conditions, you'll find him most charming.

EMMA: I must have Sasha with me.

BALABANOFF *(Dubious)*: I believe you might hold your own with Lenin—though less effectively, perhaps, if your dearest comrade is agreeing with him.

EMMA: I don't know what Sasha will say. He's in an awful state. Not wanting to believe what he knows is true. He's a stubborn man—or he would never have survived prison.

BALABANOFF: As you like, my dear. I will arrange the interview.

(Cross-fade. Balabanoff exits. Emma and Berkman are joined by an armed guard. He motions them ahead. Echoing sounds of locks and keys. A soldier shouts the names "Tovarichy Goldman and Berkman." Another guard appears and leads them to a massive door that opens from within. Lenin is seated behind a large desk. He stands as Emma and Berkman enter. Lenin holds a brochure in his hand.)

LENIN: Ah, Comrades Goldman and Berkman. *(Waving the pamphlet)* Angelica sent me a transcript of your American trial. You used your opportunity well.

EMMA AND BERKMAN: Thank you.

LENIN: It's worth going to prison if the courts can be successfully turned into a forum. But, please, do be seated.

EMMA: Thank you, comrade.

BERKMAN: We never expected the privilege of a private audience with you.

LENIN: And why not? Two such distinguished fighters for freedom!

You, Berkman—what a price you've paid! I know all about your
years in prison.

BERKMAN *(Flattered, pleased)*: You're very kind, comrade. Your praise
means a great deal.

LENIN *(Slyly)*: Perhaps you should have remained in America. Fighters
of your caliber are badly needed there.

EMMA *(Annoyed)*: The choice wasn't ours. We were deported.

LENIN *(Picking up on her annoyance; sardonic)*: You're most welcome in
the Soviet Union. Now then. There's much I want to hear about
conditions in America. When can we expect the social revolution
there? In the near future?

(Emma and Berkman exchange a look of astonishment.)

EMMA: At the moment, the situation in America isn't promising. Less
promising, say, than twenty years ago. The war destroyed much of
the radical movement in the United States—through repression
and cooptation.

BERKMAN: American workers lack social consciousness. They're apa-
thetic about their own plight.

LENIN: A temporary situation. Capitalism cannot survive for long.
What has begun in Russia will spread around the globe. Now: what
do you wish from me? Why have you come?

BERKMAN *(Flustered)*: We . . . we asked for this interview, comrade,
because we're . . . we're troubled about . . . certain matters . . .

LENIN: *What* matters?

EMMA: When we visited the great flour mill in Petrograd, several
workers told us that they were "virtual prisoners." "They even
search us when we leave the mill at night," they said.

LENIN: True. Because they've been stealing flour.

EMMA: They insist the commissars are stealing—and blaming them.

LENIN: They'll say anything to avoid responsibility. *(Turning to Berkman)* What else is "troubling" you, as you put it?

EMMA: Wherever we traveled, comrade, the suffering among the
peasants was—

LENIN *(Interrupting)*: —I was addressing Mr. Berkman.

BERKMAN *(Flustered)*: . . . Yes, the . . . the peasants, comrade . . . their dislocation . . . their—

LENIN *(Interrupting)*: —the Russian peasantry is backward and brutal, steeped in centuries of ignorance. They care for nothing but their plot of land and their religious icons.

EMMA: Excuse me, comrade, but the hunger, the outright starvation that we saw everywhere—

LENIN: —in a time of peril, the care and feeding of the masses cannot be the Revolution's top priority. *Survival* is.

EMMA: Survival of the regime? Or of the people?

LENIN: Take care, Miss Goldman. You grow impertinent.

EMMA: Shouldn't the survival of the masses *always* be the Revolution's top priority?

LENIN *(Icy)*: Such "humanitarian" sentiments doubtless win you much applause. *True* revolutionaries, of course, are not interested in applause.

EMMA: The Russian masses, who made the Revolution—

LENIN: —a few *individuals* made the Revolution. Ordinary workingmen are incapable of running political and economic affairs. That is the job of the Communist Party.

BERKMAN: Is there not a danger, comrade, that instead of the hoped-for dictatorship of the proletariat, we could get the dictatorship of the Communist Party *over* the proletariat?

LENIN: You disappoint me, Berkman. *(Cold)* What is the next item on your agenda?

BERKMAN: We . . . we're very concerned about what is happening to our anarchist comrades . . .

LENIN: Many anarchists hold important positions with us. Everything is open to them if they are willing to cooperate.

BERKMAN: I'm pleased to hear that, comrade. But why then are—

EMMA *(Interrupting)*: —why then are so many anarchists in prison? Some have been hunted down—and killed.

(Berkman audibly gasps. Lenin is unruffled.)

BERKMAN: Emma, *please!*

LENIN *(To Emma)*: You interrupted Comrade Berkman.

EMMA: We often complete each other's thoughts. *(Almost to herself)* Or used to. *(To Lenin)* I assumed you wanted me to speak frankly. Was I mistaken?

LENIN: Frankness never offends me. But ignorance does. We have *bandits* in prison—the followers of Makhno—only bandits.

EMMA: Some of our dearest friends, Aron and Fanya Baron, are being held in Taganka prison. We've *seen* them. Conditions in Taganka are appalling. No exercise or fresh air, lice more plentiful than food. We spent days trying to get a ration of potatoes or a mattress for them. To no avail. Aron and Fanya Baron returned voluntarily to Russia to assist the Revolution. And this is how they are treated.

LENIN: Conditions everywhere are appalling. You've heard, I trust, of the Allied blockade? Of the counterrevolutionary White armies that roam the land?

EMMA: Of course.

LENIN: Excellent! Then your ignorance isn't total.

BERKMAN: If I may say a word, comrade . . . ?

LENIN: If it is not more foolishness. *(To Emma)* You need to regain your revolutionary balance. Find useful work instead of dissipating your energy on trifles.

BERKMAN: We cannot consider the fate of our friends a trifle.

LENIN: I do not know these people. In a revolutionary period, the fate of individuals is not important. *(He turns to leave)* You disappoint me, Berkman. You've spent too much time in Miss Goldman's company. You need further *education*. Perhaps then your views will undergo the needed transformation.

BERKMAN: I do not think so, comrade.

LENIN *(Cold; dismissive)*: As you like. Thank you for your visit. The guards will see you out.

(As lights fade, Emma and Berkman move downstage into a spot. They hold on to each other. Emma starts to cry.)

EMMA: It's as if you wanted a child all your life, and at last, when you'd almost given up hope, it's given to you—only to die in infancy.

BERKMAN: If there was something we could do . . .

EMMA: There's no hope of being heard. We *must* leave Russia, Sashenka. Can you see that now?

BERKMAN: To say that our comrades are bandits—!

EMMA: And it will only get worse. More persecution, more dictator-ship . . . There's no hope of being useful here.

BERKMAN: . . . You're right. . . . I didn't want to see it, but you're right . . .

EMMA: Perhaps at least we can warn our comrades abroad, tell them that the Revolution's been betrayed. Or try to, at any rate . . .

BERKMAN: I'm ready to go, dear . . . *(Lights begin to fade)* Our dream of a rebirth, a liberated humanity—gone, all gone, the dream crushed, the faith broken . . . My heart is like stone . . .

EMMA: Perhaps Angelica is right after all: life destroys even the finest dreams. No—no—she is *not* right. She *must* not be right!

(Lights cross-fade as Emma and Berkman move into a room crowded with people, Emma speaking as she walks.)

EMMA: This is what we have come to England to tell you. The dream has become a nightmare, the Revolution a dictatorship as bad as any in the days of the czar. Terror has silenced the masses and the in-tellectuals alike. Those few who have spoken out have been shot in the cellars of the secret police. Our beloved Fanya Baron, our dear, splendid Fanya, radiant with life and love . . . *(Starts to cry)* existy, they called her, "expropriator." She fought to her last breath. They had to drag her, then carry her to the cellar, where the knights of the Communist state shot her through the head. . . . I make no apology for my tears. They're shed for some of the loveliest spirits the world has ever known . . .

(Tepid, scattered applause. A reception line forms. Each person introduces himself as he approaches Emma. Berkman stands beside her.)

WELLS: H.G. Wells. Revolution in a primitive country with an igno-rant populace cannot survive without drastic measures.

EMMA: *Against* the people?!

WELLS: You exaggerate, Miss Goldman. You've always exaggerated. It is part and parcel of your theatrical temperament. *(Exits)*

ELLIS: Dr. Havelock Ellis. You must understand, Miss Goldman, that social conditions must always reflect what has preceded. If that was cruel—as it was under the czars—then what follows cannot be entirely benign. In any case, Russia must work things out in her own way.

BERKMAN: England has long intervened in other countries—even swallowing them up whole. Why hesitate now?

ELLIS: Swallow Russia? Oh, come now, Mr. Berkman. *(He exits, chuckling)*

BERKMAN: Damn it! They won't pause even for a reply!

EMMA *(Scornful)*: And these are England's leading intellectuals. "Seekers after truth."

RUSSELL: Mr. Bertrand Russell. In listening to your remarks, Miss Goldman, I find myself persuaded *(Pause)*—

EMMA *(Rushing in)*: —you are?! Oh, I'm so glad—

RUSSELL: —persuaded that the anarchist vision of abolishing all government has no chance of taking root in our lifetime . . . or possibly ever. The average person requires authority and rules; they'd be at a loss without them.

EMMA: There is no "average" person. Only average opportunities. Do you really think that Russia's people *accept* Soviet authority? Would *you* "accept" starvation and misery?

RUSSELL: That is not the point. The Soviet Union has ignited a world revolution. When measured against that enormity, small considerations cannot be allowed to weigh in the balance.

EMMA: I don't consider the death of Fanya Baron—and many others—a "small consideration." You never hesitated to use your pen, Mr. Russell, in behalf of the victims of the czar. Why would you choose to be silent now?

RUSSELL *(Curt)*: You already have my answer. I will neither say nor write anything that could jeopardize the ultimate success of Russia's remarkable experiment.

(Russell exits. As the lights dim, the introductory voices become faint and echoey: ". . . Professor Harold Lasky . . . Dr. Thomas A . . .")

(Still in spots: Emma and Berkman move around the stage, stopped at every

*turn by people who stand in their path and turn them away. The sense of
exile, of wandering, of no place to rest.)*

FIRST PERSON: 1921. France. If you'd been less egotistical, you would
have cheerfully done whatever was asked of you, instead of wasting
your energy on complaint and recrimination.

SECOND PERSON: 1923. Spain. Your emphasis on Russia's sins is out of
all proportion to her gains.

THIRD PERSON: 1925. Germany. You have betrayed the international
proletariat and given ammunition to reactionary forces everywhere.

FOURTH PERSON: 1927. Sweden. Out of respect for our past friendship, it is best that we do not see each other again.

VOICE OVER: 1930. Saint-Tropez.

*(Berkman and Emma collapse into faded wicker furniture. He picks up a
large manuscript.)*

BERKMAN: I'd change the line to read this way: "Slavery is slavery. I
care not whether it be called a collective society or a capitalist one.
The only difference is in a change of masters."

EMMA: Yes, Sasha, that's much better. You're the writer. I'd never be
able to complete this without you.

(Berkman motions to the pile of manuscript.)

BERKMAN: I'd like to cut still more of it. A thousand pages! Emma, it's
unwieldy!

EMMA: My life's been that way. So should the book about it. No, old
pal, no more cuts.

BERKMAN: One or two of the love affairs could go.

EMMA: Nonsense! I hope to add a few before the book's in proofs. I'm
only sixty-one, old pal! Now take that young fisherman on the
beach who's been giving me the eye . . .

BERKMAN: He's after your money.

EMMA: He probably does think we're rich. Living here in posh Saint-
Tropez.

BERKMAN: I wish the book wasn't nearly finished. It filled up a lot of
time . . . I think you should call it *Living My Life*. You're one of the
few who's done it, old girl.

EMMA: Stop using the past tense! There's much ahead.

BERKMAN: Emma, my love, we're two homeless old people, living in a cottage with a few loyal friends paying the rent. Life's become a stupid thing . . . no place left to gain a footing, no chance to throw in our lot—

EMMA: —chances are made. With fascism spreading over Europe, two toothless tigers can do a lot of growling.

BERKMAN: No, Nietzsche was right: history is an eternal recurrence. The world learns nothing . . .

EMMA: These *are* the worst of times. But times change.

BERKMAN: Indeed they do. Now the masses are screaming their adoration of Hitler! *Nothing* has come from our years of effort. *Nothing*! We will leave without a trace.

EMMA *(Sternly loving)*: This is pure self-pity, Sasha—quite unlike you, and not at all becoming.

BERKMAN: And you, old girl, are like someone with an incurable disease. You *know* there's no cure, but you keep trying every kind of doctor, every kind of quack!

EMMA: Our work *must* go on!

BERKMAN: *What* work?!

EMMA: —you're as fanatical in your hopelessness as you once were in your optimism. You never could see more than one angle of life at a time.

BERKMAN: And you're clinging to an ideal no one wants or cares about any more. We've lived a long time—but for what? Tell me.

EMMA: For a world with less suffering in it.

BERKMAN *(Sardonic)*: You sound like the young girl I first met at Sachs's café.

EMMA *(Soft)*: That was the start of my life, Sasha. You've been the most important person in it from that moment on. You realize that much, don't you?

BERKMAN: . . . Sachs's is . . . a lost world . . .

EMMA: Our lives will end as they began: fighting.

BERKMAN: Yours, dear Emma, without doubt. I seem to have forgotten the habit.

EMMA *(Concerned)*: Why, we might even tour America again. Dreiser, Mencken—wonderful people are working for our return.

BERKMAN: It's you they want, old girl . . . you . . .

(He goes over and kisses her.)

EMMA: Why does that country keep its grip on my heart?—the land that made me suffer more than any other.

BERKMAN: Because the place is just like you: it believes everything is possible, no odds too great. You're American to the core.

EMMA: Perhaps so . . .

(Berkman sighs deeply and rises.)

BERKMAN: Whereas *I* am irreducibly Russian: the fatalist who knows when to accept . . . defeat . . .

EMMA: What?! You who went to jail to awaken the workers to their plight!

BERKMAN: *Sought* to awaken them. But on and on they still sleep . . . and will, it seems, forever . . . *(He crosses upstage, into the darkness)* Now that the book is finished . . . I feel exhausted . . . utterly exhausted . . . *(He exits)*

EMMA *(Pacing, agitated; aloud, to herself)*: I don't like it . . . I don't like it at all . . .

(The sound of a gunshot rings out. Berkman staggers back into the room. He's shot himself and collapses in a pool of blood. Emma rushes over and takes him in her arms.)

EMMA *(Distraught)*: Sasha . . . Sashenka . . . Oh, no . . . oh, no, dearest. . . .

BERKMAN *(Grim smile)*: I think I've bungled it, old girl . . . bungled it again. . . . Johann Most was right: these Russians can't shoot straight . . .

EMMA: Why have you done such a thing? . . . *(She cradles him in her arms)* Why? . . . Why? . . . Don't you know how much I need you?

BERKMAN: It's time I cleared out, old girl . . . I can't live useless . . . dependent. . . . You still have much to give. . . . Go on, dear old girl . . . go on . . .

(As he dies, lights fade and scene shifts to Emma and Helena walking along the beach. Helena bends down and examines some shells.)

HELENA: Emma——come see!

(Emma joins her.)

HELENA: Have you ever seen so deep a purple?! Like on the Kexholm, near Saint Petersburg.

EMMA: It's lovely, isn't it. Such a beautiful color.

(From across the stage, the figure of a man, Augustin Souchy, appears. He starts to run toward them. Emma and Helena see him coming and exchange an anxious look. He comes up to them, out of breath.)

SOUCHY: Miss Goldman? Is one of you Miss Goldman?

EMMA: Yes, I am.

SOUCHY: Oh, thank heavens! I was so afraid you'd left Saint-Tropez. The people in town said they haven't seen you in weeks.

EMMA: This is my sister, Helena.

(He bows.)

SOUCHY: Yes, of course. Excuse me. I mean, frightening you this way. But I was told to deliver the message personally, and I was so afraid that you'd already gone.

EMMA: Catch your breath.

SOUCHY: Thank you, yes. *(Breathes deeply)* Allow me to introduce myself. I am Augustin Souchy, secretary of the Comité Anarcho-Syndicaliste.

EMMA *(Startled)*: From Barcelona?

SOUCHY: The same.

EMMA *(Embracing him)*: My dear Souchy, what an honor! But I . . . I'm astonished . . . !

SOUCHY: I come bearing an invitation. *(Hands her a letter)* An official invitation.

EMMA *(Near tears)*: My dear Souchy—what in God's name does it say?! I can't be reading letters! I can barely keep my hands steady!

SOUCHY *(Reading)*: "Franco is determined to crush the anarchist communes in Catalonia. We are just as determined to resist. The people have thrown up barricades everywhere. The comrades ask you to come. Ten thousand workers in Barcelona wait to greet you." *(No longer reading)* Durruti himself begged me to say to you: "Emma Goldman, you must come. The ideal you have fought for all your life is here in Catalonia alive—a people without rulers, living in harmony. Come to us. We need you."

(Emma, in tears, embraces him. The three figures hurry off.)

(The narration is split among the entire cast.)

VOICE ONE: Emma Goldman gave the last years of her life to the fight in Spain against Franco.

VOICE TWO: She died in 1940 of a stroke.

VOICE THREE: The United States Immigration and Naturalization Service granted the dead exile reentry into the country; she is buried in Chicago's Waldheim Cemetery, near the graves of her Haymarket heroes.

VOICE FOUR: One day in Spain, Emma was taken high into the Pyrenees to see an anarchist experiment in education.

VOICE FIVE: She was greeted by a large banner which spelled out in bold letters the name of the colony: MON NOU: NEW WORLD.

VOICE SIX: Under it were the words: CHILDREN ARE THE NEW WORLD. AND ALL DREAMERS ARE CHILDREN.

(Stage darkens except for a bright light coming through a ship's porthole. Emma rushes toward it. She is the young woman at the start of the play.)

EMMA: Helena! Helena! I can see it. I can see the American shoreline! Come quick!

(Helena appears in the light.)

EMMA: Dear sister. We're here! We're here! America, at last! Our dream come true!

HELENA *(Looking through the porthole)*: How lovely it looks! How it sparkles in the sun! Did you think it would be so *green*?

EMMA: Oh, yes—everything!

(The two dance and happily embrace as the curtain falls.)

END OF PLAY

Posing Naked

ACT ONE

SCENE 1

(Newton Arvin's apartment on the Smith College campus, Northampton, Massachusetts. An English professor with a national reputation as a literary critic, Arvin is about sixty, articulate and charming, with a subtle, cultivated intelligence. He looks like a clerk, balding and bespectacled, an impression underscored by his sometimes tight, timorous manner. He and his guest, Ed Ford, a brilliant, good-looking young classicist who teaches at the college, have just finished dinner and are chatting over coffee. They are longtime friends and have an affectionate, teasing relationship. Ford deeply admires the older man, even while sometimes disapproving of him. The year is 1960.)

ARVIN *(Laughing)*: I was only a slip of a lad, of course, still in my teens. But Papa took my pro-socialist sympathies seriously enough to stop speaking to me. And when I announced at the dinner table one day that Emma Goldman—whom the government was about to deport—was the greatest living American, Mama stopped speaking to me, too. She later came round, but my father never did. When I graduated *summa* from Harvard, Mother wanted to come to the graduation but Father forbade it.

FORD: Nasty old cuss.

ARVIN: He took to calling me his "misbegotten" son. A disapproval, as you might imagine, more encompassing than my socialism.

FORD: Meaning—?

ARVIN: Meaning just what you think, dear. I was that unspeakable thing: a sissy. And, darling, I *was*. Combined with my oh-so-earnest politics, I was a *most* difficult child.

FORD: Trust you to blame yourself.

ARVIN: I blame "things as they are."Which includes oneself.

FORD: I'm still fond of your "earnest" politics—even if you aren't.

ARVIN *(A little indignant)*: I remain a man of the Left, thank you very much. Though these days I have more respect for "things as they are," for the *difficulty* of change. *(Pause)* How did we slip into this delphic mode?

FORD: Want a "lighthearted" change of pace? I need to appeal to your socialist sympathies yet again.

ARVIN: I know what that means. And it's fine, Eddie. You don't have to be a socialist to lend a friend money. Or to borrow it.

FORD: Thanks, Newton. It *is* embarrassing.

ARVIN: Nonsense. How much do you need?

FORD: Is this the third or fourth time?

ARVIN: I'm not keeping track.

FORD: Then I will.

ARVIN: I have plenty of money for my limited means. *(Getting up to look for his checkbook)*. Five hundred?

FORD: I feel awful.

ARVIN: I can't imagine why. Unless you enjoy feeling awful.

FORD: You're a generous man, Newton.

ARVIN: I'm the good father you never had. We all need one at *some* stage in life.

FORD: Who's providing that service for you?

ARVIN: Smith College, darling! As its *only* National Book Award winner, I can do no wrong. *(Finds his checkbook, writes out check)*

FORD: Have you started the Emerson book yet?

ARVIN: I'm still thinking. Emerson is *the* most complicated figure of the nineteenth century. Every time I think I have his persona fixed, it dissolves before my eyes.

FORD: To me, he's just another complacent patrician. I've never shared your enthusiasm.

ARVIN: Emerson's plentitude is what throws you off. The removed

Olympian, yes. But also the most egalitarian of democrats. Remember, it was Emerson who said that John Brown "would make the gallows as glorious as the Cross."

FORD: While staying safely in his study, protecting that "sovereign self" he was so fond of.

ARVIN: I vow to change your mind. See my biography—in five years or so.

FORD: That long still?

ARVIN: Now, Eddie, don't nag. After all, I spent seven years on Melville. You classicists should talk—one article every five years and you think you're being prolific!

FORD: We don't have your "plentitude" of evidence. *(They laugh. Ford picks up a plain-covered magazine from the top of a pile)* Maybe *(waving the magazine)* I should write an article on Greco-Roman loincloths—as imagined, that is, in 1960 *Physique Pictorials.*

ARVIN: That would do nothing for your career, dear heart. Now put that down till later. *(Taking the magazine from him)* Jerry's coming by to see them, too.

FORD *(Staring at the pile)* Looks like quite a haul this time.

ARVIN: Six *Grecian Guild Pictorials*! And two of them are utterly delicious.

FORD: So you've peeked, you bad boy!

ARVIN: Since *I* run the risk of having them sent through the mails, *I* get to see them first.

FORD: You, who once risked all for the Socialist Revolution!

ARVIN: *(Arch)* Ingrate! You and Jerry ought to be thankful I give you sloppy seconds. Ah, you youngsters—too many other outlets.

FORD: Oh, sure, Newton! Locked here in the woods of Northampton, surrounded by penisless Smith College coeds! Without you—*dear* mentor!—we'd have no fantasy life at all! *(Grabbing back the magazine)* Now for God's sake, let me see it! *(Arvin grabs it back)*

ARVIN: I will not have you masturbating in the living room. You're not *that* good a friend.

(The doorbell rings.)

FORD: Hoorah, Jerry! My loins are about to burst.

(Arvin presses the buzzer, goes to the door.)

ARVIN: And I'm serious about the risk I run having the stuff sent through the mails. Senator McCarthy may have left the scene, but his minions are very much with us. Did you hear about the raid at Wooster College?

FORD: Oh well—that's in Ohio, isn't it?

ARVIN: It's here in Massachusetts—not Ohio—that they've set up the new Bureau of Pornography. You haven't heard of that either, I presume.

FORD: Can't say I have.

ARVIN *(Calling down the stairs)*: My God, Jerry, I can hear you puffing from here. When *will* you give up smoking?

(A female voice, Louise, calls up the stairs.)

LOUISE: It isn't Jerry, it's Louise. And you'd be puffing, too, if you'd just had two orgasms.

(Ford jumps up and starts to hide the pile of magazines.)

ARVIN *(Calling down the stairs)*: Darling, what a surprise! *(Over his shoulder to Ford, amused)* What *are* you doing, Eddie? Louise is an avid fan of *GGP*.

(Louise arrives. She and Arvin kiss hello. She's an attractive, tart, intelligent woman in her mid-forties.)

LOUISE: Oh—Eddie! What a nice surprise.

FORD: Mutual. We were expecting Jerry. You're much prettier.

LOUISE: Jerry would never forgive you. *(She and Eddie embrace)* Am I interrupting dinner?

ARVIN: No, no. We're all finished. *(Arch)* Just chatting away about the usual subjects: art and literature.

LOUISE: Oh, I know, dears, I worry about those things all the time, too. Along with the size of the delivery boy's cock.

FORD: *Which* delivery boy?

LOUISE: Don't turn literal, Eddie. It furrows the brow.

ARVIN: And the two orgasms? Also fantasy, I presume.

LOUISE: Don't you wish, you horny old thing.

ARVIN: *Where* in the barren wilds of Northampton could you have achieved such an unprecedented double?

LOUISE: In my shrink's office.

ARVIN: In the waiting room?

LOUISE: *With* my shrink.

FORD: Very funny.

LOUISE: So much for candor. *Female* sexuality never did much interest you boys.

ARVIN: I thought it was unethical for a shrink to fuck his patients.

LOUISE: *I* initiated the fucking.

ARVIN: Ah, well, then . . .

FORD: And how was he?

LOUISE: A little rushed. The next patient was waiting.

FORD: Tends a large flock, does he? Maybe I should go for a consultation.

LOUISE: He'd never fuck you on a first visit. It took me years.

ARVIN: Oh, my, we're all getting much too brittle.

LOUISE: It's called ironic distancing. An inescapable feature of academic life. It atrophies the feelings, overdevelops the mind. Speaking of which—*(She reaches into her bag)* I'm returning Mr. Truman Capote's *Other Voices, Other Rooms.* Now, Newton, you've done more than any other critic to champion new writers, but the verdict is a decisive *no.* I am not—repeat, *not*—including this powder puff of a book in my course on the American novel. You'll pardon me, dear, but I think what you're up to here is an exercise in nostalgia.

ARVIN: Well, the book *is* dedicated to me. And I do have such fond memories of dear Truman.

FORD: I must say, I could never see the two of you together. Judging from this picture *(Gesturing to jacket photo on* Other Voices*)*, he was just as fatuous a creature then as now.

ARVIN: You're quite wrong. That first summer together at Yaddo fifteen years ago, Truman was all air and loving mischief.

FORD: Pardon me while I squirm.

LOUISE: I can remember when he used to come up to Smith and sit in on your classes.

ARVIN: He called me his "Harvard."

FORD: I'm still squirming.

LOUISE: It was embarrassing then, too. That simpering boy made you look like a child molester.

ARVIN: Truman brought out the child in *me*. He transformed me. I was actually happy. For a while.

LOUISE: Frankly, I was relieved when you finally came to your senses.

FORD: *You* left *him*?! I'd always assumed—

ARVIN: —I couldn't sustain the happiness. Too foreign to me. It's no wonder I had a breakdown.

LOUISE: Truman *was* in love. I'll give him that.

ARVIN: Well, I'm no good at it—not on a daily basis. The only thing I'm good at on a daily basis is work. Everyone needs to accept his fate. Mine is Mr. Emerson.

(The doorbell rings)

ARVIN: This time it has to be Jerry.

(Arvin goes to the door and presses the buzzer. Louise also gets up.)

LOUISE: I'm off.

ARVIN: You just arrived!

LOUISE: Darling, I know when four's a crowd. *(Gesturing to the pile of GGP magazines)* I wouldn't dream of lingering, with such urgent business on the table.

FORD: Actually, we were going to discuss the higher metaphysics. Maybe it's all one and the same.

LOUISE: Mind you, I expect to get a crack at those later. This is the only pro-sex game in town.

(Jerry Norris walks in. He's in his late thirties, owlish, nondescript in looks, somewhat muted and sullen in manner.)

JERRY: Oh—hi, Louise. I didn't expect you.

LOUISE: Don't worry, I'm leaving.

JERRY: Don't rush off on my account.

LOUISE: Oh *this* stuff's much too tame for me. All those silly body-builders in togas and spears. Once women take over, I promise you *real* pornography—mystery and danger, profusely illustrated.

ARVIN: Nothing with teeth, please.

LOUISE: What a limited fantasy life.

(He and Louise embrace affectionately at the door. Goodbyes all around. Louise exits.)

ARVIN: Some dessert, Jerry? I've got some lovely berries.

FORD: So the boys in town say.

JERRY: Just some coffee, thanks. I don't have a lot of time.

FORD *(Teasing)*: Bad news, old boy. *(Gesturing to the pile of magazines)* There's been a ghastly mistake, Jerry. Instead of our beloved *GPP*s, they sent Newton a stack of *Mattachine Reviews*!

ARVIN *(to Eddie)*: Bad boy!

JERRY: What the hell is the *Mattachine Review*?

FORD: It's the organ—pardon the pun—of the homophile movement.

JERRY: And what the hell is that?

FORD *(Fake sigh)*: You are the least political person on the planet, Jerry.

ARVIN: Compared to who? Have you actively enrolled in the Mattachine Society and forgotten to tell me?

FORD: I might yet surprise you.

ARVIN: I devoutly hope *not*.

FORD *(To Jerry)*: I made the mistake of showing Newton a copy of the Mattachine Review. I subscribe.

ARVIN: It's an incredibly dreary publication. Irretrievably earnest and dull. As for the prose *(Wrinkles his nose in mock disgust)*, it's written by people wearing thick woolen gloves.

FORD: They're not aiming at literature. Nobody else is organizing to promote our rights.

ARVIN: I have all the rights I want. To teach. To write. To cultivate my friends. The right to *no longer* try and change the world. *(Picks up a copy of GPP)* The right to share trash pseudo-pornography with my dear ones. Now let's get on with it. Eddie's been frothing at the mouth—that is, until the lust got drowned in political polemics.

JERRY *(Relieved)*: Oh, so these *are* GPPs!

ARVIN: Yes, dear. How naughty of Eddie to have trifled with your libido.

FORD: How naughty of Jerry to have one.

ARVIN: Awright, you two—I'll get the coffee while you youngsters forge ahead.

FORD *(To Jerry)*: In other words, he's already seen them.

ARVIN: And will again. In luxuriant leisure, after you scamps have gone home.

FORD: What would Ralph Waldo say . . . ?

ARVIN *(Affectionately)*: Now *that's* a low blow! I must say, Eddie, you're being uncommonly subversive tonight.

FORD: Subversive, no less! How we all do pick up the cultural lingo.

ARVIN: That's what cultures are designed for, dear: to contain the unruly.

JERRY *(Impatient)*: Could we please start. I do have another appointment to—

ARVIN: —Jerry's frothing at the mouth. You're both much too goal-oriented. It's no wonder Louise deserted.

FORD: Well, it *is* the highlight of the month.

ARVIN: Sad but true. Life in the U.S. of A., 1960.

(As they laugh, Arvin heads toward the kitchen and Ford and Jerry reach for the magazines. Blackout.)

SCENE 2

(Office of the Massachusetts State Police. Officers John Rogers and Brendan Shea, head of the State Bureau on Pornography, are questioning Michael Brown. Rogers and Shea are in their forties, Brown in his late twenties. The questioning has been going on for some time and Brown is badly shaken.)

ROGERS: Let's try it again, Brown. We're not talking about *once*. We're talking about often. You got a problem with your bladder, Brown?

BROWN: No, no . . . of course not.

ROGERS: Didn't think so, a young guy like you.

BROWN: What's the charge? That I take a piss several times a day? That I sometimes piss in a public bathroom? That's what they're there for, right?

SHEA: The men's room in the bus depot isn't an ordinary bathroom.

BROWN: What's that supposta mean?

ROGERS: C'mon, Brown, Northampton's a small town. Most people over age fifteen know about the bus depot. You are over fifteen, right?

BROWN: I'm twenty-seven.

SHEA: Fact: in the garage where you work, the toilet is not broken. Fact: your garage is two and half miles from the bus depot. Fact: right across from your garage is the Sunrise Restaurant, with five working toilets. Fact: on your sixteen visits last month to the bus depot men's room, the *least* amount of time you spent inside was eight minutes. Now unless you've got a *serious* bladder problem, Brown, something else besides a piss was keeping you busy.

(Brown is upset, agitated.)

ROGERS: Why don't you stop your dumb lying and save your ass. We're here to help you, Brown—if you can get that through your head. But before we can do that, *you* have to help *us.*

BROWN: Whaddaya talkin' about, I dunno what you're talkin' about . . .

SHEA: Officer Rogers hasn't filed a complaint on you yet. Isn't that right, Officer Rogers?

ROGERS: That's right. And maybe I won't have to. After all, a man's entitled to take a leak . . .

SHEA: Cooperate with us, Brown, and those two kids of yours won't have anything to be ashamed of. Let me ask you something, Brown.

BROWN: Yes, sir?

SHEA: Do you consider yourself a good American?

BROWN: Of course I do. Yes, sir. Senator McCarthy was one of my heroes.

SHEA: Good. Glad to hear that. *(Pause)*You ever hear of the Mattachine Society?

BROWN: The what society—?

SHEA: It's a secret group of queers, led by a bunch of Communists. They want to destroy the moral fiber of this country, beginning with a national porn ring.

BROWN: What's any of that got to do with me?

MURPHY: You ever seen a magazine called *Grecian Guild Pictorial*?

BROWN: What the hell is that?!

MURPHY: It's put out for the queers. It's got pictures, lots of pictures.

BROWN: Pictures of—what?

ROGERS *(Sarcastic)*: Now what would you guess—huh, Brown? *(Pause)* By God—you got it on the first try! Pictures of *men*, that's what! You've seen it, haven't you.

BROWN: No, I never heard of *Greek* . . . whatever you said . . .

SHEA: Where *have* you seen pictures of guys?

BROWN: Whaddaya mean, what kinda pictures, you mean naked stuff, stuff like that . . . ?

ROGERS: Oh, naked is it? Tell me about that, Brown, about those pictures of naked guys you've seen.

(Brown doesn't respond.)

ROGERS: Cat got your tongue, huh? *(Pause)* I'll bet you didn't know, Brown, that Officer Shea here is head of the new State Bureau of Pornography, now did you know that, Brown?

(Brown doesn't respond.)

ROGERS: Let's go, Brown—wake up!

BROWN *(Frightened)*: All I ever seen was . . . just some pictures of big guys . . . guys with big bodies . . . all dressed up, like they was Roman soldiers, or something' . . .

SHEA: Where did you see these pictures?

BROWN: I don't know, just around.

SHEA: You realize there's a new law in this state, Brown, that makes possession of pornography a felony.

ROGERS: You can get sent away for a long time. Your kids would be grown up next time you got to see them.

BROWN: I don't own no pornography, I just seen these big muscle guys, they weren't naked or nuthin'.

SHEA: Where did you see them? Who showed them to you?

BROWN: A couple of guys passed 'em to me, that's all. I just gave 'em a glance, that's all.

SHEA: Who? What guys?

BROWN: Uh . . . some guy at the college . . . at Smith College . . .

SHEA: You mean a professor?

BROWN: I guess so. I dunno. I guess he could be a professor. He said, "I teach the girls at Smith."

(Shea lets out a sigh of pleasure.)

SHEA: *Now* we're getting somewhere! That's a lot better, Brown.

BROWN: Oh yeah? Great . . . So you'll let me go now?

ROGERS: I think maybe it's going to be okay for you, Brown. . . . All you have to do is tell Officer Shea here a little more about this professor, like how did you come to meet this guy?

BROWN: I dunno. . . . It was a real casual thing, just in passing, along the street.

ROGERS: The street or the bus depot?

BROWN: Somewhere around there . . .

ROGERS: So you struck up this conversation, and then what happened?

BROWN: Oh, it was real casual-like.

ROGERS: Yeah, you said that already.

BROWN: He asked me if I liked "cheesecake," and I said sure, who doesn't. So he took me back to his place and showed me this stuff.

ROGERS: The magazines with Roman soldiers.

BROWN: First some girlie stuff. A lot of girlie stuff . . .

ROGERS: And then the Roman soldiers.

BROWN: Yeah . . . I guess they were soldiers . . .

ROGERS: Was this once or often?

(Brown doesn't respond.)

SHEA *(Losing patience)*: Jesus, this is pulling teeth! *(Barking, to Brown)* If we're going to help you, Brown, you have to come *clean*! You get that?!

BROWN: Yes, sir . . . yes, sir . . .

SHEA *(Calming down)*: Now it sounds to me, Brown, like you've been taken advantage of, corrupted you might say, by one of those fancy-talking, pinko intellectuals. Isn't that right, Brown?

BROWN: Yeah, I guess you could say that . . .

SHEA *(Barking again)*: Then say it! *(Pause, calmer)* He gave you a lot to drink, kept showing you those pictures, took advantage of you, you might say . . .

BROWN: Oh right, yeah! Yeah . . . he did give me a lot to drink . . .

SHEA: Very good, Brown.

ROGERS: Were the pictures of men and women, or just men?

BROWN: After a while, mostly men. Hey—they didn't turn me on or nuthin'. The guys weren't doin' nuthin', just standin' there posing. Like, if they'd been fucking women, I mean, well hell, that woulda got me hard as a rock!

SHEA: What's this professor's name?

BROWN: . . . don't think he ever said . . .

SHEA: Did he or didn't he? Think hard, Brown. This is important.

BROWN: Well, I only seen him a coupla times . . .

ROGERS: Sure, sure, Brown, we'll take your word on that. You seem like an honest guy to us. If you tell us you were just taking a leak at the bus depot, well I'm sure you were just taking a leak. Now see if you can't come up with this professor's name . . .

BROWN: Well, he never told me his name, but—*(Pauses)*

SHEA *(Interrupting angrily)*: —Goddamn it, Brown, don't you understand we can charge you with public lewdness, put you away for ten years if we feel like it?!

BROWN: —But I . . . I did find out his name later. I looked on his mailbox. His name is Newton . . . Newton Arvin. Yeah, I'm certain that was it: Newton Arvin.

SHEA *(To Rogers)*: The name mean anything to you?

ROGERS *(smiling broadly)*: Oh—yea-ah! He's the most famous professor at the college. Its star. The guy's won all kinds of awards.

SHEA: I see. . . . This has been a real help, Brown, a real help. You've done a fine, patriotic thing here today, and in acknowledgement of that, we're going to let this little matter of the bus depot just stay between us.

(Brown jumps up.)

BROWN: You mean I can get out of here, I'm all done?!

ROGERS: That's right, we're going to let you walk out of here, a free man, and we're not going to say anything more about it. But Brown—

BROWN: —Yes sir, yes sir—

ROGERS: Try to remember you're a family man, Brown, a family man and a father. You got important obligations. And from now on you better honor them. You get my meaning?

BROWN: I certainly do, Officer Rogers, I certainly do, I certainly appreciate what you're saying . . .

SHEA: Awright, get outta here.

(Brown scurries to the door.)

BROWN: Yes sir, yes sir . . . sure appreciate this . . .

(He exits.)

ROGERS: Scumbag. The guy's as queer as a three-dollar bill.

SHEA: I've seen worse: queer *and* communist: this guy's just dumb.

ROGERS: Newton Arvin . . . Sounds like we're on to something big . . .

SHEA: We've struck gold, Rogers, pure gold.

ROGERS: You mean I might get my picture in the paper?

SHEA: No question. "PATRIOT POLICE ROUND UP PORNO PERVERT."

ROGERS: No, no—"*PRIZE-WINNING* PORNO PERVERT." You'll be a captain in no time. C'mon—let's go pay the professor a little visit—and save the country.

(Blackout.)

SCENE 3

(Arvin's apartment, the following day. He and Louise are in animated conversation.)

LOUISE: No, I can't do it then. That's the Friday I'll be in New York.

ARVIN: Going to see more bad theater?

LOUISE: I'm going for a medical consultation.

ARVIN: My God, Louise—! Is something wrong?

LOUISE: I'm seriously—

ARVIN *(Overlapping)*: —what, for heaven's sakes—?

LOUISE *(Gesturing at neck and face)*: —I'm seriously thinking of some nips and tucks.

ARVIN: You scared me to death!

LOUISE: I'm desperate! I can hardly work up a masturbation fantasy any more.

ARVIN: Look at *Grecian Guild Pictorials* more regularly.

LOUISE: I'm backwards: I still need the real thing.

ARVIN: Then do what most of the world does: separate sex and intimacy. Love is for friends, lust is for pickups.

LOUISE: Another form of surgery! Besides, women don't have your opportunities. For pickups, that is.

ARVIN: All the more reason to avoid any rush to surgery. Maybe you ought to try a few push-ups before resorting to the knife.

LOUISE: Don't get moralistic. The tendency is already overdeveloped from having to deal with American literature. All that McGuffey Reader stuff disguised as fiction.

ARVIN: Perhaps you should talk over this surgical flight of fantasy with your shrink.

LOUISE: *He's* the one who suggested it!

(As they laugh, the doorbell rings. Arvin gets up to answer it.)

LOUISE: Are you expecting someone?

ARVIN: No, no one. I suppose it could be Eddie. He drops by often. I can't tell you what a comfort he is. It's like having a son.

(Calling down the stairs.)

Is that you Eddie?

VOICE: It's me, Mr. Arvin, it's Michael Brown. You remember me?

(Brown is now at the door.)

ARVIN *(Stunned)*: Why, Michael, I mean. . . . Well, this is a surprise. We were expecting someone else . . .

BROWN: Sorry to barge in like this, but it's important.

ARVIN: Why yes, of course, Michael. Do come in, make yourself comfortable. This is my friend, Louise. Louise, this is Michael— Brown, isn't it?—

BROWN: —that's right. Gee, you remember.

ARVIN: Of course I remember.

LOUISE: How do you do?

BROWN: Pleased to meet you.

ARVIN: Can I get you something to drink, Michael?

BROWN: No. I can't stay but for a coupla minutes. I just need to let you know about somethin' that happened . . .

LOUISE *(Getting up)*: Sounds like my cue. Why am I always leaving this place just as I arrive?

ARVIN: There's no need. *(To Michael)* Louise is one of my oldest friends, Michael. You can say anything you like in front of her. Louise knows all there is to know about me.

LOUISE: Now that I doubt.

BROWN: Sorry, ma'am, no offense, but this is somethin' real, well, personal . . .

LOUISE: I understand . . .

ARVIN *(Insistent)*: Now, Michael. Louise has to go over a lecture with me that she's giving tomorrow and it would not be kindly to turn her out. Speak your mind, my boy. It's quite all right. *(To Louise)* Just to clear the air: Michael and I are occasional bed partners—as if you hadn't guessed.

BROWN *(Deeply offended)*: There's no call to say that. That's private business between you and me.

ARVIN *(Patronizing)*: Oh come, Michael. There's no need to get all huffy. As I said, Louise is a dear, dear friend. And *very* understanding. Why don't you just say what your errand is.

BROWN: I ain't here as an errand boy, Mr. Arvin.

ARVIN: That's not what I meant at all, for heaven's sakes. You're being awfully touchy, Michael.

BROWN: Maybe. That's how I am, I guess.

ARVIN: Now why don't you just sit down and have a nice, friendly drink with us. I'm sure we can clear this up.

BROWN: No, I think maybe I'll just go.

ARVIN: But what is it you wanted to tell me?

BROWN: Nuthin' important. We, uh, got a good secondhand car in the shop today. You said you were lookin' for a good buy on a car. So I thought I should tell ya.

ARVIN *(Puzzled)*: Did I? Well, it's very kind of you to let me know. Perhaps I'll drop by some time this week and have a look at it.

BROWN: Okay, sure. *(He's at the door; to Louise)* Nice meeting you, ma'am.

LOUISE: Sorry you couldn't stay longer.

BROWN: Good night. *(He exits)*

ARVIN: Good night, Michael, I— *(To Louise)* Well, that was abrupt . . .

LOUISE: And rightly. You behaved very badly, Newton.

ARVIN: Did I?

LOUISE: And I thought you were an expert on the working class. You broke at least two cardinal rules: you humiliated his manhood in front of a woman. And you took it on yourself to tell *his* secrets. Very cavalier of you, I must say. You scared that poor boy half to death. And he was rather cute, too.

ARVIN: Goodness, you're probably right. Whatever got into me? . . . I must have been showing off for you, impressing you with my daredeviltry. Appalling. I'll go down to the garage where he works tomorrow and apologize.

LOUISE: I'd wait a few days. Give him a chance to recover.

ARVIN *(Musing)*: I've never said anything to him about being interested in a used car.

LOUISE: Obviously.

ARVIN: I wonder what he really came by for?

LOUISE: Sex, of course. And to see your *fabled* collection of *Grecian Guild Pictorials*.

ARVIN: Maybe, maybe . . . Somehow I think not . . .

LOUISE: Well, try and put it out of your mind for now. I *do* need help with my Emerson lecture.

ARVIN: You can't summarize Emerson in an hour-long lecture.

LOUISE: I can. Because I must.

ARVIN: Emerson and undergraduates are oil and water. Emerson's spirit was large enough to contain opposites. The simplistic undergraduate abhors that sort of ambiguity.

LOUISE: Excellent! That's just what I'll say—leaving out the "simplistic." *("Lecturing")* "Emerson was ambivalent about joining life, yet unwilling to separate from it; indifferent to circumstances, yet centrally absorbed by them." *(Arch)* I'll compare him to you, dear.

ARVIN *(Distracted)*: Don't attempt anything complicated. What could Michael have wanted to tell me?

LOUISE: A passionate declaration of love, no doubt. Seeing me, he fled.

ARVIN: Much more likely, some sort of con job. Needing money to "buy shoes for the baby," or some such.

LOUISE: Have you given him money before?

ARVIN: Goodness, I've only seen him three or four times. The last time was months ago.

LOUISE: Should I ask where you met?

ARVIN: Don't.

LOUISE: Newton, do be a *little* more careful.

ARVIN: Become an entire corpse?

LOUISE: Michael's upset you more than you realize.

ARVIN: Not upset, puzzled.

LOUISE: Have it your way. *(Starts to leave)* Good night, dear . . .

ARVIN: . . . I have this strange sense of unease, no real content to it. Maybe it's the onset of another breakdown . . .

LOUISE *(Horrified)*: Oh, Newton . . . !

ARVIN: I'm joking, of course. I've been feeling just fine lately, give or take the usual low-level anxiety called life . . . No, no, I'm not serious . . . I've been fine for years now, as you well know—
(They embrace at the door.)

LOUISE: Please stay that way. I need you.

BOTH: Good night, dear . . . Good night . . .

(Louise exits. Arvin paces the room morosely, goes to the phone, dials, hangs up. The doorbell rings.)

ARVIN: —Good lord! I suppose Louise forgot something . . . *(He presses the buzzer and goes to the door. Calling out the door)* Is that you, Louise? Hello, hello . . . Louise, is that you? *(Aloud, to himself)* Oh Lord, I wonder if it's Michael again . . . *(Out the door)* Michael, is

that you, Michael? . . . Well, *whoever* you are, will you kindly—
(He's interrupted by the appearance of Officers Rogers and Shea, who stride into his living room)

SHEA: Professor Newton Arvin?

ARVIN: Yes, yes . . . What do you want, what is the meaning of this?

SHEA: You're to come with us, please, Professor Arvin.

ARVIN: Come with you? What are you talking about?

ROGERS: I'm Officer John Rogers of the Massachusetts State Police. And this is Mr. Brendan Shea, head of the State Bureau on Pornography. You're to come with us, please.

ARVIN: I certainly will *not* come with you! What is this all about, for heaven's sakes?! Are you charging me with something?

SHEA: The charges will be detailed at headquarters, Professor Arvin. We're asking you to come with us quietly.

ARVIN *(Increasingly upset)*: By no means . . . by no means . . .

ROGERS: Very well, Professor Arvin. We are hereby placing you under arrest.

ARVIN: You're what—?! Arrest, arrest . . . ! Is this some kind of joke? If so, I can only say that I don't find it the slightest bit—

SHEA: —it's far from a joke, sir. We've reason to believe that for some time now you've headed an eleven-state pornography ring extending from New York City to Toronto, Canada, and that you've used the United States mails to promulgate this conspiracy.

ARVIN *(Near to fainting)*: A pornography ring? . . . Conspiracy? What are you saying? This is madness, absolute madness . . .

ROGERS: You are additionally charged, under the recent Massachusetts Statute 417, with being "a lewd and lascivious person in speech and behavior," as well as committing "sodomy and unnatural acts" with person or persons hereafter to be named.

ARVIN: Good God! . . . *(He suddenly sinks to the floor)*

ROGERS: Let's go, Professor Arvin. On your feet, please. We got no time for shenanigans . . . *(Grabs Arvin under the arm. To Shea)* Jesus, the guy's gone limp. I think he's out cold.

SHEA: Typical pansy. Faints dead away like some stupid woman. I guess we'll have to drag the fruitcake down to the car. *(As they start to lift Arvin and the lights begin to dim)* If you bang his head a little on the stairs, I promise not to report you . . .

(Laughing, they hoist Arvin on their shoulders and start to exit. Blackout.)

END OF ACT ONE

ACT TWO

SCENE 1

(Two days later. Arvin's room in the Northampton Asylum for the Insane. He's in street clothes, sitting in a chair. Dr. Charles Farris, about forty, officious and assured, is looking over Arvin's chart.)

FARRIS: We'll have to wait for the blood results, of course, but the physical examination reveals no significant pathology. I'd say you were in excellent health for a man your age, Professor Arvin.

ARVIN *(Arch)*: Yes, I know. I've long been told that my problems are purely psychological. This is not my first admission to a psychiatric hospital.

FARRIS *(Reading the report)*: So I see. Two suicide attempts, four hospitalizations.

ARVIN: And years and years of psychotherapy.

FARRIS: Perhaps you had the wrong therapist.

ARVIN: And are you the right one?

FARRIS: The court thinks so. Hopefully you will, too, in time.

(Lights come up cross-stage on officers Shea and Rogers jimmying the lock on the door to Ford's apartment. This silent scene plays out concurrently with the scene between Arvin and Farris. When Shea and Rogers fail to jimmy open the door, Rogers puts his weight against it and forces it open. As Arvin and Farris continue to talk cross-stage, Shea and Rogers ransack Ford's apartment. From the top shelf of a closet, they take down some large manila envelopes, open them, let out a whoop as the contents are revealed to

be "pornography." As Shea and Rogers dance a little jig, and just as Ford en-
ters his apartment to find them there, blackout.)

ARVIN: I don't need more psychotherapy. I long ago accepted that my
homosexuality is a character disorder. I also know that nothing can
be done about it. It's a psychic injury to which I have made a fairly
good adjustment. I am, after all, a functioning, even admired,
member of the community. And I am sixty years old. Not all problems have solutions—not even in America.

FARRIS: You talk like a professor.

ARVIN: All I did was say a complete sentence.

FARRIS: I'm afraid the decision about treatment is not entirely yours.
I must remind you that you're in serious legal trouble. The issue
is not whether you will be treated, but which treatment is appropriate.

ARVIN: That sounds like a threat.

FARRIS: No, a statement of fact.

ARVIN: I voluntarily committed myself to this hospital. I can leave it
whenever I want.

FARRIS: That isn't quite true. State law, Professor Arvin, allows you to
request release. The hospital may then detain you for seventy-two
hours while deciding if it considers you a threat to your own safety
or to anyone else's. You can gain release only through court action—a tedious and prolonged process.

ARVIN *(Shaken):* You *are* threatening me. Don't you realize I have a national reputation? There's no way you can hold me against my will
without causing an enormous outcry.

FARRIS: There's already been an enormous outcry. And not exactly in
your favor. Not with headlines like COLLEGE SMUT RING in newspapers around the county. You *have* seen the current *Newsweek*? *(Arvin
doesn't answer)* No? It calls—I believe I'm quoting accurately—for a
"relentless war against homosexual offenders *regardless* of who they
are, what they know, what they do for living." Nor have I noticed
the Smith College authorities leaping to your defense.

ARVIN *(Quietly):* *I* don't defend my behavior. I never have.

FARRIS: And that is precisely why your prognosis is favorable. You *do* acknowledge that homosexual acting-out is neurotic displacement, unresolved Oedipal rage.

ARVIN: I didn't realize I'd acknowledged all *that*.

FARRIS: *Because* you acknowledge that you are ill, we can enlist you as an ally in the fight for your recovery. We're on the same side: we want you to get well. I'm your friend, not your adversary, Professor Arvin. And in time I hope you'll be able to see that.

(The cross-stage scene with Shea, Rogers, and Ford concludes)

ARVIN: What are you suggesting?

FARRIS: I agree that traditional psychotherapy may no longer be useful for you. Perhaps it never was, given your skill with words. You probably out-analyzed the analyst at every turn. *(Pause)* What I would suggest instead is another course of ECT. *(Consulting Arvin's chart)* I see they gave you a series of three electric shock treatments at the time of your second suicide attempt in 1953.

ARVIN: Absolutely not! I won't hear of it! I will never, *never* subject myself to that again!

FARRIS *(Icily)*: Do try to stay calm. This is only a suggestion. Tell me why you object so strenuously to ECT.

ARVIN: I lost all ability to work. My memory was impaired—*and* my will. Without my work, I am nothing. Can't you understand that?—nothing!

FARRIS: But you did go back to work. *(Consulting Arvin's chart)* You've published widely since 1953. And apparently you're at work on a biography of Ralph Waldo Emerson. So what you mean, Professor Arvin, is that *in the short run*—a matter of only a few months—your memory and will were affected.

ARVIN: Those months were hell, absolute hell.

FARRIS: If you had *not* had the electric shock treatments, those months would have been worse still—*and* you would not have been able to return to work in the long run.

ARVIN: I'm not in that kind of shape now! My God, in '53 I was practically curled in a fetal position! *(Pause)* Yes, I fell apart at the police station—who wouldn't have, surrounded by foulmouthed cops and leering reporters?! But I'm absolutely fine now, absolutely fine! And that was only a few days ago.

FARRIS: May I remind you that we have you on Librium *and* Tofranil. And heavy doses of both. You would not be fine if you were not sedated.

ARVIN: I don't feel sedated. I feel fine.

FARRIS: Your tolerance to both drugs is unusual. But we can't keep you on such high doses for more than a week or so without risking serious liver damage.

ARVIN: I'd prefer liver damage to brain damage.

FARRIS: Electric shock does *not* result in brain damage. That's a popular misconception.

ARVIN: I can't bear the idea of more electric shock treatment. I can't bear it . . . *(He starts to sob)*

FARRIS *(Coldly)*: There, there, Professor Arvin. It's going to be all right, I assure you. . . . We'll have you good as new in no time. Better than new. This unfortunate episode may prove the best thing that ever happened to you. Though of course it doesn't seem that way now . . .

ARVIN *(Between sobs)*: With my luck, there's probably going to be an afterlife . . .

(Louise enters the room. Startled at seeing Arvin in tears, she rushes over to him.)

LOUISE: Newton, Newton, what's wrong, sweetheart, what happened, what happened . . . ?

ARVIN: Oh, Louise, thank God you're here. Where've you been, where've you been? . . .

LOUISE: I was at Swarthmore . . . giving a guest lecture . . . I only got the news this morning . . . got the first plane I could, sweetheart. . . . It's all right, Louise is here, Louise is here . . .

FARRIS: Excuse me. I am Dr. Charles Farris. I'm the attendant psychiatrist on this case. May I ask who you are?

LOUISE: Louise Albright. I'm a close friend of Newton's. . . . I also teach at the college . . .

FARRIS: You're not a blood relative?

LOUISE: Newton is my closest friend, and he mine.

FARRIS: This is a closed floor, Miss Albright. If you're not a blood relative, the visiting hours in this unit are between two and three p.m.

LOUISE: Sorry, I didn't know. I just came up in the elevator.

FARRIS: They should have stopped you at the nurses' station. I'll have to look into that. You'll have to leave now, I'm afraid. You're welcome to return at two.

LOUISE: *Please*, doctor. This is an emergency. Newton and I *have* to talk. Couldn't you make an exception just this once? I promise I won't ask again.

(Farris hesitates.)

LOUISE: I beg you, doctor . . .

FARRIS *(Reluctantly)*: Very well. I'll give you ten minutes. Not a minute more. And this one time only.

LOUISE: Thank you, thank you so much.

(Farris exits.)

LOUISE: The little fascist shit.

(She goes over and hugs Arvin again.)

ARVIN: Ooh, that feels good. A good hugger is just what I need.

LOUISE: Looks like Doctor Farris could use one, too.

ARVIN: Are you kidding? Who hugs Sherman tanks?

LOUISE: Thank God your humor's intact. I thought you'd be in a lot worse shape. I heard awful stories from Eddie over the phone.

ARVIN: They put me on a suicide watch the first night. But no, I'm not much worse in here than I was out there. It surprises me. Guess I've always felt like an imposter—"misbegotten," as my father used to say. Always felt some day I'd be caught and exposed. It's a surprising relief when that finally happens.

LOUISE: All I know is, a lot of people love you and care about you and want you well.

ARVIN: Tell all two of them that I'm much better, that I'm not going to lose my mind. I've decided that the only people who go crazy are those who *combine* excess grief with limited understanding. All I have is the grief.

LOUISE: Rational *and* epigrammatic—the academic restored.

ARVIN: Dr. Farris thinks I'm desperately ill. He's talking about electric shock again.

LOUISE: Oh no, Newton! That was ghastly for you last time.

ARVIN: The medical world despises half measures—it's either warm milk at night or a lobotomy. It's a very melodramatic profession.

LOUISE: You're not going to agree, are you?

ARVIN: I'm not sure the choice is mine. Dr. Farris seems to think it isn't.

LOUISE: You seem *fine!* What does he hope to accomplish?

ARVIN: My guess is that he wants to scare me into being cooperative with the legal authorities.

LOUISE: Meaning what?

ARVIN: It isn't clear yet. . . . I think Farris has a long-range agenda. *(Laughs)* He probably wants to "cure" my homosexuality. Like any good psychiatrist, he sees that as the root of all my problems.

LOUISE: This isn't the Middle Ages, for God's sake.

ARVIN: Would that it were! The *modern* treatment is to stand queers on an electric grid and administer shocks while flashing pictures of naked men on the screen.

LOUISE: You can't be serious!

ARVIN: Oh yes, dear—get your head out of the Victorian novel. Then they flash pictures of naked women and *omit* the shocks. This is supposed to change your sexual orientation.

LOUISE: Good grief!

ARVIN: And they're claiming *wonderful* results. Translation: most patients stop wanting sex altogether. They put those in the "cured" column.

LOUISE: We need to get you out of here.

ARVIN: In time. I'm in no hurry at the moment.

LOUISE *(Surprised)*: You're not?

ARVIN *(Deliberately vague)*: This isn't a bad solution for now, until the legal situation clarifies. Now then—before Mussolini returns—have you seen Eddie yet?

LOUISE: I'm to see him this afternoon. I've only been back an hour. But I've talked to him on the phone three or four times.

ARVIN: How's he bearing up? They won't let us talk directly.

LOUISE: Upset, of course. Worried about you, worried about himself. But he's planning to fight the charges. So is Jerry.

ARVIN: That may not be wise.

LOUISE: The police searched Eddie's apartment without a warrant! And when he wasn't home! That alone could get the case thrown out of court.

ARVIN: Aren't you just the sweetest thing—thinking anybody gives a shit about the civil rights of homosexuals.

LOUISE: Hmm. You've got a point.

ARVIN: The police have also arrested four men in town, including Michael Brown.

LOUISE: Who's that?

ARVIN: The fellow who came by the apartment while you were there.

LOUISE: Oh Lord, that poor soul.

ARVIN: He's married, with two children. So are the other men from town.

LOUISE: Do you know them, too?

ARVIN: Only biblically. Some furtive scene or other at the bus depot.

LOUISE: What are they being charged with?

ARVIN: All of us are charged with "possession of obscene photographs and literature." Additionally *I* am charged with being "a lewd and lascivious person in speech and behavior." I've been designated the ringleader, you see. The ringleader of an interstate pornography ring.

LOUISE: It makes me want to laugh—I'm sorry!

ARVIN: Well, it's made for some lurid headlines, I can tell you. And there's already been one suicide—a man in Westfield who *thought* he might be implicated. None of us knew him. It was a matter of another guilty soul pointing a finger at himself.

LOUISE: It sounds like a first-class witch hunt. This is 1960, for God's sake!

ARVIN: For God's sake indeed. Religion and psychiatry: the two cultural authorities with but one conviction: a shared distaste for homosexuality; one calls it sin, the other sickness. But it comes down to the same prescription: eradication. Which is precisely why it seems to me that meek apologetics, not bravado, may be the wisest course for now.

LOUISE: But that's tantamount to admitting guilt. You'd be playing right into their hands.

ARVIN: We *are* guilty. At least in the limited sense that we *did* possess the material in question and we *did* share the material.

LOUISE: But those tame, pathetic little *Greek Pictorials* are hardly the equivalent of a "lewd, lascivious person!" I must say, I think Eddie's tactic is a far better way to—

ARVIN: —Eddie wants to be noble. What I want is to stay alive long enough to finish my Emerson book. Nothing else really matters to me any more.

(Dr. Farris appears in the doorway.)

FARRIS: Your ten minutes are up, Miss Albright.

LOUISE: Not already?!

FARRIS: Your fourteen minutes, to be exact. You'll have to leave now.

LOUISE: But we've barely begun to—

FARRIS: —I'm sorry, you'll have to leave. Our job is to protect the patient.

LOUISE: From *me?*

FARRIS: Professor Arvin mustn't be over-taxed.

LOUISE: Having the comfort of a close friend to talk to isn't—

ARVIN: —don't fight it, dear. Doctor knows best. Frankly, I am feeling a little worn out.

(Louise looks perplexed, but gets up to leave without further protest.)

FARRIS *(To Arvin):* You're being very sensible. You're going to come out of this a new man.

LOUISE: I liked the old one. Goodbye, dear. *(Kisses him)* I'll be back later, after I see Eddie.

ARVIN: Give him my love. Tell him we must all stay calm.

LOUISE *(Mischievously):* Goodbye, Nurse Farris.

FARRIS *(Startled)*: *Doctor* Farris.

LOUISE: So sorry. These places *are* disorienting. Perhaps it was your caring manner that confused me. *(Waves)* Ta-ta.

(Louise exits.)

FARRIS: Seems a most peculiar person. You say she's a close friend?

ARVIN: She's a little overwrought at the moment.

FARRIS: Even sensible friends can interfere with recovery. I'm glad you understand the need for rest.

ARVIN: Yes. I've been reflecting a good bit on what you said before.

FARRIS *(Confused)*: What I said about . . . ?

ARVIN: —about the need to come out of this a different person. All I want from now on out of life is the peace and quiet to do my work.

FARRIS: That seems to me a most appropriate goal.

ARVIN: My work is what matters to me. I must protect my work . . .

FARRIS: Well now, I'm glad to hear you sounding so judicious. Excellent! Perhaps now a little nap is in order. I'll drop in on you again later.

ARVIN: I'll look forward to that. . . . Thank you. . . . Yes, thank you very much. . . . It's a great relief to feel I'm in the hands of such a competent physician . . .

(As Farris smiles and exits, Arvin arranges his pillows; blackout.)

SCENE 2

(A small area of the stage lights up. Officers Rogers and Shea are questioning Michael Brown.)

ROGERS: What are you trying to say, Brown, huh? You're saying we're *liars*, is that what you're saying?!

BROWN: No, no, officer, nuthin' like that. But you said I was free to go. Next thing I know I'm bein' arrested on this here porn charge. I thought you guys had promised that—

ROGERS: —That memory of yours sure does play tricks. Is that what we told him, Officer Shea?

SHEA: What we told you was that for leading us to Professor Arvin, we were going to overlook your "activities" at the bus depot and not bring you up on sodomy charges. We could have sent you away for twenty years, Brown.

BROWN: Yes, sir, I know that, sir. I much appreciate—

SHEA: —but then *(Slapping down a magazine in front of Brown)* we confiscate this filth from the campus queers. And *this* we can't overlook. You've admitted you saw this stuff, right?

BROWN: I don't know, I don't know if this is the same stuff Arvin showed me. *(He reaches for the magazine; Rogers slaps his hand out of the way)*

ROGERS: Hey, hey! Who the fuck gave you permission to examine state's evidence?! You'll get to see that in due time—in court.

SHEA: There's no point denying it, Brown. Your name's on the list.

BROWN: What list?

SHEA: Ever hear of Manual Enterprises, Brown?

BROWN: I dunno. Is that an auto parts company?

ROGERS: That's real funny, Brown. I guess for you, that's quick thinking.

SHEA: Manual Enterprises is the largest producer of gay pornography, including Professor Arvin's favorite, *Grecian Guild Pictorial*. Thanks to cooperating officers in Missouri, we now have the complete Manual Enterprises mailing list. And your name is on it.

BROWN: That can't be! I never bought nuthin' like that. I only seen the stuff when Arvin showed it to me.

SHEA: So you're admitting that you saw it.

BROWN: Yes—I mean, no—I mean . . . *(In despair)* Ooh . . . I dunno . . .

SHEA: We don't need to take your word for it, Brown. *(Holds up a cloth-bound volume)* See this? This is one of Professor Arvin's diaries. Your name's all over it, Brown. Part of those all-night porn parties the professor loved to throw.

BROWN *(Deeply shaken)*: He put my name in his diary? He gave you his diary . . . ?

ROGERS: How we got the diary is none of your business, Brown. All you need to know is that you're in deep shit. We're talking about a national smut ring. We're talking about corrupting children, attacking the family, destroying this country's very fabric. That's what *communists* want to see happen.

BROWN: I'm no commie, for Chrissakes! No, no, I'm nuthin' like that. I love my family just like the next guy. That professor sweet-talked me clear out of my mind . . .

ROGERS *(Leading him on)*: That might just be what happened, Brown. Especially since he offered you money, too, right?

BROWN *(Catching on)*: Oh yeah, absolutely. Oh yeah, he definitely offered me money if I would, like, y'know, cooperate.

SHEA: Good, good. Glad to see your memory's improving. Yeah, these pinko intellectuals, they all got plenty of money. They talk fancy and rake in the shekels. While the rest of us stiffs work for a living. *(Putting a photograph in front of Brown)* Now look at this picture, Brown. You remember seeing this picture at Arvin's house, don't you?

BROWN *(Looking at picture)*: Oh, my God, it's a coupla young boys!

ROGERS: You remember Professor Arvin showing you this picture, don't you, Brown?

BROWN: No, not this one. No, Arvin likes men, grown men. He never said nuthin' about kids.

SHEA: You're really not very bright, are you, Brown?

BROWN: Huh?

SHEA: Here we are trying to help you, and you just won't let us.

BROWN: I don't getcha . . .

SHEA: Let's try it again. Professor Arvin showed you this picture of two boys and asked you if you knew any kids in town you could fix him up with. Kids who might be interested in making a little extra cash. *He was using you, wasn't he, Brown?*

BROWN: Yeah, yeah, he definitely took advantage of me . . .

SHEA: That's the whole point, isn't it? He wanted you to do his bidding. With men, with kids, what difference . . .

BROWN: Yeah, yeah. Oh, I see whatcha gettin' at . . . Yeah, sure, he wanted me to be like a pimp for him.

ROGERS: That's it, Brown. Very good. Now we're finally getting somewhere. *(To Shea, sarcastic)* And they say police work is easy!

SHEA: There may yet be a way we can help you, Brown. Just so long as
you take your cues from us. Think you can manage that, Brown?

BROWN: Oh, I can do that, officer. Yes, sir, I can do that.

SHEA: Let's hope so, Brown, let's hope so. I mean for your sake. Okay,
let's call it a day for now. We'll get back to you when we need you.

BROWN: Yes, sir, thank you very much, sir.

ROGERS: Don't fuck up your bail. Keep your nose clean.

BROWN: Yes, sir. Sure appreciate your helpin' me like this . . . *(He
exits)*

ROGERS: A major moron. I don't know if he can remember anything
long enough to repeat it on the stand.

SHEA: Poor bastard. The Professor talked his ears—and pants—off.

ROGERS: Sick bunch. The sooner we get 'em behind bars, the better.

SHEA *(Sarcastic)*: And the quicker your picture will be in the paper.

ROGERS: Hey, if we get famous in the process, is that our fault?
(They laugh.)

ROGERS *(As he gathers up the magazines)*: You know something, Shea?
Lookin' at this stuff all day makes me wanna go home and wrestle
with my wife.

SHEA: Keep it in your pants, Rogers. Or next thing you know, Arvin'll
take a picture of it.

(As Shea and Rogers laugh, blackout.)

SCENE 3

(Ford's apartment. Ford is on the phone, Jerry is seated in a chair.)

FORD *(Into phone)*: . . . So you've heard about the case. . . . Good,
yes, that's why I'm calling . . . *(Pause)* Yes, it's been getting a lot of
publicity. None of it good, I'm afraid. . . . *(Pause)* Yes, we're all out
on bail. The trial is set for next week. That's why I'm calling . . . I
subscribe to your publication, the *Mattachine Review*, and thought

you might be able to suggest some strategies for—*(Pause)* Yes, I do like the *Review*. Very much. It's the series you did on police harassment that made me think—*(Pause)* You're welcome. Anyway, as people fighting for homosexual rights, I thought you might help us with—*(Pause)* How? Frankly, I don't know, I was hoping that maybe your experience with similar cases in the past might—*(Pause)* Oh, I see. *(Pause)* Yes, of course I understand . . . *(Pause)* Sure, we'd be glad to send you the clippings . . . *(Pause)* Right. Okay. Well, thanks very much for your time, anyway. Goodbye. *(To Jerry)* Well, that was a bust.

JERRY: No help at all?

FORD: He was very nice. But it turns out he's *it*—the entire staff. He said the *Review* has fewer than two thousand subscribers.

JERRY: A major pressure group.

FORD: He did offer to publicize the case if we send him the clippings.

JERRY: Great, we'll get 2,000 mascaraed queens picketing the courthouse. That ought to be a big help.

FORD: Jesus, Jerry—you sound as antigay as the police!

JERRY: It is *not* a bright idea to hook up with the homophile movement. We're in enough trouble without involving ourselves with militant homosexuals.

FORD: Awright, awright! . . . Maybe if there were more than two thousand, we might stand a chance of—

JERRY: —stop it! Enough—

FORD: Jerry, centrally this *is* going to be a trial about homosexuality, not obscenity. And we have to figure out how to defend against something we're not formally charged with.

JERRY: Throw ourselves on the mercy of the court: "We can't help it, we were born that way."

FORD: The courts believe the psychiatrists: queers are *made*, not born.

JERRY: Which probably means that Newton will fare better than we will. After all, the guy's been in therapy most of his life . . .

FORD: Newton's had his share of suffering.

JERRY: I'm praying that in the thirties he never actually joined the Communist Party.

FORD *(Annoyed)*: Jerry, let's try to remember that we're in this boat together.

JERRY: Well, *was* he a communist?

FORD: He was accused of it. By William Buckley's *adorable* sister, Aloise, a *major* Smith College donor.

JERRY: Oh yeah, I heard about that. Didn't she and some other wealthy crones threaten to withhold financial support?

FORD: Exactly. "Unless Newton Arvin and the other faculty 'Commies,' " as they put it, were dismissed.

JERRY: The way I heard it, Newton cooperated fully with the committee investigating Buckley's charges.

FORD: *Not* true! Newton never named names—the way some others did. *(Pause; quieter)* He did eat a little crow.

JERRY: Meaning?

FORD: He apologized for his political "naïveté" when younger.

JERRY *(Alarmed)*: So he *did* belong to the Party!

FORD: *No*, Jerry. He supported the Republican side in the Spanish Civil War. That's all. He never joined the party. In fact, during the Buckley storm he announced publicly that he "detested" communism both in theory and practice.

JERRY: Sounds a bit craven.

FORD: I suppose he didn't have much choice. Not if he wanted to keep his job. And who are you—or me—to be judging him?

JERRY: He had more choice than we do! The police took those magazines right out of our apartments. No way to avoid a guilty verdict.

FORD: The point is: guilty of *what*? Of possessing pornography? How many straight men get arrested for that? No, no, as I keep trying to explain to you, the crime is possession of *homosexual* pornography. Deeper still: *being* homosexual.

JERRY: I plead guilty to that, too.

FORD *(Suddenly getting an idea)*: You do? You will? Publicly? Jerry, that's inspired! In court we *acknowledge* our homosexuality—and then defend it.

JERRY: And our sentences go off the charts. You've been reading too many copies of the *Mattachine Review*!

FORD: Not enough of them, I suspect. What we need to challenge is the common fear of homosexuals. My God, most heterosexuals are scared to death of us! They think we belong to a secret organization, with underground cells, maybe even an army.

JERRY: Just like the commies!

FORD: They think we all *are* commies. God, heterosexuality must be fragile if it can be subverted by the likes of us!

JERRY: We should admit in court to being pornographers in the hope they won't charge us with being sodomites.

FORD *(Giving up)*: Jerry, you just don't get it. Never mind . . . *(Pause)* Did I tell you I spoke to Kenneth yesterday?

JERRY: No.

FORD: He says every queer on the Yale faculty is terrified of being indicted as well. He says Newton writes down everything in his diary, that everybody's name is bound to turn up in his diary.

JERRY: But the police can't get that.

FORD: Which is what I told Kenneth. Newton keeps the diary in a bank vault. There's no way the police can even find out it exists.

JERRY: Did that calm him down?

FORD: When Louise asked him for a contribution to our defense fund, he said he was near to collapse and going on leave to Italy for the term. That will use up every penny he has. Homosexual solidarity. Isn't it wonderful? Thank God for heterosexual Louise.

JERRY: She's been a whirlwind.

FORD: She's already seen Newton, says he's in an "altogether peculiar mood" and will tell me more later. And she's gotten an audience with President Morse.

JERRY: You're kidding!

FORD: She intends to tell him that Smith College *must* stand behind us—no matter what the verdict in court.

JERRY: Lots of luck. The Buckley handmaidens would chew Morse alive.

FORD: Louise is coming here right after she sees him. Do you want to stay?

JERRY: I can't. The lawyer wants to go over the deposition again. I'll call you later. *(He gets up to leave)* I say, old buddy, you didn't by chance salvage *one* copy of *Grecian Guild Pictorial* from the coppers, did you?

FORD: Alas, not one.

JERRY: Pity. It would have done *so much* to calm my tattered nerves!

FORD: I'm in awe of your libido. In the very shadow of the hangman! *(As they laugh and embrace, blackout.)*

SCENE 4

(Lights immediately up on another part of the stage. Louise is in heated conversation with President Morse.)

MORSE: . . . You don't seem to appreciate, Professor Albright, just how much I've already done in their behalf. Much more, I don't mind saying, than most people in my position would have done. Aloise Buckley and her friends have been constantly on the phone since the story broke, demanding that all three faculty members be *instantly* dismissed, furious that I would retain such "perverts and degenerates"—as they call them—even temporarily. I have repeatedly told her that central to our liberties is the tradition that a man is innocent until proven guilty. I think I deserve some credit for that.

LOUISE: I realize, President Morse, that you've been under intense pressure. From what I've heard, the ladies in question are quite fierce. But what do you mean by "proven innocent"? What would "innocent" mean in this case?

MORSE: Isn't that obvious? Innocent of the charges that have been brought against them.

LOUISE: Surely you already know that Newton Arvin is the furthest thing imaginable from "a lewd and lascivious person in speech and behavior"—as charged. And of course the same is true of Ed Ford and Jerry Norris.

MORSE: They are also charged with "possession of obscene photographs and literature."

LOUISE: The materials in question were for their private use only.

MORSE: So they *did* own such materials. You're confirming that?

LOUISE: Please don't force me to *feign* ignorance. *If* they possessed
such materials, that would hardly, in and of itself, confirm that they
were "lewd and lascivious persons." Surely we've all read a dirty
book or two in our day.

MORSE: No, I can't say that I have.

LOUISE: Really? How unusual. How disadvantaged, even.

MORSE: Society expects the teacher, like the priest, to be a finer being,
less subject to human frailties.

(Louise guffaws.)

MORSE: I myself do not hold that view.

(Louise looks surprised, hopeful.)

MORSE: A teacher is, finally, just a human being like everyone else.
And, like everyone else, fallible.

LOUISE: I'm glad to hear you say that. That seems to me the accurate
and humane view.

MORSE: Of course the frailty in this case is one that society finds particularly reprehensible. We view homosexuality in our culture as a
moral disorder, and we do not want such people teaching—which
is to say, influencing—our children.

LOUISE: I'm glad that you see the real issue *is* homosexuality. Had the
contents of the magazines been heterosexual, no indictment would
have been brought.

MORSE: I can't be sure of that. Nor can you.

LOUISE: Since the material was for private viewing, how could the
morals of anyone else be endangered?

MORSE: The danger comes from the disturbed nature of any individual
who'd choose to view such materials. Such a person—it is widely
believed—cannot be entrusted with the education of the young.

LOUISE: And do *you* believe that?

MORSE: My personal opinion is of no relevance here.

LOUISE: Of course it is! You're the one who will decide, finally, whether these men keep their jobs or not.

MORSE: No, the court will decide.

LOUISE: But the courts reflect public opinion. Which means that its views on pornography and homosexuality are likely to be primitive. In falling back on the court, aren't you abdicating your own responsibility?

MORSE: Would you have me *ignore* the court's decision?

LOUISE: I would ask you not to implement its prejudices automatically. There is, after all, the higher law of conscience.

MORSE *(sarcastically)*: That sounds very nineteenth century—your field of expertise, I understand. *(Pause)* You don't seem to appreciate the restraint I've already shown, Professor Albright.

LOUISE: I've expressed my appreciation. Now I'm asking you to do more.

MORSE *(sarcastic)*: You're not asking me, I presume, to announce a decision similar to the one the Regents of the University of Massachusetts issued yesterday.

LOUISE: I don't know what you're referring to.

MORSE: No, I didn't think you did. Otherwise your tone might be a bit less—how shall I say?—adversarial. The University of Massachusetts has announced that it will immediately suspend any staff member indicted under the state's new pornography law. Merely *indicted*, mind you. Not convicted. I oppose that kind of precipitous judgment. I oppose it vehemently. I will reserve *my* judgment until the court has had its say.

LOUISE *(getting angry)*: Well, at least the University of Massachusetts has issued its judgments in its own name. Whereas you appear ready to hide behind the judgment of the court—sharing its values, doing its dirty work, all the while pretending that you have no agency in what is happening, that your hands are tied.

MORSE: Allow me to caution you once more, Professor Albright, about your tone.

LOUISE: My tone? Do you mean my passion? The lives of three good and decent men are about to be ruined. I feel strongly about that, and see no reason to disguise my feelings.

MORSE: You have all but called me a coward.

LOUISE: I've expressed regret that you won't deal with the issues head-on.

MORSE: And *I* regret that you insist on seeing those issues only by your own limited lights. We have twenty-three hundred young women on this campus, Professor Albright, twenty-three hundred young women whose parents have entrusted their moral development to our care. That is a heavy responsibility. And one which I do not intend to shirk.

LOUISE: Are you so certain what is best for these young women?

MORSE: Are you?

LOUISE: I'm certain that nothing will corrupt them more than teaching them how to hate, how to despise those who are different.

MORSE: I quite agree. And would add the corollary that to be different is not automatically to be virtuous.

LOUISE: These men challenge orthodoxy by their very existence. Nothing can more valuably widen the moral horizons of Smith undergraduates. They need exposure to people who are different— richly, valuably different.

MORSE: Our faculty is already a remarkably diverse one.

LOUISE: You're mocking me.

MORSE: Given how seriously you take yourself, I thought it was perhaps permissible to err a bit on the other side.

LOUISE *(Losing her temper)*: Your famous suavity, President Morse, can't conceal the fact that you're acting like a member of the cultural police. You don't think of higher education as free inquiry. You think of it as thought control, indoctrination into middle-class values.

MORSE: I won't warn you again.

LOUISE: You won't have to. I say this to you flat out, President Morse: in my view it is you, not Professor Arvin, who is unfit to be part of a university.

(She turns abruptly and exits. Blackout.)

SCENE 5

(Ford's apartment. Louise is pacing back and forth.)

LOUISE: —he's a twerp, a sanctimonious twerp! Ed Sullivan's twin brother.

FORD: —calm down, darling, calm down—

LOUISE: —and the worst part of it is, he thinks he's a liberal hero! All puffed up with pride because he hasn't fired you *before* the trial. Wants a goddamn medal! *(Pause)* . . . Oh, Eddie, it doesn't look good . . .

FORD: All that frowning—to quote you—will give you eye wrinkles. Morse *won't* save our jobs if the verdict goes against us. That much we know. But the verdict isn't in.

LOUISE: Everyone's decided you're guilty—for being alive, it seems.

FORD: Look: the police had no warrant for entering my apartment or seizing my property. *And* they failed to inform me of my rights. *And* they questioned me without an attorney being present. The case could be thrown out three times over. The judge could easily declare a mistrial.

LOUISE: Sure, "could"—if justice reigned. But sweetheart, the police represent public opinion. And in the name of stamping out the crime of homosexuality, the public will happily let them trample on the Constitution.

FORD: But the *court* won't. Material seized without a warrant can't be used as evidence. The Supreme Court itself has ruled on that.

LOUISE: They could convict on other evidence.

FORD: There isn't any other evidence. Why *are* you so gloomy?

LOUISE: Another participant could directly incriminate you.

FORD: Who? Who's going to offer that kind of testimony?

LOUISE: One of the four guys from town. To save his own skin.

FORD *(Deflated)*: Oh . . . that I hadn't thought of.

LOUISE: And I have a candidate: Michael Brown.

FORD: Who's he?

LOUISE: A pickup of Newton's. A garage mechanic.

FORD: Oh yeah, Newton did tell me about him. Passionately queer, Newton says. A dynamo in bed.

LOUISE: And terrified of being found out. I met him for a second. He looked as if he'd disintegrate at the touch.

FORD: But if Brown testifies, he'll be implicating himself. If he says Newton—or I—showed him photographs, that would place him on the scene.

LOUISE: So?

FORD: What's he supposed to be doing in Newton's apartment?

LOUISE: Oh, that's easy. He repaired the professor's car, and—

FORD: —Newton doesn't own a car.

LOUISE: So he was thinking of buying one.

FORD: Prove it.

LOUISE: Prove he wasn't. It's Brown's word against Newton's—and Brown is the married father of two children.

FORD: I see your point.

LOUISE: So it was a hot day. The professor offered him a drink after they took a spin in the car Newton was about to buy. Brown gratefully accepted. Then the queer prof tried to get him to look at these disgusting pictures. And our upright mechanic dutifully fled. So Newton, you see, does not keep those pictures strictly for his own use. He's trying to spread the filth around, trying to get others interested in it. It's practically a case of interstate commerce!

FORD: You're depressing me.

LOUISE: I'm introducing a little reality. *(Pause)* I've got another scenario that will depress you more: Newton himself agrees to testify.

FORD: Well, of course Newton will testify. All three of us will have to.

LOUISE: Testify to the effect that the three of you *did* exchange the pornographic materials—that this is not a case of personal use but of some larger "conspiracy" to circulate the corrupting material to others.

FORD *(Scoffing)*: Why would Newton do *that*?

LOUISE: I've seen Newton in the hospital; you haven't. His two deep-

est qualities have surfaced and merged: self-loathing and tenacity.
He's decided his one justification for remaining alive is to complete
his Emerson biography. *And* that its completion will redeem his
life.

FORD: You make him sound ruthless. Newton's one of the gentlest,
most thoughtful—

LOUISE: —plus they're threatening him.

FORD: Who is? With what?

LOUISE: With "heroic" medical intervention. It's enough to make anyone cooperate.

FORD: They can't do that!

LOUISE: Eddie, your bottomless faith in lawyers and doctors is very
touching, but just a teensy bit naive. Try this on: President Morse
told me Newton had telephoned him.

FORD: When? Why?

LOUISE: Yesterday. From the hospital. Just before Morse and I met.
Newton said he wanted to express his "appreciation" for the way
Morse has handled the case thus far. He commended Morse for his
"fair, impartial" attitude. Oh, how Morse *loved* telling me that!

FORD: Newton's trying to butter him up. That's okay.

LOUISE: I must say, it cut me off at the pass. If Newton isn't protesting
Morse's attitude, then what am I doing protesting in Newton's behalf?

FORD: It's a clever move. It speaks *well* of Newton's state of mind. He's
thinking ahead. If the court does decide in our favor, he wants to be
sure Morse doesn't fire us anyway.

LOUISE *(Enigmatic)*: Or doesn't fire *all* of you.

FORD: What does that mean?

LOUISE *(Anguished)*: Oh, God, Eddie, I do love Newton. I hate thinking
these things.

FORD: What things? You've lost me.

LOUISE: Oh how I wish you could *talk* to him, Eddie! Talk to him directly, *see* him. *(Struck at the idea)* Well, why can't you, come to
think of it?

FORD: You know we aren't allowed any contact before the trial.

LOUISE: Are you going to start obeying the law *now*? Listen: I went straight up in the hospital elevator. Nobody stopped me, nobody asked me a single question. That might have been a one-shot stroke of luck. But maybe not.

FORD: You mean, sneak in to see him?

LOUISE: Of course that's what I mean! Tonight. *Now!*

FORD: Whoa!—I need to think about it.

LOUISE: No, you don't. Listen to me. We have to find out what Newton is thinking. *Why* he called President Morse. What he's planning to say at the trial.

FORD: We don't even know if he's been declared fit to testify.

LOUISE: We need to find that out, too. Put on your coat. I'll drive you there.

FORD: This is hare-brained! Aren't I in enough trouble without getting arrested for trespassing?

LOUISE: What's another five years in jail?

(Ford hesitates.)

FORD: Awright—let's go.

(As they grab their coats and exit, blackout.)

SCENE 6

(Arvin's hospital room, later the same evening. He's seated in a chair reading, as Ford enters.)

ARVIN: Good lord, Eddie! What in heaven's name are you doing here?

FORD: Sorry to frighten you. I know this is crazy—but I *had* to see you before the trial.

ARVIN: You know we're not supposed to be in contact! What if—? Didn't they stop you at the elevators?

FORD: No, fortunately.

ARVIN: This is *very* foolish. You could get me in a good deal of trouble with Dr. Farris . . .

FORD: Is he likely to come in?

ARVIN: Anyone could pop in. This is a hospital, Eddie; they pride themselves on the maximum number of pointless interruptions per hour. Don't you realize I'm entirely at their disposal? These people can do *anything* they want with me! This isn't very considerate of you, Eddie.

FORD: I simply *had* to see you, Newton. I promise I'll only stay a minute.

ARVIN: I can't imagine what's so urgent.

FORD: I'll explain as quickly as I can. Are they likely to bother you even at this late hour?

ARVIN: Well, they have brought in the night medications already. Still, there's no telling. *My* medication, of course, isn't working. *(Gesturing to the book he had been reading)* I'd just picked up my old biography of Walt Whitman, thinking it would be a good soporific. But in fact *(Excitedly)*, in fact, it's *very good*—and especially about Whitman's homosexuality! I must say, I was daring, remarkably daring. Just listen to this. *(Reading from the book)* "The fact of Whitman's homosexuality stares one unanswerably in the face. There is a core of abnormality in Whitman, but . . . Whitman is no mere invert, no mere 'case.'"

FORD: Yes, that is remarkable; you were definitely ahead of your time. *(Trying to change the subject)* Since we only have a few minutes, Newton, I think we should—

ARVIN: —mind you, I wrote that in the 1940s when every other critic was *denying* Whitman's homosexuality, when Mark Van Doren was raving on about his "eccentric and unwholesome emotion!" *(Agitated)* Yes, homosexuality is the result of psychic injury, but what glories that injury has wrought—Whitman! Melville! Capote! *(More subdued)* Well, since you are here, why not sit—no, it's better if you stand *there (Gesturing)*, near the door. If anyone comes in, you can duck behind it. They come by every twenty minutes to shine the light in my eyes.

FORD: To do what?

ARVIN: The orderly. He comes around with a flashlight to check.

(Starts chatting nervously again) I always wave to him so he'll know I'm awake. They refuse to believe how little I sleep. That's because they won't give me enough medication. Catholics, you know: the redemptive power of suffering, and all that. Next thing, they'll be telling me, just as mother used to, "Go to sleep, dear, and be sure *both* your hands are above the covers." Next, they'll be putting a spiked ring around my penis at night to discourage tumescence.

FORD *(Humoring him)*: Don't they give you anything at all to sleep?

ARVIN: One teensy pill. And they make me swallow it while they stand there. They're afraid I'll store them up and commit suicide. Oh they don't care about *me*—it's the notion of an empty bed that terrifies them.

FORD: I'm glad you haven't lost your sense of humor.

ARVIN: What I was trying to say before is that my sense of myself as a homosexual has informed *all* of my work. I've always argued that in this wasteland of a culture, it's homosexual writers who've provided what limited sense of adhesiveness—to use Whitman's phrase—exists to counteract our ruinous individualism. Every man of genius is afflicted with—

(An orderly suddenly appears. From the doorway he shines a flashlight into Arvin's face. Ford ducks undetected behind the door.)

ORDERLY: What's going on in here? What's all the racket about, Arvin?

ARVIN: *Kindly* get that light out of my eyes! *(Orderly lowers flashlight)* Nothing's going on.

ORDERLY: You were talking pretty loud.

ARVIN: I was preparing a speech.

ORDERLY: A speech? Who you givin' a speech to?

ARVIN: My peers. When the time is right.

ORDERLY: Maybe I oughta call Dr. Farris.

ARVIN: I'm fine. In fact I *am* finally feeling sleepy. I think I'll retire now.

ORDERLY: Looks to me like you retired long ago.

ARVIN: How very kind.

ORDERLY: I'll check up on you again in fifteen minutes.

ARVIN: And please do *not* shine that light in my eyes. If I ever do get to sleep, you'll only wake me up.

ORDERLY: That's my job: to shine the light . . . *(He exits. Ford cautiously reappears)*

FORD: Jesus, that was scary.

ARVIN *(Haughty)*: *I'm* the one they're trying to frighten. It's a good thing he didn't see you back there. Now let's get on with it. . . . Where was I? . . . Did I tell you Truman wrote to me from Europe?

FORD: The president?

ARVIN: Truman *Capote*. Really, Eddie, you seem quite rattled. Do calm down.

FORD: I'll just say what I have to quickly, and then get out of here . . .

ARVIN: We'll have a few minutes peace now. Yes, Truman sent me the sweetest letter. He offered me money. He said this would be a tough experience which I must meet with toughness. Dear Truman! They call him a sissy but he's stronger than anybody.

FORD *(firmly)*: Newton, what will you say at the trial?

ARVIN: Why, nothing, of course. I don't intend to testify.

FORD: But——? I thought surely we would all be called.

ARVIN: I'm not fit to testify. I'll refuse to.

FORD: Can you get away with that?

ARVIN: I'm relying on Dr. Farris to say that I couldn't tolerate the strain of a public appearance.

FORD: And . . . do you think he will?

ARVIN *(smiling)*: Ah, Eddie . . . that is certainly my devout goal. . . . Why else would I shout quotations from my own books at midnight?

FORD: Oh! I see . . .

ARVIN: I doubt if you do . . . or will . . . which is why, as Emerson cautioned, we must cultivate indifference to circumstances . . . *(Sad, serious)* Ah, dear Eddie, our communication was once so complete . . . *(Pause)* Why the furrowed brow?

FORD *(Stumbling)*: Well . . . this is difficult to say, Newton, but . . .

ARVIN: Just say it, for heaven's sakes—before the flashlight brigade returns.

FORD: Well, Louise went to see President Morse, and he told her—

ARVIN: —she did *what*—?! I'm in direct contact with Morse myself!

FORD: Yes, so he told Louise. It surprised us. I mean, the way you complimented him on how he's been handling the case.

ARVIN: Indeed I did. I told the old fool six times over what a noble role he's playing.

FORD: I *told* Louise it was a game! You're way ahead of us . . .

ARVIN *(Enigmatic)*: I've chosen a path . . . *not* paved with only good intentions . . .

FORD *(Not understanding)*: Louise thinks Morse is badly disposed toward us. That he might fire us even if the court decision goes in our favor.

ARVIN: He mentioned the prospect of a "small pension." Enough for me to live on. I could devote myself entirely to the Emerson book.

FORD *(Startled)*: Really? But then he *is* planning to retire you ahead of schedule.

ARVIN: Retiring isn't firing.

FORD: But . . . I've only been at Smith three years. Jerry has—what?—something like ten?

ARVIN: Something like that.

FORD: We can't be retired. We haven't accumulated enough service. For us it's either reappointment or firing. If Morse isn't planning to reappoint you, I can't imagine he'll reappoint us.

ARVIN: Perhaps he was only talking contingencies. Perhaps he'll reappoint us. Who can say at this point? We won't know until after the trial. Try to stay calm, Eddie . . .

(Pause.)

FORD: This conversation isn't helping . . .

ARVIN: I'm sorry to hear that . . . *(Pause; sincerely)* I care a great deal about you, Eddie . . .

FORD: I've always thought so, yes . . .

ARVIN: I would do almost anything to keep you safe. . . . I sometimes think I care more about you than about myself . . .

FORD: No one can expect that . . .

(Pause.)

FORD: What if Dr. Farris *doesn't* say you're too fragile to testify?

ARVIN: I believe he will.

FORD: And if he doesn't?

ARVIN: Well then I'll have to testify, of course. What do you expect me to do—kill myself?

FORD: Louise said they've threatened you. Some sort of medical treatment. I didn't quite get her meaning.

ARVIN: Now, now, don't worry about all of that. Louise shouldn't have mentioned it. You have enough to deal with.

FORD: If you do have to testify, what will you say?

ARVIN: What a silly question. What will *you* say?

FORD: As little as possible.

ARVIN: Precisely my own intention.

FORD: I'm glad to hear it. *(Pause)* Are they treating you all right, Newton?

ARVIN *(Smiling)*: In a way it's close to the selfish writer's vision of utopia—you know: being entirely unencumbered, entirely spared the demands of ordinary life. It's something like that in here. Give or take that orderly's flashlight . . .

FORD: The other patients don't get you down?

ARVIN: Oh, Ed—suffering is the staple of life. But it isn't, I've learned, life's meaning. Its meaning is that we can't fix *anything*. . . . There's a woman in here who walks up and down the corridor mumbling to herself day and night. "Why don't you talk to someone else for a while," she keeps saying, "I just made that *one* mistake. Just one. Why can't you leave me alone?" Over and over again: "Why don't you go talk to someone else? Why can't you leave me alone?" But the voices go right on talking to her . . . *(Pause. Arvin yawns)* You'd better leave, I think. Before our luck runs out. If you get caught here, we'll both suffer for it . . .

FORD: I'll be back. Just as soon as they let me.

ARVIN: Don't worry about me. I'm fine. I've got my books. And as you can see, I love re-reading my own words . . .

FORD: I love you, Newton . . .

ARVIN: Goodbye, dear Ed . . .

(Ford exits. Blackout.)

END OF ACT TWO

ACT THREE

SCENE 1

(The courtroom but not entirely a naturalistic setting. Some of the scene should be played in single spots, aiming for an abstracted, somewhat surreal effect. This is further heightened by making the lawyers and the judge, where indicated, offstage voice-overs rather than onstage presences. Spot up on Michael Brown descending from the witness chair, having just completed his testimony. As the spot follows him downstage left, Officer Shea steps out of the shadows, offering his hand.)

SHEA: Well done, Brown, well done.

BROWN: Oh, Officer Shea. Thank you. . . . You really think it went okay?

SHEA: You did just fine. I'd say you were completely off the hook, Brown.

BROWN: I tried to act real disgusted when they showed me that picture of the two boys, just like you told me to . . .

SHEA: You did fine, Brown, just fine . . .

(Shea exits.)

BROWN *(To himself)*: Oh shit, I sure hope so.

(As Brown starts to exit, Arvin appears. Brown involuntarily jumps.)

BROWN: I know what you're gonna say. . . . I'm tellin' ya, I couldn't help myself. I had to say that stuff. The cops told me that if I didn't—

ARVIN *(Calming him down)*: —It's all right, Michael. It's all right. I understand completely. Really I do.

BROWN: You do? You . . . you don't think I . . . betrayed you?

ARVIN: How could you betray me, Michael? We aren't even friends.

BROWN *(Confused)*: Uh . . . yeah, I guess so. But I did lie about that picture of the boys.

ARVIN: You did what you had to. As we all must. You *are* a family man.

BROWN: That's right, Professor. That's why I had to do it.

ARVIN: I do understand. Please don't think I bear you any grudge.

BROWN: Well, I sure appreciate your attitude . . .

ARVIN: And remember: you did try to warn me, Michael. I'm the one who behaved badly and frightened you off.

BROWN: Yeah, I really did try to tell you about the cops. Put you on guard.

ARVIN: See? Truth and lies. Hard to separate. Now in my case, if I tell the *truth* on the stand, I *will* be betraying friends.

BROWN: I don't follow your meaning, Professor.

ARVIN: It's complicated.

BROWN: I heard you weren't feeling too good.

ARVIN: I'm better now, much better. Thank you for asking.

BROWN: No hard feelings?

ARVIN: None at all, Michael. I wish you well.

BROWN: Thanks, Prof. Same to you.

(They shake hands, then exit in separate directions. Lights come up on Shea on the witness stand. His examination is already in progress.)

PROSECUTING ATTORNEY MOORE: . . . Since the defense is attempting to claim that the materials you took from the apartments were illegally obtained, I want you to tell the court in your own words, Officer Shea, exactly how you and Officer Rogers obtained those materials.

SHEA: The first thing we did when we arrived was to identify ourselves as police officers. We did that in all three cases.

MOORE: By "three cases," you're referring to Professors Newton Arvin, Edward Ford, and Gerald Norris?

SHEA: That is correct.

MOORE: When you first arrived in the apartment of each of the three defendants?

SHEA: That is correct.

MOORE: What followed next?

SHEA: In Professor Arvin's case, he fainted dead away.

(Laughter in the courtroom. Judge Martin bangs his gavel.)

JUDGE MARTIN: Order, order in the courtroom. Please continue, Mr. Moore.

MOORE: Thank you, your honor. *(Mocking tone)* Did all three men faint dead away, Officer Shea?

SHEA: No, sir. Professor Ford wasn't home when we arrived at his place.

MOORE: How did you gain entry then?

SHEA: The door to his building was unlocked. We looked at the mailboxes. One of them had Professor Ford's name on it. So we rang his bell. At first nobody answered. Then an old lady came down the stairs, said she'd heard us, took us up to Professor Ford's apartment. The door was wide open, so we went in. Nobody was there.

MOORE: Then what happened?

SHEA: On the top shelf of a closet I noticed some envelopes. We took them down. They were full of disgusting pictures.

DEFENSE ATTORNEY THOMAS: Objection, your honor! The officer is characterizing the material, not describing it.

JUDGE MARTIN: Objection overruled. The officer is testifying as to his opinion. To which he is entitled.

THOMAS: We wish to note, your honor, that Officer Shea by his own testimony has admitted that the initial entry to Professor Ford's apartment took place without a legal search warrant. And that once inside the apartment, Shea and Rogers seized private property, again without warrant. The defense therefore wishes to go on record as making automatic objection to each and every attempt to exhibit material in this courtroom that was seized in an illegal search.

JUDGE MARTIN: So noted, Mr. Thomas. Be advised that the court will overrule you in each instance, in the name of reserving its overall judgment on the legality of the search and seizure until the conclusion of testimony. You may proceed, Officer Shea.

SHEA: I asked Professor Ford if he wanted us to go get a search warrant, and he said not to bother.

MOORE: When did you ask that of Professor Ford?

SHEA: When he came back to his apartment. We were standing there looking through the envelopes when he walked in. I showed him my badge and asked him if the pictures belonged to him. He said yes. Then he asked me if he needed a lawyer. I told him if he wanted a lawyer, he was entitled to call for one. He said, "I just don't know what this is all about." We asked him to come down to the police station, and he agreed.

MOORE: And what happened at the station?

SHEA: We questioned him.

MOORE: Did you take notes on what he said?

SHEA: Yes, sir. May I consult my notes, sir?

MARTIN: If they will help you answer truthfully.

SHEA: I wouldn't answer any other way, Your Honor. *(Reading from his notes)* "I asked Ford if he had accumulated all of the confiscated material while living here in Northampton. He said yes. I then asked him if he was gay."

JUDGE MARTIN: Was what?

THOMAS: May we approach the bench?

JUDGE MARTIN: No, you may not.

SHEA: Gay, Your Honor. That's an expression, or terminology. It's another word for queer.

JUDGE MARTIN *(Embarrassed)*: All right, go ahead.

SHEA: "And Ford said, 'I refuse to answer that question.' "

MOORE: Excuse me, Officer Shea, but going back, you did say, didn't you, that Professor Ford acknowledged that the confiscated material *was* his, isn't that right?

SHEA: Yes, sir.

THOMAS: Objection, your honor. I'm renewing my objection to the presentation of any material seized in an illegal search.

JUDGE MARTIN: You may object on each occasion, and I shall overrule you on each occasion. To repeat—and for the last time—I will consider the issue of illegal search *following* the completion of testimony. I make rulings, Mr. Thomas; I don't debate them. You may continue, Officer Shea.

SHEA: "So then I asked where he got all this stuff. He said, from a 'party' here in Northampton. I asked him who that party was, and he said, 'I refuse to answer that.' "

MOORE: Did you press him on that point, officer?

SHEA: Yes, sir. One of the envelopes we confiscated had an individual's address on it.

MOORE: And what was the name of that individual?

SHEA: The envelope had the name Newton Arvin on it, Prospect Street, Northampton.

MOORE: And what was in that envelope?

SHEA: Well, that particular envelope had in it what they call muscle magazines, male physique stuff, that kind of stuff.

THOMAS: I object, Your Honor. I object to—

JUDGE MARTIN: —objection overruled. Please continue, Officer Shea.

SHEA: Most of the magazines were called *Grecian Guild Pictorial*. Some of the other titles were *Manual*, *Physique Artistry*, *Man Scan*, and *Gym*.

(Laughter in the courtroom. Judge Martin bangs his gavel.)

JUDGE MARTIN: Order in the court! Order in the court! The court will not tolerate these outbursts. If there is any further disruption, I will clear the courtroom. Proceed, Officer Shea.

SHEA: Then I asked Ford directly if Professor Arvin had given him the materials. He said, "I won't answer that question. I refuse to implicate anyone else." Then I asked him if he had ever shown the pictures to other parties. He said he had, on maybe four different occasions.

MOORE: Did he identify any of those people?

SHEA: No, sir. He refused to give anybody else's name.

MOORE: Did he tell you anything about the people, whether they were friends or casual visitors?

SHEA: No, sir. Professor Ford was very reluctant to answer any more questions. Seeing as how he wasn't going to cooperate any further,

I placed him under arrest on a charge of "possession of obscene pictures and literature."

(Spot fade on Shea. His words become increasingly indistinct.)

SHEA *(As voice fades under)*: I also charged him with "possessing the material for purposes of exhibition . . . for showing the material publicly" . . . him having admitted to circulating the magazines on at least four occasions to persons other than himself . . .

(Lights come up on Louise and Ford, conferring in a corridor of the courthouse. Double scene: Shea, on the stand, still visible, but not audible; cross-stage, Louise and Ford in conversation.)

LOUISE: . . . But what I'm telling you is, I saw him myself, as I was coming out of the bathroom. He was simply wandering around the corridor.

FORD: By himself? Wasn't Dr. Farris with him, or an attendant?

LOUISE: No. He was alone. Or seemed to be. I called out to him, but I may have been too far away.

FORD: I guess that means he *is* going to testify.

LOUISE: It's all very peculiar. He hasn't sat in on any of the other testimony. I can't imagine why he didn't let us know . . .

FORD: He probably didn't want to alarm us, thinking he might still get out of it at the last minute.

LOUISE: Dear Eddie: always ready with the generous interpretation. Frankly, I have a sick feeling in the pit of my stomach.

(Ford looks at his watch.)

FORD: I have to get back. I'm next up.

(Shea steps down off the witness box and exits.)

LOUISE: Good luck, sweetie. I'll be rooting for you.

FORD: If you find Newton, try to get him to sit in on my testimony. I'm not going to say anything he has to worry about.

LOUISE: I don't think that's the danger, love.

(They kiss quickly and hurry off. Blackout. Spot comes back up slowly on Ford seated in the witness box, his testimony already in process. We hear Ford's voice before we see him.)

FORD *(Voice-over)*: . . . At the police station Officer Shea gave me a long lecture about the evils of pornography. He seemed to have memorized some speech Postmaster General Summerfield gave somewhere. He quoted it to me at length.

(The spot is now up on Ford.)

THOMAS: Do you remember any part of what Officer Shea said?

FORD: I'll never forget one line: "One million children this year will receive pornographic filth in the family mailbox."

THOMAS: Why do you remember that line?

FORD: Because I protested it. No children had seen the materials in my apartment. They were strictly for use by adults in the privacy of their own homes. Besides, they weren't "filth"; they were for erotic stimulation. The two are not the same.

MOORE: Objection, Your Honor! This line of questioning is irrelevant to the issues in the case.

THOMAS: Your honor, that is precisely what I'm establishing: that children have nothing to do with this case, that the issue is a red herring.

JUDGE MARTIN: Objection sustained.

THOMAS: Professor Ford, do you know who the "old lady" is who Officer Shea claims let him into your apartment?

FORD: I don't believe an old lady lives in our building. There are only ten apartments. I would know if an old lady lived there.

THOMAS: The hallway leading to your apartment is very clearly a private entrance to a private apartment, is it not, Professor Ford?

FORD: Yes, sir.

MOORE: Objection, your honor! Counsel is leading the witness.

JUDGE MARTIN: Objection sustained.

THOMAS: Are you in the habit of leaving your door unlocked, Professor Ford?

FORD: I lock it automatically. I always have. It's a reflex reaction.

MOORE: Objection, your honor. Counsel is again leading the witness.

JUDGE MARTIN: Objection sustained.

THOMAS: When you arrived home, Professor Ford, please describe what you saw.

FORD: The door to my apartment was wide open. When I went inside I saw Officers Shea and Rogers standing in my living room going through material that I keep in my hallway closet. They were dancing a kind of jig. Like excited kids.

THOMAS: Did they identify themselves?

FORD: Yes, they did.

THOMAS: Did they show you a search warrant?

FORD: No, they did not.

THOMAS: Did you ask to see a search warrant?

FORD: No, I did not.

THOMAS: Why not, Professor Ford?

FORD: I really don't know. That seems strange to me now. I suppose I was too rattled. Before I had a minute to think, they were plying me with questions and accusations. And then they took me down to the station house.

THOMAS: Did they ask you why you had the materials in question?

FORD: Yes. I told them I kept them for my personal enjoyment—words to that effect.

THOMAS: Did they ask you where you got the materials?

FORD: Yes, they did. I told them I wouldn't answer that question, wouldn't implicate anyone else. Then they asked me if I had ever shown the materials to anyone else and I said that I had, three or four times in my own apartment. When I refused to tell them who I had shown the pictures to, they placed me under arrest.

MOORE: Objection, Your Honor!

JUDGE MARTIN: On what grounds, counsel?

MOORE: The witness is not competent to testify as to why Officer Shea placed him under arrest.

JUDGE MARTIN: Objection overruled. Proceed, Mr. Thomas.

THOMAS: We come now to the content of the materials, Professor Ford. Is it accurate to say that the materials are homosexual in content?

FORD: The materials show men in various poses of near nudity, but they do not portray sexual acts of any kind.

MOORE: Objection, Your Honor! The specific content of the material is irrelevant. The 1959 pornography statute talks only in general terms about the crime of procuring or exhibiting obscene—

THOMAS *(Interrupting)*: —of course the content is relevant, Your Honor! Homosexuality is *precisely* what is on trial. It is sheer hypocrisy for the prosecution to claim—

MOORE *(Interrupting)*: —Your Honor, Your Honor!

JUDGE MARTIN *(Banging gavel)*: —Order in the court! I will not tolerate both counsels speaking at once, is that clear?

MOORE: May I argue the law, Your Honor?

JUDGE MARTIN: You may. And without interruption.

MOORE: Thank you, Your Honor. The Supreme Court's 1957 ruling, *Roth v. the United States,* defined something as obscene if—and here I quote directly from the decision—"its predominant appeal is to prurient interest, that is, a shameful or morbid interest in nudity, sex, or excretion." In other words, Your Honor, nudity or near nudity is *alone* sufficient grounds for an obscenity indictment.

FORD: As is an interest in sex. To say nothing of our bowel movements. Doesn't that make us all indictable?

JUDGE MARTIN: The defendant will kindly refrain from gratuitous comment.

MOORE: The Supreme Court went on to say that any material—and again I quote—"that went substantially beyond customary limits of candor in description or representation" could also be considered obscene. Here, the gender of the figures portrayed *could* be considered relevant. After all, depictions of men posing in suggestively scanty clothing does indeed go beyond "customary limits of candor." But that would be to convict twice over. The Supreme Court's inclusion of nudity or near nudity in its definition of obscenity is sufficient to convict, without any need to discuss or debate the gender of the figures portrayed. The homosexual content of the materials is *not* germane to the indictment.

THOMAS: Your Honor, counsel knows full well that if the materials did not depict male figures, we would not be in court today. Officer Shea has himself testified to the effect that he would not arrest a husband showing so-called obscene pictures to his wife. *That*, Office Shea said, "would be interfering with the sanctity of marriage." Now surely, Your Honor—

JUDGE MARTIN *(Interrupting)*: ——the court will not listen to *ad hominem* argument. The objection is sustained. I order the preceding testimony about the homosexual content of the material stricken from the record as irrelevant.

MOORE: Thank you, Your Honor. May I argue one final point of law?

JUDGE MARTIN: You may.

MOORE: The *Roth* decision also ruled that obscenity is *not* protected by the First Amendment. Obscenity, the Supreme Court has said, "is not speech." It is therefore—like libel and blasphemy—subject to statute imitations *without* compromising the protections of the First Amendment.

THOMAS: May I respond, Your Honor?

JUDGE MARTIN: You may.

THOMAS: We have an older tradition in this country that predates the *Roth* decision. Namely, that an individual's fundamental rights as guaranteed in the Bill of Rights may be infringed upon only where a compelling reason exists for doing so, only when public safety itself is at stake. Since the materials Professor Ford kept were for his private use, it can hardly be said that he represents a threat to the public safety.

MOORE: Liberty, Your Honor, is not license. As we learned from the decline and fall of the Roman Empire. When a people is complacent in the face of moral laxity, they will be destroyed. The Supreme Court, Your Honor, has provided us with a standard whereby we can defend ourselves against the further deterioration of our country's moral values.

FORD: May I be heard, Your Honor?

JUDGE MARTIN: For what purpose, Professor Ford?

FORD: Well, I guess you might say to provide expert testimony . . .

JUDGE MARTIN *(Snide)*: Are you an expert in obscenity?

FORD: An expert in the classics, sir. I'm a professor of classics.

JUDGE MARTIN *(Hesitating)*: Well, I . . . this had better be relevant, Professor Ford.

FORD: I believe it is, sir.

JUDGE MARTIN: Very well then. But be brief.

FORD: Thank you, Your Honor. Speaking as a classicist, Your Honor, I want to note that in the ancient world gymnasts practiced in the nude, and the leading male citizens of the town would gather to admire and comment on their beauty. Since the ancient world is the source of our moral values in the West—surely no one disputes that—how can nudity be equated with obscenity or—

MOORE *(Angrily interrupting)*: —Your Honor, *please!* This outburst is entirely irrelevant. It matters not a whit whether Professor Ford and his privileged friends *agree* with the assumptions behind the *Roth* decision. *That decision is the law of the land.* And the law is the law—for everyone. I therefore ask that Professor Ford's statement be stricken from the record.

JUDGE MARTIN: So ordered. *(Turning to Ford)* I wish to ask you one question directly, Professor Ford: you admit showing the materials in question to three or four people. Were any of them minors?

FORD: I cannot answer that, Your Honor.

JUDGE MARTIN: Do you have a voice and a memory, Professor Ford?

FORD: Yes, Your Honor.

JUDGE MARTIN: So in fact you *can* answer, but are *choosing* not to. Is that correct?

FORD: Yes, Your Honor.

JUDGE MARTIN: Will you tell the court whether the three or four people alluded to were casual or longtime friends?

FORD: No, Your Honor.

JUDGE MARTIN: You are refusing to answer that question as well?

FORD: Yes, Your Honor.

JUDGE MARTIN: And for what reason, Professor Ford?

FORD: I do not wish to implicate others.

JUDGE MARTIN: May I suggest, Professor Ford, that you are placing loyalty to individuals above loyalty to your country.

FORD: I hope so, Your Honor.

JUDGE MARTIN: Beg pardon?

FORD: I hope, as E.M. Forster once said, that I would always place loyalty to friends above loyalty to country.

JUDGE MARTIN: Who is E.M. Forster?

FORD: A writer, Your Honor.

JUDGE MARTIN: An American writer?

FORD: No, Your Honor.

JUDGE MARTIN: I thought as much. The witness may step down. The court is adjourned until tomorrow morning at nine a.m.

(Blackout. In the darkness, we hear Arvin's voice. It should not be clear at first whether he is giving a speech or testifying in court.)

ARVIN *(Voice-over):* . . . For those who live in the age of absolutist states, of secret police, of brutal mind control, Emerson's confidence in the power of the untrammeled human spirit against the forces that would enslave and if possible annihilate it, is more necessary than ever before. The Emerson, I mean, who taught us that our basic purpose in life is to become "a system instead of a satellite." The self-reliant human being is not against society, but beyond it. The only society worth having is that which emerges naturally from the sum of all the individual rejections of society.

(Lights back up in the courtroom. Arvin is on the stand.)

JUDGE MARTIN: Are you addressing the court, Professor Arvin?

ARVIN: Yes. But not solely.

JUDGE MARTIN: You are not being responsive to counsel's questions.

ARVIN: I will try to do better, Your Honor. I am enraptured by fact. By the facts of universal experience.

JUDGE MARTIN: Counsel: repeat your question to the witness.

MOORE: Are you now or have you ever been a member of the Communist Party of the United States of America?

ARVIN: I am not now, and never have been.

MOORE: Did you support the Republican side in the Spanish Civil War?

ARVIN: I did.

MOORE: Did you write articles in the *New Masses* magazine?

ARVIN: I did.

MOORE: Did you join a group in the 1930s called the National Committee for the Defense of Political Prisoners?

ARVIN: I did.

MOORE: Your Honor, I submit in evidence this list of seventeen organizations of which Professor Arvin was a member. All seventeen have been cited by the Attorney General as communist or communist-front organizations.

JUDGE MARTIN: You have seen this list, Professor Arvin?

ARVIN: I have.

JUDGE MARTIN: And you acknowledge your membership in all seventeen of these organizations?

ARVIN: I do.

JUDGE MARTIN: I order the list entered as evidence, marked "1A."

ARVIN: Do not confuse a piece of evidence with the entirety of truth.

JUDGE MARTIN: Do you wish to be heard, Professor Arvin?

ARVIN: As Emerson said, "The things that are seen are temporal; the things that are unseen, are eternal."

JUDGE MARTIN: The court wishes you to speak in your own words, Professor Arvin.

ARVIN: Those are my words. Emerson's and mine. We both understand that virtue is not a matter of behavior, but of surrendering to nature—to the nature of one's own being.

MOORE *(Interrupting)*: I object, Your Honor. The witness is not being responsive.

JUDGE MARTIN *(To Arvin)*: I must caution you, Professor Arvin. You are facing serious charges.

ARVIN: My quarrel, as Emerson once said, is not with the State of Massachusetts but with the state of Man. Or with the state of most men, those who refuse to let their real natures unfold, fearful of marching to a different drummer. The laws of right and wrong have no authority compared to the authority of one's inner voice.

JUDGE MARTIN: Which seems to mean that you place your individual judgment above that of the community.

ARVIN: You understand me very well.

JUDGE MARTIN: That is a prescription for anarchy.

ARVIN: No, men are in all ways better than they seem.

JUDGE MARTIN: How can one have an orderly society, Professor Arvin, when each citizen is following what you call his own "inner voice"?

ARVIN: I will relinquish it if you will show me the fountains of the Nile.

JUDGE MARTIN: Come, come, Professor Arvin, you're speaking in riddles.

ARVIN: I must be relieved of responsibility for a Universe I do not use.

JUDGE MARTIN: Are you mocking the court, sir?

ARVIN: Not at all, Your Honor. I am merely doing my calisthenics. As Mr. Emerson said—

JUDGE MARTIN *(Angry)*: —I have cautioned you once already, Professor Arvin, about quoting from somebody else. I won't do so again. The court wishes only to hear your own words.

ARVIN *(Continuing to quote from Emerson)*: —Society is a masked ball where everyone hides his real character and reveals it by hiding.

JUDGE MARTIN: Continue your questioning, Mr. Moore.

MOORE: Do you acknowledge, Professor Arvin, that *(Gesturing to bound volumes on the table)* these diaries are yours?

ARVIN: I do.

MOORE: Do you acknowledge that you freely turned these diaries over to the police?

ARVIN: I do not.

MOORE *(Surprised)*: You do not?

ARVIN: I acted under constraint.

MOORE: Are you claiming that the officers forcibly took the diaries from you?

ARVIN: No, I am not.

MOORE: Then you surrendered the diaries voluntarily.

ARVIN: I was not in my normal state of mind. I do hope you'll forgive my use of that much controverted word.

MOORE: Mind?

ARVIN: Normal. Though "mind," too, now that you mention it.

MOORE: How would you characterize your state of mind at the time you turned over your diaries?

ARVIN: Distraught.

MOORE: How did the officers even know that such diaries existed?

ARVIN: I told them.

MOORE: So you voluntarily apprised the officers of the existence of your diaries.

ARVIN: As I've already said—and His Honor does not care for repetition—I was not myself.

MOORE: Who were you?

ARVIN: Ah, a genuinely interesting question at last. I was probably my father.

MOORE: Are you saying you were out of your mind?

ARVIN: My father was entirely sane. Excessively sane, one might say— that is, if we reserve the designation "sane" for those people, and only those people, who can be counted on to agree with the opinions of their neighbors.

MOORE: Is it true, Professor Arvin, that you are currently under treatment in the psychiatric hospital?

ARVIN: Treatment? I am being housed there.

MOORE: Your physician, Dr. Farris, has testified to your improved condition.

ARVIN: Then it must be true. Dr. Farris is an excellent physician.

MOORE: Do you agree with his estimate?

ARVIN: His estimate of what?

MOORE: His estimate of your mental condition.

ARVIN: I have no opinion on that subject.

MOORE: Are you feeling less distraught than when you turned your diaries over to the police?

ARVIN: Oh, you're asking about my *emotional* state.

MOORE: Yes.

ARVIN: But you previously said my "mental condition."

MOORE: That is correct.

ARVIN: *What* is correct?

JUDGE MARTIN: Kindly answer the question, Professor Arvin.

ARVIN: Gladly, sir. But what *is* the question? The mind and the emotions are not to be equated. Though of course they influence each other profoundly.

MOORE: Never mind, Professor Arvin. Let us turn to another matter.

ARVIN (*Chuckling; almost to himself*): Never "mind." Another curious usage.

MOORE: Do you acknowledge, Professor Arvin, that the materials found in your home belong to you?

ARVIN: I do.

MOORE: And do you acknowledge that you shared those materials with others?

ARVIN: I do.

MOORE: Please tell the court who you shared them with.

ARVIN: With several men who live and work in the town. And with several of my colleagues as well. I believe this is all in the diaries.

MOORE: Please tell the court the names of those colleagues.

ARVIN: I shared the magazines and pictures with Professor Gerald Norris and with Professor Edward Ford.

MOORE: Did you share the materials once or often?

ARVIN: More than once.

MOORE: And did Professors Norris and Ford ever share material of their own with you?

ARVIN: The material originated with me. Mostly.

MOORE: Did they *ever* share material with you?

ARVIN: Yes.

MOORE: *That* fact is *not* in the diaries.

ARVIN: Not every petty event of a given day makes its way into a diary, Mr. Moore.

MOORE (*Putting evidence in front of Arvin*): Are these some of the pictures Norris and Ford shared with you?

(*Pause. Arvin laughs.*)

MOORE: You find the pictures amusing, Professor Arvin?

ARVIN: Vastly. They're so artificial, you know. The men seem quite uncomfortable.

MOORE: You don't find the pictures—how should I put it?—sexually arousing?

ARVIN: An individual's erotic appeal hinges on a lack of vain self-consciousness. Such people are rare, and rarely attainable. Thus one settles *(Pointing to the pictures)* for what *is* available. These men, however, are monumentally self-conscious, not in a natural state.

MOORE: It will be up to the court to define what is or is not erotic or obscene.

ARVIN: Obscene? My dear sir, I have the utmost contempt for all moralizing that pretends to derive from universal standards. Morality means only one thing: obeying the voice of God in the soul.

MOORE: So you do believe in God?

ARVIN: In the long run, fate is not arbitrary. I seek a natural freedom because I believe in supernatural perfection. That is precisely why we must cultivate indifference to circumstances: in the long run, there can be no calamities. What looks like disaster is in fact necessity—the necessities of our natures.

MOORE: So you're defining God as a reality external to yourself.

ARVIN: Cogently summarized, sir. I am enraptured by the romance of infinitude. Life itself perpetually promises us a glory we will never attain.

THOMAS: Your Honor, I object, strenuously object, to the entire line of questioning that has developed here. I fail to see how questions relating to God, fate, morality, and the like are germane to the issues of law in this case.

ARVIN: Do you not, Mr. Thomas? How very surprising.

JUDGE MARTIN: Since I cannot *follow* the line of questioning, Mr. Thomas, I must assume its irrelevance. Objection sustained. *(Turning to Arvin)* Now Professor Arvin: allow me to caution you again, sir. I will be forced to terminate your testimony, sir, if you do not address yourself *concretely* to the issues.

ARVIN: But the one issue is always character.

JUDGE MARTIN: I am asking you to be responsive, sir, to the questions asked.

ARVIN: I am responding—with my real self. And my real self is my whole contradictory nature.

JUDGE MARTIN: I'm warning you, Professor Arvin.

ARVIN: I'm very fond of my own equivocations. Because I'm fond of my whole nature. Surely that alone proves me a uniquely sane man.

JUDGE MARTIN: I see you *will* persist, sir. Very well: you're ordered to step down from the witness stand.

ARVIN: Then my testimony is concluded?

JUDGE MARTIN: Yes. Such as it was.

ARVIN: I'm sorry it didn't please. All our testimonies are partial, don't you agree?—the result of our mortal limits.

JUDGE MARTIN: *Kindly* step down, sir.

ARVIN *(As he steps from the witness box)*: Never mind. I have grown up at last.

(The spot dims and follows Arvin as he moves off and quietly sits downstage left. Judge Martin begins his summation. As he proceeds, his voice gradually fades out.)

JUDGE MARTIN: After due deliberation, the court finds that the defendants did, by their own admission, have in their possession pictures, images, and printed matter that can appropriately be defined under State Statute #417 as indecent or obscene. As for the issue of illegal seizure, the court views it as warranted in this instance due to overriding issues of public safety and morality. *(Voice fades)* The court further finds that the defendants exhibited these materials. "Exhibition" is taken to mean the showing or quasi-public display to third parties. Professor Arvin's testimony has indisputably established that such an incidental purpose *was* present. He has freely admitted that he showed various items to Professors Norris and Ford, and that Professors Norris and Ford, in turn, showed various items to him . . . *(Voice now nearly inaudible; the spot on Judge Martin fades)* . . . even when indecent materials are primarily for one's own use . . . even an *incidental* purpose to show . . . to others . . . sufficient grounds for conviction.

(Arvin's figure remains visible. Louise and Ed Ford appear in separate spots.)

JUDGE MARTIN *(Voice-under; the spot fades out)*: . . . The nature of the materials seized . . . so heinous a nature as to deprive . . . defendants of the ordinary safeguards provided by the First . . . Fourteenth . . .

(Louise takes a tentative step toward Arvin.)

LOUISE: Newton . . . Newton, are you all right?

ARVIN: Yes, dear. Of course I am.

LOUISE: Oh, Newton, Newton . . . I don't understand . . . How could you have . . . ? Why did you ever agree to testify?

ARVIN: I tried not to. But Dr. Farris "advised" it. *Strongly* advised it. He said it was the only way I could convince *him* that I didn't need electric shock, and convince the authorities of my sanity.

LOUISE: So cooperating with the state makes one sane?

ARVIN: It's an ancient definition, dear. An essential part of western culture.

LOUISE: You'll forgive me, but I found your testimony—shall we say—bizarre in the extreme. Hardly a guarantee that you'd be found "sane."

ARVIN *(Amused)*: A bit too "enigmatic," eh? But rather mystically eloquent, wouldn't you agree? Dare I say, "Emersonian"?

LOUISE: No, you don't dare. I don't want to hear that man's name evoked again for as long as I live!

ARVIN: As you wish . . .

LOUISE: And the diaries, Newton? Couldn't you have retracted the diaries?

ARVIN: You mean deny I had written them?

LOUISE: Deny their right to use them.

ARVIN: Take the police to court?

LOUISE: Oh, Newton, stop it! Enough games! How did the police *get* the diaries?

ARVIN: As I testified, I was distraught. . . . Do you want me to repeat my entire testimony? . . . *One part of me* volunteered them . . . not the part I like best, but the same part, oddly, that will push ahead with the Emerson biography . . .

LOUISE: Your intelligence?

ARVIN *(Snorting)*: *Really*, Louise! . . . No, my dear loyal friend: my wish to be left alone . . . that bottom-line feature of my character . . . the hermit seeking his cave.

LOUISE: But you *love* Eddie!

ARVIN: Yes . . . it *is* a tangle. . . . As I said, Doctor Farris told me that
if I refused to testify, he'd assume that I was seriously ill. He'd then
have no choice but to prescribe *multiple* treatments of electric
shock therapy—since the limited, earlier courses had obviously
not succeeded.

LOUISE: Not succeeded in turning you into a vegetable.

ARVIN: A flowering cherry tree is, I believe, the preferred outcome.

(Judge Martin's voice is now once more audible.)

JUDGE MARTIN *(Voice-over)*: . . . The court therefore pronounces the
following sentences: Professors Gerald Norris and Edward Ford
. . . one year each in the House of Correction. Professor Newton
Arvin . . . out of feelings of compassion for his age and health . . .
a suspended sentence and a fine of one thousand dollars . . .
Michael Brown . . . probation for a period of two years . . .

*(Judge Martin's voice fades to inaudible. Louise steps out of the spot, Ford
into it.)*

FORD *(Sardonic)*: Congratulations, Newton! You're off the hook.

ARVIN: Not in any way that matters.

FORD: You're not going to jail. That matters.

ARVIN *(Quietly)*: Yes, it does . . . *(Pause)* What will you do, Eddie?

FORD: Do? Appeal, of course. I have no intention of sitting in jail for a
year because of *your* treachery.

ARVIN: I know you must see it that way.

FORD: Is there another way?

ARVIN: You're young, Eddie, in time this will all—

FORD *(Flaring)*: —do you mean the trivial little year I face in jail, or
the fact that my entire career has been—

ARVIN: —I had no choice, I tell you, no choice . . .

FORD: There's always a choice. You made the selfish one.

ARVIN: I was just trying to stay alive. To be of use to anybody else, one
has to stay alive.

FORD: Who can you be of use to now? Who would have you? Those
cute little Emersonian riddles on the stand can't cover up the fact
that you were betraying your friends.

ARVIN: And if I had courageously destroyed myself . . . ?

FORD: You don't betray friends! Not if you have feelings for anyone else.

ARVIN: It's true I don't seem to feel much any more. Not for a long time; perhaps, maybe, as far back as Truman. . . . Maybe that's when I froze over once and for all. Maybe that's how I survived . . .

LOUISE *(Stepping back into the spot)*: Word has come from President Morse. . . . The Board of Trustees has voted that *(To Ed)* you and Jerry are dismissed from the faculty as of today. You, Newton, are immediately "retired." A small income will be provided until your pension begins in eight years, when you turn 68.

FORD: Congratulations, Newton. Your strategy worked. You'll be as snug as a bug. But do you know what? You'll never finish your Emerson biography. You'll fester. You'll sink into depression and, finally, suicide.

ARVIN: Oh, my: just like one of your Greek tragedies, eh? What a romantic you are, Eddie.

FORD: Newton Arvin succeeds in outwitting the State—and ends up destroying himself. *(Pause)* Goodbye, Newton. I hope my prediction doesn't come true.

ARVIN: That's kindly of you, Ed.

FORD: Oh, I'll always love you, you despicable old man. But I'll never see you again.

(He exits.)

LOUISE: Oh, Newton, Newton . . . Why didn't you tell him about Dr. Farris? About the threat of electric shock?

ARVIN: I didn't want to rob him of his anger. He'll need that to survive.

(Pause.)

LOUISE: I love you, too, Newton. But you don't make it easy.

ARVIN: I know: such a ruthless old man. So intent on staying alive. What's to love?

LOUISE: I have to keep telling myself that you didn't set the terms for survival. I'll reserve my anger for those who did—for those who made you chose between friendship and life.

ARVIN: You're a generous pal, old dear. Much more than I. *(Pause)* Well, all I want now is some peace. Maybe I'll take to planting long rows of beans and corn . . . with occasional interruptions from my friend Louise to remind me that Mr. Emerson awaits . . .

(Louise takes his arm, as the stage lights dim.)

LOUISE: You've mentioned him again. Once more, and I'm gone! *(They chuckle)* Since when did you become a gardener?

ARVIN: On the day I realized all the free hours I'll have now that *Grecian Guild Pictorial* is no more . . . *(They again laugh)*

LOUISE: You are unquestionably an enemy of the people.

(Pause.)

ARVIN: I'll miss Ed.

LOUISE: And he'll miss you. But you'll never see him again.

ARVIN: I know.

LOUISE: I have to tell you, Newton, that on balance, I go with Ed.

ARVIN: Of course. So do I, my dear. So do I. . . . That's why I have to keep repeating to myself over and over: there are no calamities. There are only necessities of nature. Which may even be true . . .

(As they move off, arm in arm, blackout.)

END OF PLAY

Visions of Kerouac

ACT ONE

SCENE 1

(Lights up on Allen Ginsberg's apartment, 1944.

The apartment is filthy, cramped; cushions and mattresses are scattered on the floor. A sign is tacked over the stove: WE JELL PLOTZ. *Onstage with Kerouac is Allen—about twenty, short-haired, clean-shaven, intense, hyperverbal, brilliant, given to sudden shifts of mood from mournful to manic—but with his essential sweetness and generosity always showing through. He looks like one of the Three Stooges—the tender, lovable, vulnerable one. Also present are:*

Gregory Corso: in his early twenties, he looks and often acts like an Italian Dead End Kid; given to wild flights of lyrical fantasy, bursts of fury; always horny; usually unpredictable.

Ruth Heaper, Kerouac's girlfriend, in her early twenties; pretty, warm, good-natured.

William Burroughs, pale, lanky, laconic; about ten years older than the others.)

ALLEN: Jacky—the days of wrath are coming! It's 1944—there's a war on! And all *you* want to do is bum around the country, looking for hincty sweets on village greens. *Believe me,* I know what's best for you—you've got to *stop reading Thomas Wolfe*!
KEROUAC: Allen, how annoying you do get.
CORSO: He's right. Read more Celine, all Dostoevsky!
ALLEN: —let me talk!

KEROUAC *(Amused):* When *don't* you, little Allen?

ALLEN: Jack, I specifically asked Will to come over tonight to—
(Turning to Burroughs) Will—*please* explain to Jack that—

BURROUGHS *(Laconic):* —later, later, Allen. Talking can ruin a good
high.

CORSO *(Growling at Burroughs):* No good Times Square junkie freak!

BURROUGHS: We all have our visions, Gregory.

ALLEN: Don't mind Gregory. Deep down he's very gentle.

BURROUGHS: I hope you make it to the bottom alive. I've read his poetry.

CORSO: I'm gonna get you gang-raped, Burroughs, open up that ass of
yours!

BURROUGHS: Splendid! Perhaps we can get the same gang to close
your mouth.

RUTH: This is the crowd that's going to save American literature?

ALLEN: World literature! We have a Blakean message for the Iron
Hound of America!

RUTH: I'm sorry! I'm sorry!

BURROUGHS: So are Van Doren and Trilling.

ALLEN *(With mounting fervor):* How can the East have respect for a
country that has no prophetic poets? The Lamb of America must be
raised! Big trembling Oklahomas need poetry and nakedness!
Wheat's got to be sent to India!

CORSO: Enough, enough! I gotta get laid!

ALLEN: Gregory—shut up!

CORSO: Yeah? Well, I may give up the poetry racket altogether, paint
religious murals for Mafia bars. I wanna heart-shaped moat like
Dali's! Triplex pigeons on the roof! A villa on Capri!

ALLEN: You write a poem every time you open your mouth, Gregory.

RUTH *(Mimicking Allen):* "You are a great prophetic bard!" *(Getting ready
to leave)* Unfortunately, *we* have to get to the Laundromat before it
closes.

KEROUAC: Aw, c'mon, babe . . . have another beer. . . . Wanna beer,
Will?

BURROUGHS: Nothing for me . . . uh, unless you have a little codeine cough syrup?

CORSO: How about a dozen suppositories!

RUTH: Jack, let's go . . . please . . .

ALLEN: Ruthie, I *have* to talk to Jack. . . . So many complex, interesting, illuminating things have happened while he was in the merchant marine.

RUTH: You've been talking his ear off for *hours!*

KEROUAC *(To Allen)*: I can come back tomorrow.

ALLEN: This is *urgent!* Very serious!

KEROUAC *(To Ruth)*: I'll call you later, hon . . .

RUTH *(Angry, heading toward the door)*: I've hardly talked to you since you've been back!

KEROUAC: I told you I had to see the boys.

RUTH: You've seen them. When do the girls get a turn?

ALLEN: No fighting! No fighting! You're all wonderful people—and great writers!

RUTH: Don't be compulsive about loving everyone, Allen. It shows a lack of discrimination. Drop me off, will you, Gregory? If you can tear yourself away from the boys.

CORSO: Dee-*light*-ed, my dear!

RUTH *(To Kerouac)*: Let me know when my turn comes around again.

KEROUAC: I'll call ya later, hon. I promise . . .

RUTH: I won't hang on it. *(Ruth exits)*

(Corso starts to leave.)

ALLEN *(To Corso)*: And where are you going?

CORSO: To hang out. Waiting on the street corner for no one—*that's* true power!

(Corso exits.)

ALLEN: Will, *why* haven't you been talking more? Jack *has* to decide what he's going to do with his life, and you're the *only* person who can tell him. Will—*tell* him!

BURROUGHS: Tell him *what?*

ALLEN: I showed you a chapter of his novel.

KEROUAC *(Startled)*:You did? Whaddya think of it?

BURROUGHS: Good, good . . .

   (Pause.)

KEROUAC: But whaddya think of it . . . specifically?

BURROUGHS *(Pursing his lips)*:Why . . . I don't specifically *think* of it. I just rather like it, is all.

KEROUAC *(Hurt)*:Well, it was fun writing it.

BURROUGHS: I daresay. . . . Now tell me—how would I get papers if I wanted to join the merchant marine?

ALLEN *(Astonished)*: Join the wha—?

BURROUGHS: —shush, Allen. So much need to be noticed. Now about the merchant marine . . .

KEROUAC: What was your last job?

BURROUGHS: Summons server in Newark.

KEROUAC: Before that?

BURROUGHS: Exterminator in Chicago. Of bedbugs, that is.

KEROUAC: Well . . . you got to get your Coast Guard pass first, down near the Battery . . .

BURROUGHS: Precisely *where* near the Battery?

ALLEN: Will hates confusion.

BURROUGHS: Also liberals and cops. *(Charming smile)* You see, I'm really a Kansas minister.

ALLEN *(Adoring)*: *Tell* us about it, Will. *Please!*

BURROUGHS: Allen, do let Jack talk.

ALLEN: Jack doesn't like to talk.

BURROUGHS *(To Kerouac)*:Very sensible of you. 'Tis a finkish world. *(He starts to leave)* Go to the movies a lot. And don't let Allen bother you with *literary* matters. I'll give you a bang of morphine—much better for you. Why, when I was your age . . .

KEROUAC: —how old are ya?

BURROUGHS: Thirty-two.

KEROUAC: You're only nine years older than me.

BURROUGHS: But I'm an agent from another planet. Unfortunately, I haven't gotten my orders clearly decoded yet. . . . Well, must fill some new prescriptions . . .

ALLEN: Be careful, Will—you'll get in trouble.

BURROUGHS: Always careful. Unlike the riffraff. *(Burroughs exits)*

ALLEN: Do you realize *everyone* we know is a genius? Especially Burroughs.

KEROUAC: You think all your friends are geniuses.

ALLEN: Burroughs is *über*-genius! He knows *exactly* what's happening. *(Gesturing toward window)* . . . The great canvas of disintegration . . .

KEROUAC: —Allen?

ALLEN: —Jack, if you go on interrupting me, how will you ever understand what's going on? It's the great molecular comedown. All character structures based on tradition will slowly rot away, people will get hives on their hearts, great crabs will cling to their brains . . .

KEROUAC *(Nervous laugh)*: You're goofing . . .

ALLEN: Marijuana fumes will seep out of the Stock Exchange. College professors will suddenly go cross-eyed and start showing their behinds to one another.

KEROUAC: Allen, why don't you go back to becoming a radical labor leader, like you always wanted?

ALLEN: Burroughs will help you see it. He's helped me see *everything*. Of course he *loves me* . . . *That's* what I have to talk to you about, *very* important!

KEROUAC: That's enough, Allen, I gotta go. I gotta find Ruthie.

ALLEN: *Now?* You're leaving *now*, just when I was—

KEROUAC: Allen—I got things to do, places to go! I didn't quit Columbia to sit around all day and *talk*!

ALLEN: It's true you're not very good at it . . .

KEROUAC: I wanna see where the rest of those lights on the highway stretch to! Prowl and roam, study the real America!

ALLEN: *More* Thomas Wolfe romantic posh! *(Pause)* Jack, are you in love with Ruth?

KEROUAC: Huh?

ALLEN: Stop acting like you don't understand the language! Those Canuck "huhs" only work in *polite* society.

KEROUAC: I like Ruthie, yeah. She's a good kid.

ALLEN: Then why do you mistreat her?

KEROUAC: Do I?

ALLEN: You won't *connect*. You keep veering off—

KEROUAC: —stop analyzing me! You're like the priests in high school.

ALLEN *(Giggling)*: I'm a black monk. Gregory says so. *(They laugh. Pause) (Deeply felt)* Jack—I love you.

KEROUAC *(Perfunctory)*: I love you, too, Allen.

ALLEN: No, I mean: I *love* you.

KEROUAC: Awww, Allen . . .

ALLEN: I love you and I want to sleep with you, and I really like men, and that's part of what's changed, and I—*(Takes a deep breath)* and I want to sleep with you.

KEROUAC *(Confused, sad)*: Oooooooh, no . . .

ALLEN: I don't mean *now*, or tomorrow. . . . There's no hurry, things happen. . . . I just wanted to let you know . . .

KEROUAC: But you know how much I like girls, Allen . . .

ALLEN: Of course I do. And I respect that. Just as *you* accept *my* soul with all its throbbings and sorrows and—

(A sudden shaft of light as the apartment door opens. A young man— Neal—is silhouetted in it.)

ALLEN: Hello . . . Who are you?

NEAL: Hunkey gimme this address. Said to come here when I got in from Denver. *(Peering in Kerouac's direction)* That you, Hunkey?

KEROUAC: I'm Jack.

NEAL: Oh . . . whaddaya say, Jack!

ALLEN: I haven't seen Hunkey in months. . . . I'm Allen. Do you want to come in?

NEAL: Sure—no place else to go. *(He pulls a young girl into the light)* This here's my wife, Marylou.

ALLEN: Marylou . . . that's a nice name.

MARYLOU: Yeah? I don't like it . . . common.

ALLEN: Well, come on in. We got lots of room. We're a cornucopia of roomy rooms. *(Marylou giggles)*

NEAL: Appreciate that.

ALLEN: My name's Allen, Allen Ginsberg.

MARYLOU *(Giggling)*: Everything's sure funny here.

ALLEN *(Beaming)*: You sense it immediately, eh? Ah, yes—there's much serious joy and gloom here. I myself am a big dignified poet, with only one important ambition in life: *to have a voice in the supermarket.* *(Marylou giggles)* No—*two* ambitions: to arrange at *once* for the publication of all my friends' writing!

NEAL: You're all writer-fellas, huh?

ALLEN: We're big international traveling authors. We sign autographs for old ladies from Ozone Park! *(To Neal)* And you're—you're Abner Yokum! Or is it Gene Autry?

NEAL *(Laughing)*: Nah, I'm just the son of an old Okie Shadow . . .

ALLEN *(Excited)*: What, what? Another archetype? Another type for the Ark?

KEROUAC *(Mock disgust at the pun)*: . . . Allen!

NEAL: Yassir, born in a jalopy as my folks were makin' their way from Iowa to L.A., eyes fixed anxious on the road . . . where I been ever since . . .

KEROUAC *(Excited)*: You really been around, huh? . . .

NEAL: Seen it all, m'boy . . . shiny swath of headlamps shimmerin' astral-like down the road . . .

ALLEN *(Delighted)*: My God! An Ode from the Plains! A wild yea-sayer!—what a *find!* *(Hopefully)* Were your parents . . . uh . . . *real* Okies?

NEAL: Nah—Pa had a barber trade—till Ma died when I was ten. Then he became the most totterin' bum on Larimer Street. He and me hoboed all over the Southwest.

KEROUAC: Wow! That's what I'm gonna do!

ALLEN: I'll bet you've never been to *school!*

NEAL *(Annoyed)*: Why, sure I been to school! Spent *all* my time in the library—'cept a'course for a few innings out in, how you say, the pool hall and jail. First-class altar boy, too. Priests loved me—and I mean *loved* me, know what I mean?—in every Catholic church in Colorado!

ALLEN *(Overcome)*: How did you *get* here?

NEAL *(Proud)*: Drivin' a '32 Pontiac clunker, the Green Hornet. . . .
Didn't have to steal it, neither. Marylou here turns a trick now and
then.

ALLEN: You're going to *love* New York!

NEAL: Hey, man—you think you could rustle us up a little grub? Got
any eggs maybe we could fry? Ain't had a bite all day and Marylou
here's about to faint on me.

MARYLOU: Am not, either.

NEAL: Now, darling, here we are in New York and it is absolutely
necessary to postpone all those leftover things concerning our
personal lovethings. . . . *(To Allen)* Did you say you had somethin'
to eat?

(Allen jumps up and heads for the kitchen.)

ALLEN: Yes! All sorts of things! Cloverleaf jam, zwieback crackers,
hundred-year-old Chinese eggs—we'll pour all kinds of good
things into you. . . . *(Allen exits)*

NEAL *(Calling after Allen)*: So long's I can get this li'l old gal something
to *eat*, son, ya hear me? I'm *hungry*, I'm *starving*, let's *eat right now!*
(To Kerouac) You don't seem to say much, man. Cat got your tongue?

KEROUAC *(Stunned)*: . . . Uh . . . Allen does most of the talking . . .
I'm . . . I'm not much of a talker.

NEAL: Well, I know what you mean, yass, absolutely. . . . Marylou's a
lot like that, aren't you, darlin' . . .

MARYLOU: Ah dunno. . . . Ah just try to get along. . . . Ah—

NEAL: —'cause you do, darlin', now you just come over here, honey-
thighs, you sit next to me, 'cause now is the time and *we all know
time!* *(Marylou moves away)* I've pleaded and pleaded with Marylou
for a peaceful sweet understanding of pure love between us forever
with all hassles thrown out. But her mind is bent on something
else.

KEROUAC: *(Dumbfounded)*: . . . Uh-huh . . . Yes, women aren't easy to
understand . . .

NEAL: We blame on them and it's all our fault. *(Marylou suddenly plops
down on Neal's lap)* But peace will come suddenly—see, now?—and
we won't understand it when it does.

KEROUAC: You been to California, too?

NEAL: Well a' course—sweet zigzaggin' every side . . .

KEROUAC: That's what I gotta do . . .

MARYLOU: Ah like Denver better . . .

NEAL: Now darlin', it is absolutely necessary at once to begin thinking of our specific worklife plans!

ALLEN *(Yelling in from the kitchen)*: I'm heating chop suey! On its way!

NEAL: Wonderful, perfect! Now, damnit, look here—we all must admit that everything is fine and, in fact, we should realize what it would mean to us to *understand* that we're not *really* worried about *anything*? Am I right?

KEROUAC: How old are you?

NEAL: Almost twenty! Marylou here's only a child—mah child bride of fifteen.

MARYLOU: . . . Told you I dint wanna get married . . . jes no point to it . . .

NEAL *(Laughing)*: Oh honey Marylou, how sweet you musta been at *nine!* Think of all that time we coulda been back of the garage.

MARYLOU: Ah don't like New York . . .

NEAL: When I see a sidewalk, never can resist the urge to—

(Allen reappears.)

ALLEN: Come and get it!

NEAL: *Wheeoo!* Here it is, darlin'! *(Oratorical)* I can't think of nothin' in my interior concerns but caterin' to the amazement and gratitude I feel for you fine people!

(Marylou and Allen exit to kitchen. Neal starts to follow, realizes Kerouac is lingering, turns back to him, grinning.)

NEAL: Why, man, we'll roll it *coast to coast!*

KEROUAC *(Delighted, stumbling)*: What . . . what's your *name?*

NEAL: *Neal*—Neal Cassady. Fastest man alive! Jes leapin' with love-looks! C'mon—*let's eat!*

(Blackout.)

SCENE 2

(Early morning. Wooded area. A battered old car is barely visible to the side. Ruth and Marylou are curled up in sleeping bags. Neal and Kerouac, just awake, are enjoying the sunrise, making some halfhearted efforts to clean up the campsite.)

NEAL: —Yup, that trail to heaven is a long, long trail. But y'see m'boy, there's no need to worry—'cause we're already *there!*

KEROUAC: Sure feels that way this morning. *(Looking around happily)* Never seen such beautiful country.

NEAL: Lots of it—and we're gonna see it all.

KEROUAC: I sure hope so!

NEAL: Deprived mill-town youth. Y'lucky Ah come along, boy, got you outta that tiny li'l life, eh? You diggin' this sun, Jack? Damn! Bam!

(Neal dances around maniacally.)

KEROUAC: Shush, Neal . . . you'll wake the girls.

NEAL: No way, m'boy. Not after last night's workout. That is— *(Laughs)*—if they got as confused as *we* did! Ah swear at one point there Ah had sweet *Ruthie* in mah arms, while you and Marylou were—

KEROUAC *(Embarrassed)*: —what am I gonna say to Marylou? What am I gonna say to *Ruthie?* We've never done anything like *that* before . . .

NEAL: *Never* done—?! *(Heads toward the women)* Wahl, Ah guess you need a little more practice, then!

KEROUAC *(Grabbing Neal)*: Stop!—wait! We got to slow down . . . got to get my bearings . . .

NEAL: Thas jes what you're doin!—travelin' around with me and becomin' a big artist-type writer. Right, m'boy?

KEROUAC: Pa says, "No Kerouac was ever an artist. . . . Never was such a name in the artist game."

NEAL: Wha—?! He want you to talk and write jes like everybody else?

KEROUAC: Neal, you understand completely.

NEAL: A'course Ah do. Always have. It's my amazin' intu-ee-tive power.

KEROUAC: Thing is, ya see, my folks always had it tough. Pa workin' in other men's printing shops, Ma spending most of her life in a shoe factory or as a maid in—

NEAL *(Interrupting, emphatic)*: —'cause they let the world *catch* 'em! The secret, m'boy, is to *keep movin'*! *(He starts dancing around again, yelling Indian war whoops)* Like a young idjit Injun in the sagebrush! Whoo! Whoo!

RUTH *(Sticking her head out of sleeping bag)*: I thought Tonto and the Lone Ranger had gone off the air? What a sight to start the day . . .

KEROUAC *(Starting toward Ruth, embarrassed)*: Hey, Ruthie . . . uh. . . . Mornin', m'love. . . . Got some breakfast over here, if—
(Marylou slowly sticks her head out of her sleeping bag. She's naked from the waist up.)

MARYLOU *(Grumpily)*: —Chris' sake! Ain't you two got nuthin' better t'do 'cept croak away like two dumb bullfrogs? . . .
(Neal leaps over and dives onto Marylou's sleeping bag.)

NEAL: Honeythighs, I got *lots* better things to do! Jes shove your sweet little ass right on over there and Ah—

MARYLOU *(Pushing Neal away)*: Ah'm *finished* with you, hear me? *(To Ruth, indignant)* Why, that no-good cracker sex fiend put Lady Parker Cold Cream all over mah sweet little—

NEAL: —Honeythighs, you know you scored that jar all by yourself last week in the A&P—*(Interrupts himself)* —uh-oh . . . Don't look now, me pretties, but . . .
(A uniformed state trooper walks toward them.)

NEAL: An offisah-type fella jes jumped outta the piney woods . . . sha-zola! *(To Marylou)* Quick—put on the overcoat!

MARYLOU: It's wedged between—where's mah clothes, where's mah clothes?—

RUTH: —*under* the sleeping bag. Here, let me—
(They freeze as the Trooper saunters up.)

NEAL *(unctuous, ridiculous)*: Hi there, offisah, beautiful day, eh? Sure is wonderful country you got in these parts—

TROOPER *(Southern accent)*: Mighty glad y'all like it. We're famous in Texas for our—hospitality.

NEAL: Yass, exactly, thas jes what I was tellin' my friends here—in Texas, I told 'em, why, people can't hardly do enough for ya, they's just about *the* most cordial, friendliest folk in—

KEROUAC *(Trying to shut Neal up)*: —didn't think they'd be any harm in our camping out for just one night, officer. That's our car right over there and we'll be heading off in less time than it—

TROOPER *(To Marylou)*: —if those are your clothes Ah passed on mah way down here, ma'am, you best stay in that sleeping bag. You see, we got a statewide ordinance in these friendly parts 'gainst what we call "indecent exposure"—public nudity?

MARYLOU *(Mumbling)*: He mean me? *(Indignant)* Well Ah never in all mah born days—

KEROUAC *(Interrupting)*: —hush up, Marylou . . .

NEAL *(To trooper, pretending to be dumbfounded)*: Bless my soul, how customs do change from place to place!

TROOPER: You folks from these parts?

MARYLOU: We're from Colorado. Them two's *(Pointing to Ruth and Kerouac)* from New York—

NEAL *(Trying to shut her up)*: —oh my, *no!* See, we been travelin' 'round, jes goin' here and there. . . . With that sun beatin' down Ah said to them, "Now you all do as I'm doin', disemburden yourself of them clothes, jes open up your pretty bellies as we drive into that sun . . ."

TROOPER: Mmm . . . does get hot in these parts. *(He reaches down and picks up the jar of cold cream)* But applyin' this to your bodies, jes gonna make you hotter—know what I mean? *(Marylou giggles)* Especially if these young ladies do the applyin'—

KEROUAC: That's mine, officer. I got this rash, you see, and the doctor told me—

TROOPER: —well, a' course he did. Mighty easy to get a rash travelin' 'round in mixed company. You folks got a destination—a place y'all plannin' to stop on your way to the sun?

NEAL: Destination *Mars!* That's it, *Mars!*

MARYLOU: Ma's—mah ma's.

RUTH: We're on our way to see her mother in Santa Fe.

TROOPER: Uh-huh. Little surprise, eh?

KEROUAC: That's right, we're heading straight outta Texas, officer, straight on out . . .

TROOPER *(Serious, laconic)*: Well . . . I'll tell ya what Ah think . . . *(He slowly replaces the jar on the ground)* Ah think . . . what with these two beauties sittin' round naked, that you boys 'bout the luckiest sons of bitches Ah seen in a long time. *(Tips his hat)* Now you look for the diner when you get *over the state line*. Reckon you can manage that *before* breakfast?

KEROUAC: Yes, sir!

TROOPER: Good day, ladies . . . *(Trooper exits)*

(They all roar with delight, then quickly start gathering up their things.)

NEAL: Whoo! Hot damn! It's jes like Allen sez, see—the whole world's turnin' upside down! Oh, the ramifications, the infinite ramifications—but no time now, no *time!*

MARYLOU *(holding up the overcoat that had been covering her)*: Ech—cold cream *every*where!

NEAL *(As he exits, followed by Marylou)*: Let's *go*, me pretties!

(Ruth holds Jack back.)

RUTH: Jack—wait.

KEROUAC: Huh? *C'mon*, Ruthie, we gotta get out of here!

RUTH: Where to now?

KEROUAC: Who knows—that's part of the fun.

RUTH: Fun, is it . . .

KEROUAC: What's the matter? I thought you were having a good time.

RUTH: I have been. But is this supposed to go on forever?

KEROUAC: Aw, Ruthie, don't start again . . . Traveling around with Neal like this—what could be finer? We're seeing America!

RUTH: We're seeing Neal.

KEROUAC: I thought you liked him!

RUTH: He's the most amazing con man I ever met. And the most exhausting. I'd like *some* time alone with *you*. Threesomes are *not* my ideal way of life.

KEROUAC *(Misunderstanding)*: Oh, listen, Ruthie, I'm sorry about last night—I swear, that'll never—

RUTH: —I'm not talking about sex. I'm talking about love. I feel like I'm in a contest for your affection—and that I'm losing.

KEROUAC *(Getting irritable)*: I guess I don't know *what* you're talking about.

RUTH: Mmm. Maybe you don't. Or don't want to.

KEROUAC *(Angrier)*: What the hell's wrong with you? Here we're been having this great old goof-bang of a time in—

RUTH *(Sarcastic)*: —as Neal would say.

KEROUAC: Yeah, as Neal would say. So what? I *like* what Neal has to say—*and* how he says it.

RUTH: You're beginning to sound like him.

KEROUAC: Oh yeah? Well that's good, that's fine.

RUTH: I liked your own voice.

KEROUAC: I'll make you a record. *(He starts to leave; pauses)* You coming?

RUTH: Only as far as Dallas.

KEROUAC: What's that mean?

RUTH: It means in Dallas I'm taking a train back home.

KEROUAC: Women—they'll drive you nuts! What the hell do you *want*!

RUTH: What everyone wants.

KEROUAC: What *I* want is to be on the road.

RUTH *(Resigned)*: And so you are. Me, I want to be with someone. *With* them, you understand?

KEROUAC: Well you *are*, for cryin' out loud. We're in this together, movin' ahead like one person. We're with old superman himself, Neal Cassady—the King!

RUTH: You and Neal—it's what you want. Though my guess is, you'll be the last to know.

(She quickly exits. Lights fade on Kerouac, alone and confused.)

SCENE 3

(Several years later. Denver. Neal's living room. Benny Carter music is playing softly in the background. Lights slowly up. Kerouac is typing. He pauses periodically to puff on a joint and sip beer.)

KEROUAC *(Reading from page in the typewriter)*: Have you ever seen anyone like Neal Cassady? If you've been a boy and played on dumps you've seen him, all crazy-full of glee-mad powers, giggling with pimply girls back of fenders and weeds till some vocational school swallows his ragged blisses . . . I've known Neal four years now. . . . We been East Coast, West Coast, most places in between, concentrated energy *goin'* somewhere, a swinging group of American boys intent on *life!* Neal's by far the greatest man I ever met . . . but he's also a devil, an old witch, thinks he can read my thoughts and interrupt them on purpose so I'll look on the world as he does. *(Neal comes breezing into the room. He stops when he sees Kerouac working.)*

KEROUAC: And jealous, all over. "If anything I can't stand," Neal says, "is people fucking when I'm not involved. That is, not only in the same room, but the same floor or house or world—"

NEAL: —*time!! (Kerouac jumps)* Whatjadoin'?

KEROUAC: What the hell does it look like?

NEAL: Looks like you're getting stoned! *Now:* we gotta move fast! M'God, boy, I'm almost twenty-*four.* And you—*wah!* No end to the things to be done—and Carolyn's gonna be home soon. First we gotta go see that sweet baby-pussy Marylou, then over to Allen's basement, move on to—

KEROUAC: —you gotta stop seeing Marylou.

NEAL: Why? Because I'm married?

KEROUAC: Well—yes. Married and a father. You got responsibilities, man!

NEAL: Uh-oh, here comes the Catholic bishop! Why, everything's sweet and fine! Marylou and Carolyn talk together over the tel-e-phone 'bout the ee-normous size of mah dong.

KEROUAC: Doesn't sound like the Carolyn *I* know. You got a fine, up-standing woman there . . .

NEAL *(Suddenly distracted by the music)*: Did you hear that riff? Chu Berry used to blow like that . . . They all learned from Chu. . . . Who's that, the Hawk?

KEROUAC: Benny Carter.

(Neal starts peeking at the page in Kerouac's typewriter.)

NEAL: . . . Yass, yass . . . Everythin's workin' out jes fine. . . . No hassles, no infant rise of protest . . .

(Kerouac shields the page.)

NEAL: You writin' about me again?

KEROUAC: Uh-huh . . .

NEAL: Tellin' the tale of my spermy disorderliness, eh? Hee, hee . . . All you done since you got to Denver is *write.* Why you been practi-cally celi-bate, 'cept for me gettin' you and Carolyn together now and then so I could watch. You puttin' Carolyn in the book, too? Tellin' how she makes me sit up straight when I watch *Gang Busters?*

KEROUAC: I'm sayin' you gave Frank Sinatra his very first kiss, and in all probability are the uncredited composer of "Laura."

NEAL *(Grinning)*: Thas fine . . . but be sure and tell the lit-rary folk Ah'm the possessor of the very biggest dork in the en-tire West. Ex-cept that bum who used to sleep with me and pa in the shanty-town—he'd wake up mornings with this big-piss hard-on, you know, and I was stupefied by the size of it, see—'cause I was only nine and noticin' those things . . . *(Sensing Kerouac's unease)* C'mon! *(Pulling Kerouac to his feet)* I'll tell you all about it on the way to Allen's, m'boy. Allen and me are embarked on a tree-mendous season together, just like when we were in New York. We're build-ing our relationship, he says, like a l-o-n-g Bach fugue, see, where all the—

KEROUAC: —you and Allen gonna kill yourselves with those all-night benny sessions.

NEAL: Why not, man? A'course we will if we want to.

(Carolyn enters the room. She's in her late twenties, warm, full-blooded, direct.)

CAROLYN: Well—both husbands! Nice.

NEAL: Well, yass . . . Hi, darlin' . . . We're *about to leave! (Looking at his watch) Time!* You don't realize or notice—it's passin' us by this very minute! No end to the things to be done! Got to pick up the car, pick up Allen—

CAROLYN: —pick up the laundry, pick up the groceries . . .

NEAL: Ain't you got 'em?

CAROLYN: No, I don't. You said you'd pick them up, since I had to work today. Remember work?

NEAL: Now, darlin', you know and I know that beyond the furthest abstract definition in metaphysical terms or any terms you care to—

CAROLYN *(Irritable):* —Oh, *stop* Neal! Not today. I'm too tired for any more *babbling!*

NEAL *(Hurt):* Babbling, is it? That's not nice, Carolyn, that's not the fine, tender girl I married.

CAROLYN: Then we're even. You're not the fine, upstanding lad *I* married. Or thought I was, before I started hearing about the debts, the jails, the—the girls . . .

KEROUAC *(Uneasy):* Now don't start fighting, you two. You sound just like my pa and ma.

CAROLYN *(To Kerouac): Your* trouble is you sit on your feelings. Neal talks too much, you talk too little. Maybe that's why you like each other.

NEAL: Now, darlin', I have one concrete, non-babbling question to ask you: are you sorry we tied the knot? 'Cause if you are, I can assure you that we—

CAROLYN: —to tell the truth, yes. Sometimes I am sorry. And lately the times are growing. I *do* get sick of all the shenanigans. I mean, for somebody born a Catholic—

NEAL: —but not a *guilty* Catholic! Thas jes what you love most about me, am I right or what? You love me for *not* being a Kerouac-like uptight bishop!

CAROLYN *(Wistful):* Jack and I were meant for each other. . . . Well, next time maybe . . . *(Throws up her hands in good-natured surrender)* All right, you two, all right! What's your goddamn schedule?

NEAL *(To Kerouac)*: You see how fine she is?! *(To Carolyn)* Here we go, darlin'! *(Consulting his watch)* It is now exactly six fourteen. I shall return at exactly ten fourteen, for our hour of sweet reverie together, darlin', and then, strange as it may seem but as I thor-ro-ly explained to you—

(The lights begin to dim.)

CAROLYN: All *right*! Enough words! I'll see you two later. Try not to get into a wreck, or thrown into jail . . . *(Carolyn exits)*

NEAL: Let's *go*, m'boy! Time's run-n-*ning*! *(They start to head out)* Why even as we're diddlin' away, Saturn's turned course three more times toward the moon, and by the time we get on outta here, the moon'll be turnin' two more times toward the—

(They've exited. Blackout.)

SCENE 4

(Three hours later, Allen's basement apartment in Denver, empty except for a burning candle, an old chair, a makeshift icon, a bed. As lights go up, Neal and Kerouac are entering the apartment, Neal still talking at fever pitch. Allen jumps up.)

NEAL *(In mid-conversation with Kerouac)*: —yass, m'boy, it all goes to develop respect for the unconscious properties of the soul—

ALLEN: —where *were* you?! You said eight o'clock—

KEROUAC *(To Neal)*: —that's right! Got to reinvent everything.

ALLEN: —I got so worried, I wrote *three* new poems—*bad* poems!

(Neal throws his arm around Allen.)

NEAL: —Now, *Allen*, when we reach the planet Saturn—where ol' Jack here will promptly turn into a *rock*!—*(Neal starts to laugh)*— dependin', a'course, on the Savior's higher grace—

ALLEN: —Neal, *calm down*!

KEROUAC: How can we calm down when we're inventing a whole *new way*?

NEAL: Right, m'boy!

ALLEN *(To Neal)*: How can we have our session if your soul is so agitated with excitement?

NEAL *(sidling up to Allen like Groucho Marx)*: Can you shoot pool? Can you cheat at poker?

(Allen starts to giggle.)

NEAL *(Following up his advantage)*: You can't? You don't? Then how you gonna make a *living*?—tell me *that*!

ALLEN *(Giving up, joining in the goof)*: We'll freelance as writers for hate mail! We'll go to Paris! We'll buy islands!

NEAL: *Now* you're talkin'! Got to be hot-rock capable of everything at the same time! Got the bennies?

KEROUAC: Got any beer?

ALLEN: You want beer *and* benny?

KEROUAC: Dunno—sure.

(Allen goes to check for beer.)

NEAL: Got to meet our earned fate. . . . Jesus knew he was assigned to die for the sake of the eternal safety of mankind . . .

KEROUAC: —Of all sensing beings.

NEAL: No—not flyin' ants. Knowin' it, Jesus does it, dies on the Cross—dig what that means.

(Allen comes back.)

ALLEN: Yes . . . we have *some* beer.

KEROUAC *(Enthusiastic, as he moves to chair)*: Aw-*right* now! I'm gonna sit m'self down over here and listen to you two guys talk magical words in the air!

NEAL: Beautiful, man! Jack's gonna write it all down!

ALLEN *(Slightly annoyed)*: Like always . . .

KEROUAC *(Happily)*: Yup, yup . . . just an ambitious paranoid . . . scribblin' away to keep myself company . . .

NEAL: C'mon, Allen, open the tubes!

ALLEN *(Cautious)*: . . . Then, Jack, you . . . you *are* staying?

KEROUAC *(Surprised)*: Huh? Sure—why not?

ALLEN: Well, frankly, Jack, it . . . it might interfere with Neal and me becoming absolutely honest and complete with one another . . .

NEAL: Allen—open the goddamn tubes! What difference does it

make, anyway? Jack watches me and Carolyn, too . . . matter
a'fact—hee, hee—I sorta dig it when Jack watches, it's like
havin' a—

KEROUAC *(Suddenly catching on, stunned)*: Wha—? I thought you guys
just *talked!*

(Allen hands some soaked cotton from the Benzedrine tubes to Neal.)

ALLEN: We do whatever we feel like doing—

KEROUAC: Wait a *minute!* Are you trying to tell me that you two
actually—

ALLEN: —and don't start acting like some shocked priest warning the
boys to keep their hands above the covers at bedtime.

*(Kerouac turns away, shaking his head in disbelief. Neal hands Kerouac
some of the cotton.)*

NEAL: You *got* to start takin' your clothes off at the orgies, Jacky
m'boy. . . . Got to *burn*—and *burn!*

KEROUAC: Lemme be . . . just lemme be . . .

ALLEN *(To Kerouac, much softer)*: Ah, Jack, your big funny mind . . .

KEROUAC *(Also softening)*: You two keep this shit up, I may go back to
Ruthie.

NEAL: Marriage is *not* the name of your karma, m'boy. . . . Allen,
gimme another tube. . . . *C'mon!*

*(Allen puts his arm gently around Kerouac's shoulder. Kerouac wiggles
loose, embarrassed.)*

KEROUAC: I can't keep up with you two . . .

ALLEN: Come sit on the bed with us.

KEROUAC: . . . No, no . . . I'll rest over here . . . doze . . .

ALLEN: Old Romeo Sadface . . . you got the biggest soul of all.

KEROUAC: Awright, just get on with it . . . whatever the hell it is.

NEAL: Yass! . . . The time has *fi*-nally come for us to get *with* it! *Now*:
the first thing I got to talk about tonight, since Carolyn sees me as
some no-good sex fiend, and Marylou as the biggest hammer in the
West, is my early sex life and early life in general . . .

(Kerouac takes out a notebook, occasionally scribbles in it.)

ALLEN: We can't talk exclusively about matters sexual or Jack will fall
into his dumb-show-avoiding-slumber.

KEROUAC *(Flaring)*: Stop trying to control everything, Allen! *(Quieter)*
. . . Just talk . . . I'll be asleep in no time . . .

NEAL: Yass . . . well . . . we'll talk about *cars*! Every time I stole a car,
I'd let the clutch out too fast and snap the universal joint—

ALLEN: —That's *beautiful*, Neal, the way you put that.

NEAL: —Not even a dream machine, not even a 1940 Cadillac Eight
banger, can you be sure you won't crack the cam, too—whoo!

ALLEN: You could be the greatest poet since Rimbaud—if you'd stop
rushing out to see the midget-auto races.

KEROUAC: Slow down a little.

ALLEN: Serious talkers don't have time to fool around with form.

KEROUAC: How about writers?

ALLEN: Great writers depend on amazement, not words. That's why
you're a great writer, Jack, you're always so amazed.

NEAL: —So many things to get down! Why, you could teach me to
write, too—whoo!

ALLEN: —No more grammatical fears, modified restraints—

NEAL: —Yass! You can't make it with geometry!

ALLEN: The bennies are glowing in our hearts!

NEAL: Blowin' in our bladders!

(Neal and Allen are now sitting on the bed facing each other.)

ALLEN: All part of the spontaneous flow!—you do remember we
talked last time about the spontaneous flow?

NEAL: A'course, and it started a train of my own that I had to tell you.
. . . When I stole that last car, the only reason I stole it was because
I had to find out if *I* was traveling or just the *car* was traveling, or
was it just the *wheels* were rollin', or the ball-bearings ball—

ALLEN: —closer, Neal . . . I have to look directly into your eyes
while hearing these sweet true heart sounds. . . . *(Very serious)* My
need to be loved is my last attachment to the possibility of fixed
states . . . though I know all that is dinosaur futile and must be left
behind.

NEAL: Yass, yass, absolutely . . . no such thing as dependable love, not
even sex, not even *cars* . . .

(The lights begin to dim.)

ALLEN: Closer, Neal . . . closer . . .

NEAL: The thing is not to get hung up. God exists without qualms. As we roll along this way, I am positive beyond doubt that everything will be taken care of for us. . . . No need to run to God, 'cause we're already there . . .

(As the lights fade, Allen and Neal wrap into each other's arms. Seeing them, Kerouac averts his eyes. Lights out for several beats, then slowly back up. Allen and Neal are sprawled on the floor.)

ALLEN: Are you being honest—I mean honest with me to the bottom of your soul?

NEAL: Why do you bring that up again?

ALLEN: That's the one last thing I have to know.

KEROUAC *(Quietly, from the corner)*: That "one last thing," Allen, is what you can't get. . . . Nobody gets that last thing.

NEAL: —That crazy cat's been awake all night! What were you thinkin', Jack, I mean especially the cor-por-eal aspects of—

ALLEN: —Jack, you have to stop listening in on other people's lives!

KEROUAC: Why?

ALLEN: Because it's . . . it's *bad* for you!

KEROUAC: I just don't know what you two are trying to get at. I know it's too much for anybody.

ALLEN: No, no, no . . . negative Catholic Jesuit again. You know very well—but you don't like it.

KEROUAC: Well what *is* it you're driving at?

ALLEN *(To Neal)*: Tell him.

NEAL: You tell 'im.

ALLEN: . . . Conclusive coming together . . . energies meeting head-on . . .

KEROUAC: See—there's nothing to tell. You're very amazing maniacs, but I'm gonna tell you somethin'—you keep this up, you'll both go crazy.

NEAL *(Smiling)*: Should we let you know what happens along the way?

KEROUAC *(Starting to lecture)*: Now, listen, Neal, I—

(A knock at the apartment door.)

NEAL: OO-eee, I'll bet it's Carolyn!

ALLEN: I'll bet it's Ruthie, come to reclaim her football hero.

KEROUAC *(Angry)*: That's enough, Allen . . .

(Neal opens the door. Carolyn hurries in.)

NEAL: Now lissen, darlin', before you get upset and start worrisome things about which no one has any control other than—

CAROLYN: —Neal, shush. There's bad news, Jack. A telegram from your mother. Your father's very ill. She wants you to come home.

KEROUAC: Pa?—my Pa? Oh, Christ!—Oh, no! . . .

NEAL: Hey, ol' buddy, take it easy now—*(He puts his arm around Kerouac's shoulder. Kerouac recoils violently, shoves Neal away)*

KEROUAC: No—NO! Get your fucking hands off me! This is what comes of all this—see? *SEE!*

(He runs out.)

NEAL *(Calling after him)*: Jack! Jack, it's okay, ol' buddy. . . . It's gonna be okay . . .

ALLEN: Oooh, I don't like it . . .

CAROLYN: Come on, you two. We got to get him on a plane. Anybody got any money?

NEAL: I'll get him there on my back . . .

(Fade-out as the three of them start to leave. Lights up on opposite side of stage.)

SCENE 5

(The Kerouac living room in Lowell, Massachusetts, a few days later. The interior is spotless but shows borderline poverty. Catholic religious objects are much in evidence, including a plastic statue of Sainte Thérèse, surrounded by devotional candles. As lights go up, Leo Kerouac is sitting in an armchair, wrapped in blankets. In his fifties, he's volatile and loud. Like his wife, Gabrielle, he speaks with a French-Canadian accent.)

LEO: Sure I feel good this morning! I tell ya, the crud's healin' *itself*. It can happen, you know. . . . It could happen . . .

KEROUAC: You look good today, Pa. You musta made a killing on the horses.

(Leo points energetically to some scrap paper on the table.)

LEO: Gimme those, gimme those, Jacky!

(Kerouac hands the papers to Leo. Gabrielle Kerouac enters. She's about the same age as her husband, and has the same "peasant" build. An explosive, canny, often mean-spirited dynamo, Gabrielle adores her son, tolerates her husband. She always wears a religious medal pinned prominently to her dress.)

GABRIELLE: Eh, *maudit*! Losing all our money, eh?

LEO: I got these horses beat so bad, I'm gonna *buy* Hialeah!

GABRIELLE *(Sardonic)*: We're gonna be millionaires. Again. *(Putting on her coat)* I'll be late to the shop. . . . Make him more coffee, Jacky.

LEO: He makes mud. Can't do nuthin'—except play the Carlson all day. Chekooski—*all day* yesterday!

KEROUAC: Tchaikovsky, Pa.

LEO: Sure—correct me again! I forgot how good you were at *that*!

GABRIELLE: Dr. Schwarz will be here at three.

LEO: He's not drainin' me again! I'm not havin' no more needles stuck in my belly!

GABRIELLE: You know he's got to get the water out. If you'd go to the hospital it wouldn't hurt so. *(Exasperated; almost to herself)* Why should I care?! Pretty soon I'm gonna be wavin' ya-ya-ya . . .

LEO: Who said it hurt? I'm sick of Jewish doctors playin' with my belly, that's all. Jewish doctors, Russian Chekooski—it's a goddamn foreign takeover!

KEROUAC *(Annoyed)*: Just 'cause they're foreigners, Pa, doesn't mean they—

GABRIELLE: —they're still complaining about Hitler!

KEROUAC *(Confused)*: Who is, Ma?

LEO: The damned Jews—who else? Hitler shoulda finished the job . . .

GABRIELLE: —Jacky! Jacky! . . . I saw all those big words you pinned up on the bedroom wall. Whoever uses such words? Leo—they all begin with "U." "U-bee-quee-tu." "U-reen."

KEROUAC: Ubiquitous. Urine.

GABRIELLE: Means what? *Je suis tu dumb?*

KEROUAC: *Ubiquitous* means "everywhere." *Urine* means . . . uh . . . you know, pee-pee.

GABRIELLE *(Amazed)*: *Gidigne?* Dingdong?

LEO: Respect for your mother, Jacky!

KEROUAC: Not the dingdong, Pa. What comes out of the dingdong.

GABRIELLE: Ay, now I know who uses them words—that Allen Ginsberg and them other New York bums—

LEO: —the ugliest puss I ever saw. He looks like a cockroach. A cockroach with pimples.

KEROUAC: You're as good as Milton Berle.

LEO: I warned you about hanging out with those nonathletic Jewish kids. That's why you quit Columbia, threw it all away. The chance to make *real* contacts in the world!

GABRIELLE: What does that Ginsberg know how to live? All you need is good food, good beds—*la tranquilité qui compte!* Make yourself a *haven*, and heaven comes after.

LEO *(Grim chuckle)*: Sure, heaven is great. It better be, anyway . . .
(Gabrielle kisses Leo on the forehead.)

GABRIELLE: I'll be back at six. *Six heures* . . .

LEO *(Quietly)*: Angie—? *(She turns back) Cette maudite vie*, eh?

GABRIELLE: *Oui, cheri . . . oui . . .* at six . . . *a six heures* . . .
(She motions for Kerouac to follow her to the door. They step into the corridor.)

GABRIELLE *(Picking at a rip in Kerouac's collar)*: Now you're home again, I fix that. Who buys your clothes now, ay? You don't even know what size your collar is . . .

KEROUAC: Aw, Ma . . .

GABRIELLE: It's good you're back, Jacky. You come with me to Sainte Agnes, eh? We say a novena together . . .

KEROUAC: Sure, Ma . . .

GABRIELLE: "Aw, Ma," "Sure, Ma"—I don't know why you learned English for all the talking you do! Listen, *Ti Jean*, you'll never be sorry if you always live a clean life, like a real French-Canadian boy, the way I brought you up.

KEROUAC *(Playful)*: "Aw, Ma . . . sure, Ma." *(She laughs)*

GABRIELLE: Gimme a kiss, eh? *(They embrace)*

GABRIELLE: And here—here's a five spot . . .

(Kerouac tries to push the money away, but Gabrielle persists until he pockets it.)

KEROUAC: No, Ma. I don't need that. I'm okay . . .

GABRIELLE: *Weyondonc!* Five dollars ain't no silverware china bazaar! *(She embraces him) Ce soir, mon pousse . . .*

KEROUAC: *. . . A six heures . . .*

(Gabrielle exits. Kerouac turns back into the living room.)

LEO *(To himself)*: Ay . . . It takes too long. . . . Well, dyin's all I got left, why rush it, eh?

(He winces with pain.)

KEROUAC: You okay, Pa?

LEO: Ai, mauva—!

KEROUAC: What is it, Pa, what's causin' the pain?

LEO: The philosopher wants to know what causes pain, eh? If you hadn't quit Columbia, you'd have the answers to those questions. *(He winces again)* Ai! . . . *birth* causes all pain, sonny, that's what—*birth!* That's why we're born, so there can be dyin'. Put that in your book, sonny . . . *(Subsides)* . . . Ah, better . . . It's better . . .

KEROUAC: I'll make coffee for you.

LEO: I don't want no goddamned coffee! It makes water. . . . It's awright—I'm awright now . . .

KEROUAC: Does Ma always leave so early?

LEO: That poor girl—works in the shoeshop all day while I sit here figuring the horses. . . . In the hospital they got no radio, you can't figure the horses, you just lie there doin' nuthin' . . . *(He slaps the armchair with frustration)* . . . If I had done the right thing! . . . So many things I could've done! What I got to show for it, eh? *(Holds up his hands)* Ink stains, that's what I got to show . . . *(Tearful)* Oh, God, how short it all is . . . just a snap of the fingers . . . I want to be in the *middle* of life . . .

KEROUAC *(Mournful, embarrassed)*: Aw, Pa . . . please, Pa . . .

LEO *(Furious)*: Whatsa matter?—I can't cry?—'cause I'm not some fancy Russian composer, some Chekooski? You told me he'd just throw himself on the bed sometimes and cry—"wonderful!" you said, "wonderful!" Hah!—it means a hell of a lot when *they* cry . . . 'cause he's a famous man and they all write about him . . .

KEROUAC: C'mon, Pa!—I never said that!

LEO: Ah, you damn kids—you think you can do what you want *all* your life! . . . *(Sadly)* Then you learn how men—how things—can break . . . Jacky, it's *hard* to make a living!

KEROUAC *(Quietly)*: I don't want a living. I want life.

LEO: You're just playing with words, sonny—words you learned in books . . . *(Weakening)* . . . I had all the time, all the time—and no more . . . *(Starts to doze off)* What a chunky little kid you were . . . strong as an ox . . . smiling, always smiling . . .

KEROUAC *(Choked up)*: . . . I'm—I'm still smiling, Pa . . .

LEO: . . . It's them niggers and Jews you gotta watch . . . that's right, my poor little boy . . . that's . . . the . . . most . . . important . . . *(His head drops; Jack doesn't see. He paces, then turns to face Leo.)*

KEROUAC: Listen, Pa . . . I been wanting to tell ya . . . I mean, Pa, why can't you and me ever . . . Oh, Pa, *listen* to me for once! *(Kerouac grabs Leo's arm, suddenly realizes he's dead.)*

KEROUAC: Pa! . . . Pa! . . . *(Yelling at the walls)* . . . Somebody . . . My father's dead! My father! What was his sin? . . . Somebody help me—PLEASE! *(Blackout.)*

SCENE 6

(Gas station washroom on the road to Mexico City. Neal and Kerouac are pissing in adjacent urinals. Kerouac's mood is sullen.)

NEAL: —Nothin' like being back on the road, huh, m'boy? Why, we could go right on to South America! Think of it—where the Injuns are seven feet tall and eat cocaine on the mountainside!

KEROUAC: Worldwide band of wild fellahin beggars . . .

NEAL: And all in this sun! Are you diggin' this Mexican sun, Jack? It makes you high—whoo! I want to go on and on—this road drives *me*!

KEROUAC: How far to Burroughs's place, do you think?

NEAL: Ah, well . . . *(Laughs, W.C. Fields accent)* Now you're askin' me impon-de-rables—ahem! . . . We'll be kissin' señoritas b'dawn!

KEROUAC: Hope Allen and Gregory got to Will's okay. They should be there ahead of us.

NEAL: Don't know why Allen took that bus. Gettin' awful cautious, yass, cautious. He's gettin' too many poems published, you all are, makes you cautious and calculatin'.

KEROUAC: Makes *you* crazier. *(Pause)* Hope Allen brings the reviews—hope the book *got* reviewed.

NEAL: Relax, relax! You got it published, dintya? Wanna be like queer old Proust hisself, writin' eighty-seven volumes? Relax!

(Neal finishes, starts washing his hands at the sink.)

KEROUAC: Hey, Neal—dig this trick! *(Kerouac stops pissing, moves to the next urinal and starts to piss again)*

NEAL: Yes, man, that's a very good trick . . . but awful on your kidneys . . . awful kidney miseries for the days when you sit alone on park benches . . .

KEROUAC: I'm no old fag, you got to warn me about my kidneys.

NEAL *(Amazed)*: No old—? Whoa, m'boy!

KEROUAC: ". . . Queer old Proust hisself . . ."

NEAL: Why, man, a no-account little joke that—

KEROUAC: —I don't want to hear any more about it.

NEAL *(Hurt)*: . . . Well, how about that . . . Here we been havin' this real goofbang time together, no hassles . . . I'm surprised at you, Jack . . .

KEROUAC: Just 'cause I let Allen suck me off now and then . . . persistent little pest . . .

NEAL: Oh, man, that's your favorite thing, ain't it, jes lyin' back and lettin' somebody else—male, female, don't much matter—moisten up that pole?

KEROUAC *(Angry)*: Better'n bein' a rapist, like you.

NEAL: Being' a *what*?!

KEROUAC: You heard me. Carolyn and Allen both say the same thing about you. The only thing you're good at is jammin' it in . . .

NEAL: Is that a fact? Well, I'll tell ya what, passive little muffin boy, maybe I oughta jam it into *you*! Somethin' tells me you might jes like that . . . especially if you were dead drunk and could tell yourself it never happened . . .

KEROUAC: You ever lay a hand on me, Neal, and they'll find your body floating down the Hudson.

NEAL: Especially if I touched you tender, right? Oh, fuck it . . .

(Neal kicks open washroom door, walks out into the sun. Kerouac follows.)

KEROUAC: You gotta stop thinking up new gags about my kidneys . . .

NEAL: . . . Oh, man . . .

KEROUAC: You take more bennies than I do! I can't help it if my legs start to swell. . . . You shouldn't make fun of your friends . . .

(Neal shakes his head sadly.)

NEAL: No man, no man, you got it all wrong, completely wrong . . .

KEROUAC: Come on—you're just mad . . .

NEAL: Believe me, Jack, really do believe me . . .

KEROUAC *(Subdued)*: Ah, shit, Neal . . . I don't know what to do with . . . how to be close to . . . don't know what to do with these— feelings. I hold them in my hand like . . . like pieces of crap and don't know where to put 'em down. . . . Not even with my *father* . . . my *father*, when he was dyin' . . . I didn't know . . .

NEAL: . . . Yes man, yes man . . .

KEROUAC: It's not my fault. . . . Nothin' in this lousy world is my fault!

NEAL: . . . 'Cause it isn't . . .

KEROUAC: . . . All those catechisms . . . fucked up my brain . . .

NEAL: No pitch, man, I only want you to know what's happenin', I—

KEROUAC: —I *do* believe you, man . . .

(Pause.)

NEAL: Now hold out your hand . . .

KEROUAC: Huh?

NEAL: C'mon, c'mon!

(Kerouac opens the palm of his hand. Neal places a crystal in it.)

NEAL: That's for you, Jack. Traded my wristwatch for it!

KEROUAC *(Touched, embarrassed)*: Aw, Neal, I can't—

NEAL: —Shush! It's the wildest, strangest of all the crystals, probably the soul of the big chief himself. Traded for it with that little Indian girl come up to me on that mountain road while you were relievin' your, ah—kidney—ahem!

KEROUAC *(Looking at the crystal)*: . . . It's a beautiful thing, Neal . . .

NEAL: A'course it is! And that dear child picked it from the mountain jes for us . . . Ah, Jack, she broke mah heart, murmurin' all those loyalties and wonders . . .

(He closes Kerouac's palm over the crystal.)

NEAL: And now the big chief hisself has got it back again. . . . Yass, yass, it's all workin' out jes the way it should . . .

KEROUAC *(Near tears)*: I'll cherish it . . . cherish it all my years . . .

NEAL: Now, Jack, we're goin' to leave behind us here this little trouble we had . . . *(Peering into the distance)* . . . Think of this big continent ahead of us, and those Sierra Madre mountains we saw in the movies, jungles all the way down . . .

KEROUAC: Right, old buddy . . . We're on the same route of old American outlaws skippin' the border to Monterrey . . . Picture that grayin' desert, Neal, the ghost of an old Tombstone hellcat making his lonely gallop into the unknown . . .

NEAL *(Smiling)*: Now you're seein' further again! C'mon—we gotta find the local whorehouse, or I'll be whacking off all the way to Burroughs's. Let's *move!*

(Blackout.)

SCENE 7

(Lights up on split set: Burroughs's living quarters and its backyard, outside Mexico City. Dusk. Neal is asleep on the ground. Kerouac and a Mexican woman, Tristessa, are curled up together. Loud police whistle from offstage.)

KEROUAC *(Alarmed)*: Huh?—who's there?

NEAL: What? What? . . . Where?

(Voice from behind tree; fake Spanish accent.)

VOICE *(Allen)*: Geev up, Americanos! Geev up! Es policia, policia!

VOICE *(Gregory)*: You—are—surrounded!

(Allen and Gregory jump out from behind trees.)

ALLEN: We have come to arrest you crazee Amer-ee-can poets!

NEAL: Allen! . . . Whoopee!

(Everyone shouts delight and greetings. Neal and Allen embrace.)

KEROUAC: Where ya *been*? You're three days late!

ALLEN: Gregory's been writing big mad poems all the way down from Tijuana about the doom of Mexico . . .

CORSO: I don't *like* it here—it's too damn hot!

NEAL: Ah, but the girls, Gregory—wait'll I tell ya about the girls!

CORSO *(Sardonic)*: You're writin' Carolyn all about them, too, I suppose.

NEAL *(Belligerent)*: Don't worry your empty head about me and Carolyn. . . . She's just as fine as fine can be . . . understands me *com*-pletely.

CORSO *(Mumbling as he walks away)*: Yeah, some people have a real thing for sociopaths . . .

TRISTESSA *(Frightened, to Kerouac)*: Who these men? Crazy men, no?

KEROUAC: . . . My brothers . . .

TRISTESSA: . . . Brothers? . . .

ALLEN: . . . Just what I like to see, boys and girls—and boys—all curled up together!

CORSO: Who's the gorgeous doll?

KEROUAC *(To Tristessa)*: . . . This is Tristessa—she's a friend of Will's—

ALLEN: Where *is* Will?

CORSO *(Looking at Tristessa)*: Ah, Jack, you have all the luck.

(Burroughs enters the yard from the living quarters.)

KEROUAC: Will's taking a nap.

BURROUGHS *(Sleepily)*: *Was* taking a nap. Such carnivorous shouting
. . . I knew it had to be you . . .

ALLEN: Will!——We're here, we're here!

(Allen embraces Burroughs, who's pleased but holds to his mocking posture.)

BURROUGHS: Welcome, welcome . . .

CORSO: Why is it so hot?

BURROUGHS: This is the cool season, Gregory. You'll adjust in a year
or two.

KEROUAC *(Shy)*: Hey, Allen, did you bring, uh, any of the reviews? . . .

ALLEN: Oh, Lord, yes!——I almost forgot!

(He rummages in his duffel bag.)

BURROUGHS: Ignore reviews, Jack. They ruin concentration.

ALLEN: Here——the *Times*, the *TIMES*! *(Reading)* " . . . In sum"——that's
all I can read now, Jacky, or Will might go back to sleep——"Jack
Kerouac's *The Town and the City* is a rough diamond of a book . . .
not at all an unpromising performance for a first novel . . ."

*(Kerouac excitedly takes the review from Allen and starts reading it to
himself.)*

ALLEN: Of course they don't understand the book! It's not a novel, it's
a big hymn, an epic poem!

BURROUGHS: Stop inciting Jack. Sounds like a quite decent review for
a first book. Anything *more* favorable and Jack would go on writing
in the same style.

NEAL: That's right, Will! Tell him, you tell him . . .

KEROUAC *(Exuberant)*: By the time I'm done, I'll write down everything that ever happened on the earth *in detail*!

BURROUGHS: That's still Thomas Wolfe, pseudo-lyrical insatiability.
Don't bore me with your New England dreams . . .

NEAL: Yeah——borin' . . .

ALLEN: Never mind! You'll be dancing naked on your fan mail in no
time!

CORSO: When I peed in my sheets as a kid, I knew it was all gonna be creepy.

KEROUAC: Without you, Allen, I wouldn't have got this one published.

ALLEN: I hereby predict the new one will be out *within* a year! Even idiot publishers must see that *On the Road* is a big mad book to change America!

CORSO: *On the Road*? Is that the title? Sounds like a Dorothy Lamour movie.

BURROUGHS: Why does Gregory always yell?

ALLEN: That's the way he talks. It's just as good as silence.

CORSO: Good as gold.

NEAL *(Angry)*: You wanna know the first sentence of *my* book? *I take my friends too seriously!* That's the first sentence of *my* book!

KEROUAC: Great . . . what's the second sentence?

NEAL: *Either that or I don't like life anymore.*

CORSO: Next sentence: *Church music, that's best, just like Artie Shaw said.*

BURROUGHS: A little codeine cough syrup, anyone?

NEAL *(Quieter, to Kerouac)*: *On the Road* is the one about you and me, right?

KEROUAC *(Embarrassed)*: Yeah, sorta . . . our adventures and your . . . your rhythm . . .

ALLEN: *Into* the experience, not around it.

NEAL: Runnin' up and down the changes—like how we *live*!

BURROUGHS *(Dry)*: It's not how *I* live.

NEAL: Or how we *usta* live—before lit-er-a-ture took the reins.

ALLEN: It's time for the *poets* to influence American civilization!

BURROUGHS *(Laconic)*: If you'd seen a vision of eternity, Allen, you wouldn't care about "influencing American civilization." Now sit down . . .

ALLEN *(Respectfully)*: Have you been writing, Will?

BURROUGHS: I have limited energy. I write *or* talk.

NEAL: Good for you, Will.

ALLEN: Don't be mean, Will. . . . Look, we're all here together again . . .

BURROUGHS: Together? Autocratic people can only fall in love with themselves.

KEROUAC: Or the image of what they'd like to be . . .

BURROUGHS: Some people get high on drugs, others on introspection.

CORSO *(Yelling)*: *Burroughs!* I wanna find some girls, I wanna swim in lakes, buy straw hats, I wanna—

BURROUGHS *(Dry)*: —Oh my, so many *wants* . . . *I* want morphine . . . *(Tristessa reacts to the word.)*

TRISTESSA: *Morphina?*

BURROUGHS *(Beaming)*: Si, si . . . Mexico has *wonderful* doctors!
(Tristessa and Burroughs exit to the living quarters, start boiling down morphine tablets in spoons. It's now almost dark in the yard.)

CORSO *(To Kerouac)*: You and Allen are off eating international roast beefs—me, I'm suppos'ta stick to great horror poems on gutters and tenements!
(Burroughs and Tristessa bend over cotton, hypodermics, et cetera, with absorption.)

NEAL *(Calling out)*: Think I'll join your crowd, Will. *(Almost to himself)* All these urgencies anxious and whiny.

KEROUAC: You talkin' to me, Neal?

NEAL *(Angry)*: Now, man, that's profoondified.

KEROUAC *(Bewildered)*: Huh?

CORSO *(To Kerouac and Allen)*: You two think you're the only ones—

ALLEN: *No*, Gregory—we're *all* originating a whole new way, innocent go-ahead confession, no redoing, no—

CORSO: —Don't gimme that "spontaneous" bullshit! You write too fast! You need *craft*!

BURROUGHS *(To Tristessa)*: Looks like pretty good stuff.

KEROUAC: Craft is crafty.

NEAL *(Yelling out to Burroughs)*: Hey, Will—you got an ice-cream soda? *(Almost to himself)* What am I doin' down here?

ALLEN *(Startled, goes over to Neal)*: To be with me, of course.

NEAL: Well and yes, a'course, wanted to see you—glad of you—love you as ever . . .

ALLEN: We're going to work on regularizing your energy. You have to learn to control those forces in you.

NEAL: Thas jes what Carolyn says when *she* wants somethin' outta me.

BURROUGHS *(Feeling the veins on his arm)*: . . . No, it's raw. I'll have to try the leg again . . . *(He searches for a spot on his thigh, then sinks the needle in)*

ALLEN *(Hurt)*: It's for our ongoing opening-up.

NEAL *(Cynical)*: So we can be straight in our souls. . . . Right, Jack?

KEROUAC *(Distracted, reading review)*: Huh? . . . Oh, sure, ol' buddy . . .

NEAL: Yeah, sure, ol' buddy . . . Everybody openin' up—to wrap-around *words*! The *pull* of that lit'rary Mars, man . . .

(Kerouac looks up and sees Neal and Allen standing close to each other.)

KEROUAC: Hey, you two . . . Don't start that "sweet-true-heart-sounds" shit again.

(Burroughs and Tristessa return to the yard. Both lie down.)

NEAL *(Angry)*: What the hell difference does it make to you? *You* got no life except as a writer. You're gonna end up an empty orphan, sitting nowhere, sick and alone. . . . Betta be careful, Jack . . .

KEROUAC: I'm warnin' you and Allen, that's all.

NEAL: Nobody *warns* me, m'boy. Ah live m'own life. That's *it* for Neal!

(He abruptly starts to leave. Allen runs frantically after him.)

ALLEN: Neal, what's the matter?—Wait . . . There are lots of good things ahead!

NEAL: Not for me. I'm splittin'. *Right now*! Where's my satchel . . .

(He goes offstage to look for it)

ALLEN *(Following Neal offstage)*: Wait . . . Oh please, wait! . . .

CORSO: Looks like the cowboy's off to a new frontier. *(Yelling)* Hey, Allen—I keep tellin' ya—ya can't get everyone in the same bathtub together!

(He laughs, slumps in hammock, nods off)

BURROUGHS *(Mumbling)*: . . . Allen always did overestimate the charm of . . . being human . . . *(He passes out. Neal returns with satchel, Allen hanging on his arm)*

ALLEN: . . . It'll all work out . . . you'll see . . . we'll work it out!
(Neal throws off Allen's arm, starts to leave)

KEROUAC: Neal—hey! . . . Wait a minute . . .

NEAL: No way, man, I'm catchin' a freight tonight . . . going back to Carolyn, straight on through . . .

KEROUAC: . . . All that again?

NEAL: . . . Goin' back to mah *life* . . . *(He turns to leave)*

KEROUAC: Why? . . . Why ya goin'?

NEAL: I come, I'm gone . . . Neal's tired of cultured tones, dainty explicity. . . . Nuthin' more for me here. *(Directly to Kerouac)* You got my rhythm, got your book—that's all you really wanted, right?

KEROUAC *(Upset)*: Whoa, Neal, that ain't fair!

NEAL: "Fair?!" You *steal* mah life, and you talk "fair"?! *(He spits in disgust)* You no better'n a cow rustler, that's what. Back home we usta string up men like you!

KEROUAC: You got your goddamned nerve talkin' to me like that! I put you in my books, gonna make you *famous*, and that's the thanks I get for—

NEAL: —and here all along, I thought you were puttin' me in your *life*! Sure fooled me, boy . . .

KEROUAC: —*now* what the hell you talkin' about?

NEAL: Nuthin' you would understand. Nuthin' you'll *look* at. *(Bursting out)* —*feelin's*, man, that's what I'm talkin' about, *feelin's* . . .

KEROUAC *(Evading)*: . . . Don't know what the fuck you mean. . . . Don't know *what* you want . . .

NEAL: Now *there* is truth! 'Course you don't know. And what's more, never will. I can see that now, plain as day. . . . Never shoulda come down here . . . *(Starts to leave)*

KEROUAC: . . . Yeah, well . . . sorry you had to make the trip . . .

NEAL: Wahl, can't talk it no more . . . makin' logic when there's only sorrowful sweats. . . . Don't kick around the gong too much, fellas . . . *(He turns to face Kerouac; deeply felt)* Old fever Jack . . . goodbye . . .

(Neal exits. Allen goes wailing after him, but stops at the edge of the yard.)

ALLEN: . . . Neal . . . Neal! . . . *(Pause; Allen sinks to the ground, crying)* Oh, God . . . my heart's broken . . .

KEROUAC: . . . Gibberish, that's all Neal talks, just gibberish . . . 'tsall settled . . . all settled . . .

ALLEN: . . . Why? . . . why did he go?

(Kerouac grabs a bottle and starts to chugalug it.)

KEROUAC: We should all go home . . . lie down . . . rest . . . *(Laughs)* I wanna eat Wheaties by my Ma's kitchen window. . . . Ooh, I feel like a giant cloud leanin' on its side . . .

ALLEN *(Tearful)*: . . . I wish I was a giant cloud . . .

KEROUAC *(Drunken)*:

Girls are pretty
But their cherries are itty
And if they ain't got cherries . . .

(He kneels down and shakes Tristessa) S'funny, I'm so horny. . . . Hey, Tristessa? . . . Tristessa? *(She moves and groans)* Hey, babe, you and me . . .

TRISTESSA *(Barely audible)*: . . . Mmm . . . si . . . dormiendo . . .

KEROUAC: Ah, Tristessa, you're like a madonna. . . . A madonna of suffering . . . Hey, Allen, what's gonna become of us, huh? . . .

ALLEN: . . . It would have worked out. . . . We could have worked it out . . .

KEROUAC: Whaddaya talkin' about now?

ALLEN: Oh, Jack—you know Neal and I were lovers! . . . Don't be such an ostrich.

KEROUAC: . . . Yeah, sure, I know . . . Neal'll fuck anything that walks . . . *(Laughs crazily)* . . . Male, female, need to fight the man off . . . *(Kerouac nudges Tristessa harder)* Think it would be wrong if I took her when she's out cold?

ALLEN: Yes.

KEROUAC: Mmm . . . So do I . . .

ALLEN: I wanted classical angels . . . hand in hand . . .

KEROUAC *(Flaring)*: You *still* on that shit? Gregory's right—you're all crazy! I'm tired of all this *love* shit between grown-up men . . .

ALLEN: Love is love. . . . You went to church too much.

KEROUAC: Allen, *shut up!* . . . It's unnatural . . .

ALLEN: *Not* being able to love, *yes* . . . Who do you love, Jack?

KEROUAC: Listen, little Allen, don't think you can say *any*thing to me—

ALLEN: —can't I?

KEROUAC: Just 'cause you're a smart-assed little Jewish queer—you and your aching fairy woes—

ALLEN: —you and your lumberjack tears . . . buried and bereft American man . . .

KEROUAC *(Angry)*: I'm gonna stick it to her!

ALLEN: No, you're not. . . . *That's* unnatural.

KEROUAC: Oh, yeah?—*(He wheels around to face Allen)*—then why don't you just stick it in your face!

(Pause.)

ALLEN: Jack . . . I'll blow you . . . I love you, Jack . . .

(Kerouac hesitates a beat, then walks toward Allen.)

KEROUAC: . . . What the hell . . . You always did have a big mouth . . .

(Blackout.)

ACT TWO

SCENE 1

(A shabby apartment in Richmond Hill, Queens, 1955. The same religious objects are visible as in Act One, Scene 5—for example, the statue of Sainte Thérèse. Kerouac is alone, seated cross-legged in the middle of the room, meditating. He's shabbily dressed and has aged noticeably—hair receding, the beginning of a paunch, et cetera. Periodically, he winces with pain, pulls up a trouser to rub his leg for relief—revealing that the leg is bandaged. Gabrielle enters the apartment carrying a cake box. Seeing Kerouac cross-legged on the floor, she frowns, then slams the door with extra force. Kerouac jumps.)

KEROUAC: —Wha—? . . . Oh, *mémère* . . . the factory close early?

GABRIELLE *(Angry)*: Early?—It's six-thirty! You're in a trance again . . .

KEROUAC: It helps the phlebitis, Ma . . . my brain discharging the Holy Fluid . . .

(She bangs down the cake box.)

GABRIELLE: Holy?—*Envi d'chien en culotte!* *(Softening)* For dessert—cakes from Cushman's . . . Try the white one, vanilla . . . *(She sinks into a chair, exhausted) Ai—cette maudite vie!* . . . What's gonna happen? . . .

KEROUAC: Nobody knows . . . *(He suddenly winces with pain.)*

GABRIELLE: *My* legs have to pain—standing ten hours! Yours you *make* pain! A true Kerouac . . .

(Kerouac uncrosses his legs and gets up.)

KEROUAC: It's good for me, Ma . . . holds my body to a dead stop . . . not even the shred of an "I-hope" or a Loony Balloon.

GABRIELLE: So who wants to get rid of hope? Whadda you, an old man? Thirty years old and he's—

KEROUAC: —Thirty-three.

GABRIELLE: —Bon! Thirty-three! . . . And you gotta stop hoping?

KEROUAC: Pa said life is what you smell in the Bellevue morgue. Detachment's the one salvation, to go apart and—

GABRIELLE: —Jesus is salvation! I brought you up to know right from wrong and what God wants of you!

KEROUAC: —It's awright, Ma, Jesus and Buddha are tellin' us the same thing.

GABRIELLE: Then why don't you stick to the religion you were born with, why should you need another religion?

KEROUAC: They both teach life is an illusion—empty arrangements of things that seem solid.

GABRIELLE (Agitated): Whaddaya mean, empty? (She grabs her pocket-book) This is a pocketbook, ain't it? I'm holdin' it! And it ain't empty. (Drops it in disgust) Aw, shu'. (Starts toward kitchen)

KEROUAC: Dinner's ready. I heated up the fricassee.

GABRIELLE: You shouldn't have to do that.

KEROUAC: Makes me feel good to do somethin' around here. You shouldn't have to work in the shoe factory.

GABRIELLE: Tiens! I did it before, I do it again . . . Besides, I like to be with people. We got a lot to say.

KEROUAC: I guess I should go out more, find me a woman. But they all look like airline hostesses, with mock teeth.

GABRIELLE: You don't need a girlfriend. They're all whores these days. Can't even cook. You stay here. You got me for company.

KEROUAC: You're the woman that wants me most, Ma.

GABRIELLE: Did you write today?

KEROUAC: Sure . . . like always.

GABRIELLE (Teasing): More dirty stuff you won't let your old lady read, eh?

KEROUAC (Moody): It would be nice to have somebody reading them.

. . . Eleven books since *Town and the City* . . . eleven books . . . and not one published.

GABRIELLE: Try not to think about it. . . . It makes you drink. . . . We make out, don't worry . . .

(Pause.)

KEROUAC *(Cautious)*: Got another letter from Allen today. He says California's fulla good young writers. . . . whole new scene out there . . .

GABRIELLE: You're the best, you're here.

KEROUAC: No, no, Allen says Gary Snyder's the best, the best young poet in California. Gary Snyder. Only twenty-three . . .

GABRIELLE: Such names, such people . . .

KEROUAC: Ruthie's out there, too. Remember Ruthie? She's a photographer now.

GABRIELLE: A slut! One of the worst . . .

KEROUAC: She wrote to me, too . . .

GABRIELLE: I already read the letter . . .

(Kerouac laughs.)

KEROUAC: You know all my secrets, Ma.

GABRIELLE: You told me I should open the mail, keep all those bums away . . .

KEROUAC *(To himself)*: Well, *most* of my secrets . . .

GABRIELLE: What?

KEROUAC: Just thinking about Neal . . . He's out in California, too.

GABRIELLE: Neal *ye plein d'merde!*

KEROUAC: Ma!—what language for a Catholic lady!

(Gabrielle crosses herself.)

GABRIELLE: Believe me, he's worse than that.

KEROUAC: Allen says Neal doesn't hang out with the new crowd. He's workin' hard on the railroad, buyin' things for Carolyn and the kiddies.

GABRIELLE *(Impressed)*: Eh? Good for Neal! Maybe he's not so crazy.

KEROUAC *(Sad)*: Wonder how he is . . . Haven't heard from him in *(Figuring in his head)*—Huh! Years . . . *(Almost to himself)* I should be out there, see what's goin' on . . .

(pause.)

GABRIELLE: Eh, Jean . . . why not?

KEROUAC: Huh?

GABRIELLE: Why not California? I need a rest from "Holy Fluids" and Buddhas . . .

KEROUAC: Would you really be okay? . . . I mean, if I went for just a little while?

GABRIELLE: Whadda you, some big-time entertainer? All I hear is junk about empty pocketbooks!

KEROUAC: You'll miss me, you'll see . . .

GABRIELLE: You'll be back. I know that. I'm the only one you don't run from.

KEROUAC: I could carry everything I need, Ma, right on my back! A regular kitchen and bedroom . . .

GABRIELLE *(Smiling)*: Don't worry. *(She pats her belly)* I got a little saved. In the corset, like always!

KEROUAC: Aw, Ma! . . . It won't cost much to hitchhike, and *(Quieter)* . . . and when I get there, maybe . . . maybe I could stay with Neal and Carolyn.

(He pours himself more liquor. Gabrielle heads toward the kitchen.)

GABRIELLE: *Vas*, Jean, *vas!* But don't forget Jesus, eh? *(She exits)*

KEROUAC *(Calling after her)*: I'll pray all the time, Ma, pray for all living creatures . . . *(To himself)* Only decent activity left . . . just rest and be kind . . .

GABRIELLE *(Calling out from kitchen)*: You want milk, Jean?

KEROUAC: Sure—*du la chocolat* . . . My stuff'll get published some day, Ma. . . . then I'll buy you lots of good things!

(Gabrielle re-enters.)

GABRIELLE: Mmm . . . a li'l home of my own again. But who cares! Remember my motto: "Be glad for little favors, suspicious of big ones."

KEROUAC *(Smiling)*: Gary Snyder told Allen I'm a great Bodhisattva.

GABRIELLE: Great what?

KEROUAC: Great wise being . . . great wise angel.

GABRIELLE: Buddhists got angels, too? You're too old to be an angel.

KEROUAC: Aw, Ma, ain't it the truth!

GABRIELLE *(Exiting again to kitchen)*: Go tell it to those bums in California!

(As the lights fade out, Kerouac raises bottle in a toast.)

KEROUAC: To *mémère*, who's already entered perfect sainthood—and the proof is, she doesn't know it! *(Blackout.)*

SCENE 2

(A coffee shop in San Francisco, 1955. A poetry reading is in progress. Stage dark.)

ALLEN *(Reciting; voice-over)*:

. . . *What angry horde shadows your doorways, crumbled, disheartened,*
     its features erased—?
Wailing of Children!
Wailing of Mothers!
Wailing of all the blue-suited men!
Wailing, America, flung in your doorways.
Wailing in tenement prisons of Grace.
Jailhouse of nations, sorrowing freedoms,
Lost in the maelstrom,
Lost in the last ship,
Lost on the voyage, last of our journey,
Lost, O America, maker of Men!
(Applause, noisy enthusiasm, lights up. People are crowding around Allen congratulating him. We hear an occasional few words: "Astounding poem!"; "What a night!"; "Changes the entire scene . . ."; et cetera. Ruthie is prominently in evidence, happily taking pictures of everyone. Kerouac, looking forlorn and bewildered, is wandering around, holding out a hat.)

KEROUAC: . . . For the wine, folks . . . Need a contribution for the wine, everybody. . . . Gotta kick in a little somethin' for the wine . . . *(He collides with Rexroth)*

REXROTH: You drink too much, Kerouac.

KEROUAC: Better'n to be "cool" like you, Rexroth. You and your dainty poems!

REXROTH: Since I can't use your abuse, Kerouac, you can have it back. What's important is that Allen's reading tonight marks the first explosion: it'll transform American poetry. And it's happening *here*, in San Francisco.

KEROUAC: Allen's from New York.

REXROTH *(Ignoring the point)*: The poem will make Allen famous from coast to coast. He and Gary Snyder have taken the lead.

KEROUAC: If Gary's smart he'll disappear into Central Asia with a string of yaks, selling popcorn and safety pins. *(Starts to wander off)* . . . Money for the wine, folks . . . money for the wine . . .

REXROTH *(Sardonic)*: Gary tells me that you're "into" Buddhism now. He'll help you move on to the important texts, though for *that*, of course—for *Zen* Buddhism—you'll have to actually learn an Oriental language.

(Gary Snyder—young, intense, direct—enters and hears the two snarling at each other.)

KEROUAC: I'll leave the indoorsy abstractions to you, Rexroth—you and your little pansy friends.

(Snyder leaps into the air, lands near Kerouac.)

SNYDER: Yaaaah! How ya doin', old Bodhisattva?

KEROUAC: Hey—Gary!

REXROTH: You're just in time, Gary. Mr. Kerouac is about to recite one of his earthy epics about freight trains and the *wonder* of exchanging cigarette butts with bums.

(Snyder pulls Kerouac away.)

REXROTH *(Calling after them)*: . . . You're a fine *historian*, Kerouac . . . taking down verbatim what *others* do and say . . . *(Rexroth exits)*

KEROUAC: Lots of big-shots around here, Gary . . . no wonder m'buddy Neal stayed away . . .

SNYDER: Yeah, old Neal doesn't take much to this crowd. You going to see him and Carolyn while you're out here?

KEROUAC: Dunno. . . . Gimme another slug of that jug . . .

(Allen suddenly joins them. He's in an exuberant mood from the triumph of

the reading. As he and Gary start to exchange Zen aphorisms, Ruthie comes up and starts snapping pictures of them.)

ALLEN: Gary is the thunderbolt!

SNYDER *(Taking up the playful spirit)*: Ants and bees are communists! And trolley cars get bored!

ALLEN: An ant is bigger than you think!

SNYDER: A horse's hoof is more delicate than it looks!

KEROUAC *(Disgusted; angry)*: . . . Aw, balls! What is all this bullshit?

RUTHIE *(Tenderly)*: Cheer up, Jack . . . just Zen Lunatics yelling poems that come into their heads for no reason. . . . It's just fun.

KEROUAC: . . . "'tsall famous twaddle . . .

SNYDER: What would you say, Jack, if someone asked the question, "Does a dog have the Buddha nature," and they answered, "Woof!"

KEROUAC: I'd say it was a lotta Zen bullshit.

SNYDER: *Perfect* answer, absolutely *perfect*. You're already a Zen master.

ALLEN: But not a red as a tomato.

KEROUAC: Wish to hell Neal had come. . . . Mighta gotten some sense around here . . .

SNYDER: You're vexed, Jack, you're lettin' the world drown you in its horseshit.

ALLEN: *Om mani Pahdma Hum.*

KEROUAC: Sure—you're all excited about being Orientals, and over there real Orientals are reading Darwin and wearin' Western business suits.

SNYDER: East'll meet West. And it's guys like us who started the whole thing.

KEROUAC: All you need to know is Sakyamuni's first noble truth: All life is *suffering* . . .

SNYDER: Jack, I do appreciate your sadness about the world, but—

KEROUAC: —we kneel down and drink from soundless streams. . . . Christ looking down on the heads of his tormentors . . .

ALLEN: Oh, no—don't start preaching Christianity, Jack!

KEROUAC *(To Allen, yelling)*: You got somethin' against Jesus?

ALLEN *(Shocked)*: —Jack! What's *happened* to you?!

RUTHIE *(Trying to change the subject)*: What are you writing these days, Jack? Are you writing any poetry? I used to love—

KEROUAC: —you're the only one out here writes poetry, Gary. . . . Your voice is as tender as a mother's.

ALLEN *(Hurt)*: Didn't you like *my* poem, Jack?

KEROUAC: Sure, sure . . . eloquent rage of old Jewish prophets and all that . . . but what was that shit about "granite phalluses," or whatever the fuck you said . . .

ALLEN: Jack, you're getting downright sullen! *(Turns to Ruthie)* C'mon, Ruthie. Time for yabyum.

KEROUAC: Time for *what?*

ALLEN: You wouldn't like it, Jack. Everybody gets naked and joyful, and we do what we feel like. Just like the good old days with Neal. Remember?

(Kerouac groans. Allen exits. Ruthie calls after him.)

RUTHIE: I'll be right there! *(She kneels down gently next to Kerouac.)* Jack . . . can we . . . can we maybe have some dinner later? . . . Just the two of us, to catch up on each other's—

KEROUAC: —naw, Ruthie, naw . . . too much rotgut in me . . . Couldn't talk any sense to you, Ruthie. Tell Allen I'm sorry, will ya? He's the best friend I got. . . . Don't know what's wrong with me . . .

RUTHIE: I'll tell him, Jack, I promise. He'll understand. . . . We all do . . . We love you, Jack . . . We'll always love you . . .

(Ruthie exits.)

KEROUAC: . . . I'm fulla hopeless electric snakes . . .

SNYDER: Jack, what you got to do is go climb a mountain with me soon. The secret of climbing, Jacky, is *Don't Think.* Just dance along. Easiest thing in the world, easier than walking on flat ground.

KEROUAC: Leave all my pills and booze behind, huh? . . . Empty and awake . . . Be reborn as a teetotalin' bartender . . . *(He reaches for wine bottle)* Hey, Gary—tell me another of those haikus.

SNYDER: Well, let's see. . . . How's this?

The sparrow hops along the veranda,
with wet feet.

That's one by Shiki. *(Kerouac laughs happily.)* You like that one, huh?

KEROUAC: . . . So much sufferin', Gary . . . Always readin' about some tar-paper shack burnin' down. . . . Even the kitty burned. . . . It's all too pitiful. I ain't gonna rest till I find out why. . . . *Why*, Gary, *why*?

SNYDER: In pure Tathagata there is no asking of the question "Why?" *(Laughing)* You better find a woman, Jack—have half-breed babies, homespun blankets—

KEROUAC: —yeah, that's what Ruthie once . . . I know that. . . . She's after me. . . . Hell, I had hundreds of lover girls when I was young. . . . Every one of 'em I betrayed in some way. . . . We oughta go back to the days when men married bears and talked to the buffalo, by gawd!

SNYDER: Hang on, boy, the ecstasy's general. Somethin' good's coming outta all this.

KEROUAC: Good comin' outta *what*?

SNYDER: Out of all this energy focused into the Dharma.

KEROUAC: Oh, balls on that old tired Dharma! . . . I'm too old for young idealisms. I can't even get my books published. . . . Rexroth's probably right about me. . . . I'm just a spy in somebody else's body. . . . Neal's body, maybe . . .

SNYDER: Jacky boy, don't give me that . . .

KEROUAC: Ah, lousy me, I'hse so tired. . . . You know what I'd like? A nice big Hershey bar. Even a little one. A Hershey bar would save my soul . . .

SNYDER: How about moonlight in an orange grove?

KEROUAC: A Hershey bar . . . with nuts . . .

SNYDER: When we gonna climb?

KEROUAC: Huh?—Oh yeah . . . I dunno. . . . I gotta see Neal . . . gotta find out what's happened to Neal . . . *(He starts to doze)*

SNYDER: You'll see in the mountains, Jack, see this vision of a great rucksack revolution, millions of young Americans goin' up the mountains, makin' children laugh and old men glad, makin' young girls happy and old girls happier. Jack, by God, we'll have a fine freewheeling tribe, have dozens of radiant brats, live like Indians in hogans, eat berries, read—*(Kerouac snores out loud. Gary stops in mid-sentence and chuckles. Lights dim)*

SNYDER: Yep . . . leapin' the world's ties and sittin' among white clouds . . .

(Blackout.)

SCENE 3

(The following week. Cassady living room. Evening. Chu Berry's music is playing on the phonograph. Carolyn is sitting on the couch with five-year-old son, Timmy, who's staring at a light bulb in the ceiling. Neal and Kerouac, both high, are trying to play along with the music on toy flutes.)

KEROUAC *(Laughing):* . . . Trouble, trupple, tripple—whoo! *(To Neal)* . . . See you got my drink!

NEAL *(Teasing, holding Kerouac's drink out of reach):* You said you gave all that up in the mountains!

KEROUAC: Yeah, changed m'life—but not m'thirst! . . . Special occasion, m'boy . . . big reunion with old hellcat buddy . . .
(Neal gives Kerouac his drink back.)

NEAL: What we gotta have is another flute for Carolyn Honey-thighs!

CAROLYN: I'm fine. . . . Calm down. . . . I know it's been five years, *but*—

NEAL: —nope, nope, nope . . . gotta have a trio . . . Timmy, son, where's sister's piccolo, mmm? *(Timmy continues to stare at the light-bulb)* Child seems absorb-ed in otherworldly aspirations . . .
(Neal picks up an ocarina, hands it to Carolyn.)

NEAL: Here, darlin' . . . You play the sweet potato, Jack'll play the white piccolo, I'll play the—

CAROLYN: —sweetheart, you know I can't play this thing. Why don't I get you two some coffee?

KEROUAC: . . . Assailed from all sides!

NEAL: Terrible feelin', man . . . terrible feeling . . . *(Provocative)* *But*—still no time for feelin's, right?

KEROUAC: . . . Sure, sure . . . peaceful feelin' on . . . Mount Hozomeen.

NEAL *(Slight irritation)*: You *told* us 'bout the mountain, Jacky. . . . Yass, yass . . . that bee-u-ti-ful Void—uh, life—Gary-fary found in the mountain-laurel air . . .

KEROUAC: . . . That Gary's somethin' else . . . not twenty-four years—

NEAL: —just lost mah thought . . . *lost mah thought!* . . . Terrible when people don't listen to ya . . .

KEROUAC: . . . Saw Ruthie, too . . . at Allen's big-time, bit-time, reading. She was tryin' to get me to go off with her . . . or somethin' . . .

NEAL: Ruthie would be good for you. 'Cept, a'course, you'd never stay. Rather be alone. . . . Trouble is, you don't like your own company much, either . . .

KEROUAC *(Interrupting)*: —Shush, shush! *(Shifts his chair nearer to the phonograph)* . . . You're talkin' so loud, can't hear my boy Chu . . . guy's so soft, can't seem to get close enough . . .

CAROLYN: Coffee, anyone? Last offer.

NEAL: . . . Uh, no darlin' . . . My nerves are too jangled as is . . .

TIMMY: Daddy . . . daddy . . . ?

NEAL: Huh—what, child?

TIMMY: Can we go hiss the villain again?

(Carolyn and Neal laugh.)

KEROUAC: Does that little angel mean *me*?

CAROLYN: It's the local theater group I do sets for. . . . Neal and I took the kids to see an old 1910 play about villains foreclosing the mortgage, mustaches, calico tears . . .

TIMMY: Uncle Jack come, too?

KEROUAC: Why, sure, Timmy, I'll go hiss the villains with you anytime.

TIMMY: Thanks, Uncle Jack. *(He goes back to staring at the lightbulb.)*

NEAL: Timmy, darlin', aren't you ever goin' to bed? Sister's been asleep two hours, son.

(Timmy doesn't answer) What are you thinking, man?

KEROUAC: He's high on that light. . . . All he wants to do is stare at that light.

CAROLYN: It's too *strong*. Bad for his eyes. I'll put him to bed. *(To Timmy)* C'mon, sweetheart, Mommie'll read to you.

(Carolyn takes Timmy by the hand. He kisses Neal good night.)

NEAL: Mmm . . . yummy . . .

TIMMY *(To Kerouac)*: You're not going to go away, Uncle Jack, are you?

KEROUAC *(moved)*: . . . No, son, no . . . I'll . . . I'll see you in the morning.

(Timmy breaks into a big grin, then skips off with Carolyn.)

NEAL *(proud)*: Now ain't he weird? Ain't that the weirdest kid?

KEROUAC: You sure got a range of graduating golden angels there.

NEAL: Yass, yass, all truly lovely . . . Love 'em more'n I can say. . . . Only trouble comes when the sun goes down. . . . A man's still got to bat around now and then lookin' for a little ecstasy . . .

(He fiddles with the phonograph. "Them There Eyes" starts playing.)

NEAL: That new one I was tellin' you about . . . Ooh—a gone little body! . . . Wanna be sub-beau for another of me beauties, boy?

KEROUAC: Double husbands, eh?—just like old times. We gotta be the two most advanced men friends in the world, right?

NEAL: Yeah . . . except you Canucks save your spit in your watch pocket.

KEROUAC: What's that mean?

NEAL: Oh, goin' around containin' yourself . . . even when you're high, you know?

KEROUAC *(Evading)*: All I hope, Neal, is some day we'll live on the same street with our families and get to be a couple of old-timers together.

NEAL: That's right, man—I pray for it completely, mindful of the troubles we had. And the troubles comin'. . . . But you better start makin' that family, boy . . . or *somethin'* . . . *(Sly)* Last time Allen wrote, he said somethin' about Old Jack havin' a daughter. . . . Is that true?

KEROUAC *(Angry)*: What the fuck—?! That girl's not mine! *Mémère*

made me see *that*. The kid's bitch mother had a spic lover the whole
time we were together. . . . That kid looks practically black!

NEAL *(Deliberately provoking him)*: Allen says she looks *exactly* like you
. . . that there's no mistakin' it. . . . You can't refuse to know your
own child, Jacky.

KEROUAC *(Furious)*: Sure—join the chorus! Well, I'm not payin' no
goddamn child care, you hear me? Five fuckin' dollars a week—
that's a fuckin' fortune! That's two quarts of Jack Daniels!

NEAL: . . . Okay, 'ole buddy, okay . . . Sorry I brought it up . . .

KEROUAC *(Simmering down)*: . . . Stay apart . . . Pass through . . .
Learned that in the mountains . . .

NEAL: But *that's* always been your trouble, man.

KEROUAC: . . . No more gnashin' . . . or tears . . .

NEAL: Hey, Jack! You hearin' me?

KEROUAC: Huh?

NEAL: I'm talkin' now about *you and me*, Jacky . . . or tryin' to . . .

KEROUAC: Oh yeah—double husbands! Sure, I heard ya . . .
heard ya . . .

NEAL *(Serious)*: You know, Jack, lots of people still care about you. . . .
I do. . . . But they—well—we get tired of waitin' . . .

KEROUAC *(Evasive)*: Whew, you know—I'm feelin' real drunk. . . .
Feel like an old fool . . .

NEAL: Well, I feel pretty foolish, too . . . like back when Allen and me
usta have our "sessions" . . .

KEROUAC: Aw, Neal, ya can't fight nature!

NEAL: Thas what I said to ol' Allen the first time!

KEROUAC: —nature made you all cheekbone . . . impenetrable as
steel . . .

NEAL: Yah!—sure fooled me! It was them Nembutals Allen fed me.
Hit me just like that—bam! I was completely outta norm—outta
control. . . . Was all I could do to hit the bed. . . . And that ol'
Allen was jes amazin'! We kept renewin' the supply after that!
(Pause) You know: you can't trust people once you give 'em exactly
what they want.

KEROUAC: Huh? . . . what you mean? I don't—

NEAL: Sure you do. . . . No? . . . Okay. Let it pass. Like always. Anyway, I got better control now than I used to . . .

KEROUAC *(Listening to the record):* . . . Oh, that's fine . . . fine . . .

NEAL: . . . It got so, finally, I couldn't stand for Allen even to touch me.

KEROUAC: Huh?

NEAL: See, only touch me . . . I never been "that way," you know. . . . At least, didn't wanna be for too long with Allen. *(Laughs)* Now with *you,* Jacky, it mighta been a different story. . . . It ain't fatal, you know, no matter what your mama told ya . . .

KEROUAC: What's *in* that tea? . . . Can't understand half of what you're sayin' . . .

NEAL *(sly):* Wahl, half oughta be enough. . . . The thing is, I think your mind is *too* much on the writin'. Keeps you from sittin' down and goin' into this . . . this thing between us . . .

KEROUAC *(Trying to laugh it off):* Allen says they call you the Preacher now.

NEAL: . . . You gotta watch the shell, man. I been noticin' that in you . . . a shielding, a coverin' over.

KEROUAC: Well, I got news for you, Neal, something has come of nothing, and that something is Dharmakaya, the body of True Meaning.

NEAL: The hell with all that Buddhist bullshit—just cut it out, and *live!*

KEROUAC: All *you* want to do is run out there and get laid . . . get banged around by samsara. You'll deserve it, too . . .

NEAL: That's not nice, Jack. Eveybody's tryin' to live with what they got. Your Buddhism's made you mean.

KEROUAC: . . . All I want is a shack in the woods. . . . Wise old Thoreau, sittin' in my cabin . . . I'm startin' a new life.

NEAL: New words, yass . . . but nuthin' else, Jack, no new *human* thing—'cause you won't look at the old ones . . .

KEROUAC: Don't know what's got into you . . .

NEAL: What's always been there.

KEROUAC: Well, I'll tell you straight, old buddy, I don't like it. You're actin' just as weird as Allen.

NEAL: Weird to *you*, 'cause you're tryin' to find your heartbeat on some mountaintop—

KEROUAC: I know my heart's not in my balls.

NEAL: That's jes what you *don't* know—

KEROUAC: —that's enough, Neal!

NEAL *(Turning to face Kerouac directly; near tears)*: Dammit, Jack! I love you, man, you've got to dig that; you've got to *know*—(Carolyn *comes back in)*—got to *know* about our love, you great ol' Jocko Jerk!

CAROLYN *(Softly, concerned for both of them)*: . . . You'll never guess who I met downtown. . . . Remember that older woman at the Edgar Cayce meeting last week?

NEAL *(Overlapping; to Kerouac)*: Well, we'll all meet in hell and hatch another plot. . . . *(To Carolyn)* 'Course Ah do, darlin', truly spiritual-type person . . .

CAROLYN: Well, it turns out she's a secretary at Firestone! *(To Kerouac)* Neal starts working at Firestone next week.

KEROUAC *(Still in shock)*: You startin' at the railroad again?

NEAL: Naw—gonna wear goggles this time, work like Vulcan at his forge.

KEROUAC: Huh?

CAROLYN: He's going to work at Firestone, Jack.

NEAL: Thas right . . . throwin' tires all over the place with mah fantastic strength. . . . *(Sarcastic)* While all you got to do is sit around and write insensible little ditties.

KEROUAC: Yeah, big-time writer, that's me. . . . Stare at the stars, and they stare right back . . .

NEAL: Well, I'm just your average dope, go to work and go home, go and try to get a girl, or girls . . .

KEROUAC: You can't be average because I've never seen you before.

NEAL: Why, sure—just a normal young kid—Carolyn'll tell ya!

CAROLYN *(Laughs)*: Normal!—

NEAL: Well, normal-*seeming*, anyway . . . *(He starts toward the bathroom)*

Got to 'scuse me now, y'all, gonna take my gorgeous-makin' Joy bubble bath, then get out my new magenty-slamenty Jeepster and join the Mongol horde for the Saturday-night beehive slam . . . hee hee hee . . .

CAROLYN: Neal, what in the name of—? Jack's stayin' overnight! You are, aren't you, Jack?

NEAL: 'Course he is, darlin'—he promised Timmy. Jack's a man of his word . . . *all* his words. We'll have us a flapjack sausage jamboree come first thing mornin'. But tonight I got to celebrate my new job and this bee-u-tee-ful reunion we jes had. . . . Seein' you, goo me I'm gushy all over. . . . My heart is jes OVER-flowin' . . . *(He exits)*

CAROLYN: —Of all the crazy—! I haven't seen him *this* wild since— *(Neal sticks his head back in.)*

NEAL: —Oh, darlin'—I have in the second drawer mantel the *last*, yet most perfect, of all black-haired seeded packed tight superbomber joints in the world—which I want you to light up for you and Jack while I'm tossin' bubbles to the ceilin', and while you two talk about *me and Allen and the bed that broke*—"Ee-dee-fy his mind with the grand actuality of *FACT*," as dear ol' Will Burroughs used to say . . . *(He exits again)*

CAROLYN: Poor Jack, I bet you wished you'd stayed wherever you were.

KEROUAC *(Quietly)*: Neal, the Holy Goof.

CAROLYN: Sometimes I get so disgusted I just want to gather up the kids and. . . . But then there are those other days, when Neal's just as sweet and tender as—oh well—you want that joint?

KEROUAC: Sure . . . why not?

CAROLYN: You and me again—like old times.

KEROUAC: My best pal and my best gal.

(She hands him the joint.)

CAROLYN: You and I were made for each other, Jack . . . but it's my particular karma to serve Neal in this particular lifetime. I'll get you in the next one, though.

KEROUAC: What?—me running up the eternal halls of karma tryin' to get away from you?

CAROLYN: And what's more, I'll make you very happy. *(She puts her arm around Kerouac)* Ah, Jack, it's nice you're here. . . . Why don't you just stay a while and rest?

KEROUAC *(Sadly)*: Too late, I guess . . . *(Almost to himself)* Don't know *what* Neal was tryin' to tell me . . . Great Snake of the World coiled out there . . . closer and closer to breakin' through the crust . . .

CAROLYN: What?

KEROUAC: I will, Carolyn . . . I will . . .

CAROLYN: Great Snake of the World?

KEROUAC *(Trying to be lighter)*: That Catholic background of mine . . . Gotta watch myself every minute. What'd Neal mean about Allen and the bed that broke?

CAROLYN *(Laughing)*: Oh, you know . . . a few years back when he and Allen—

KEROUAC: —Neal told you *that?*

CAROLYN: Oh, sure.

KEROUAC: Didn't you . . . *mind* that they were—

CAROLYN: —oh, what can I tell you, Jack, I try to take Neal as he is, though it isn't easy, and there yet may come a day when—

KEROUAC *(Preoccupied; as if talking to himself)*: —I can't believe he told you about him and Allen. I mean *all* of it, the whole sick, perverted—?

CAROLYN: —I don't understand, Jack. The way Neal tells it, for years you and Allen also—*(Kerouac jumps up. His chair hits the floor)* Jack— what the—what did I say—?

(Neal appears upstage. Kerouac doesn't see him.)

KEROUAC *(Yelling)*: They were *lovers*! Not a blow job, Carolyn— *LOVERS!* He told you that, too, I suppose—huh, HUH?

(Neal comes downstage.)

CAROLYN: Jack, please, I—

NEAL: —yeah, Ah told her. Got nuthin' to hide, man. Never have. *(Direct, hard) You* got nuthin' to show.

KEROUAC: Is that right?—

CAROLYN: —will you both *please* calm down. What in the world started all this—?

NEAL: —anything else you wanna say—behind my back?

KEROUAC: Yeah, plenty—plenty to say! Mexico!—"I come, I'm gone!
I come, I'm gone!" Just up and leave, up and leave, whenever it
suits *you*!

NEAL: You never gave me any reason to stay.

KEROUAC: . . . Never shoulda come back here . . . too late . . .
shoulda known it was too late.

NEAL: I think maybe that's right, ol' buddy . . .

CAROLYN: It's *not* right! We're Jack's oldest friends! You *belong* here,
Jack!

NEAL: Jack don't belong nowhere . . . doesn't want to. . . . Rather sit
around wonderin' where to go . . . and all the time it's right in
front of him . . .

KEROUAC *(Yelling)*: All *you* know about is gettin' *laid*!

(Timmy, frightened, appears at the doorway in his bathrobe.)

TIMMY: —Daddy?

NEAL: —no, son!—go back, son! *(To Kerouac)* See what you done,
man, scared my little boy, scared my little Timmy!

KEROUAC *(Overlapping)*: —laid, man—*LAID*!

CAROLYN *(To Timmy)*: Come here, darlin' . . . *(Timmy runs over to
Carolyn. She holds him)*

KEROUAC: I'm sure he's seen worse! *Lots* worse, lots worse!

NEAL *(Blowing up)*: Get outta here, man!—get *outta here*!

CAROLYN: Neal, please . . . You're frightening Timmy . . .

NEAL *(Yelling)*: Buddhist bullshitter—go daddle with your *kidneys*!

TIMMY: Is Uncle Jack the villain, should we hiss Uncle Jack?

CAROLYN: Shush, Timmy darlin', shush . . .

KEROUAC *(Screaming)*: You fucking eternal piece of meat! Cunt's all
you ever cared about—cunt!

NEAL *(Enraged)*: Does that include *you*?!

*(Neal goes for Kerouac, lands a hard punch on his jaw. Neal then quickly
retreats, turns his back, pounds one fist into the other in frustrated despair.
He grabs up Timmy in his arms.)*

TIMMY *(Crying)*: . . . Bad daddy . . . hiss, hiss, bad daddy . . . bad
daddy . . . hiss . . . hiss . . .

NEAL (*Overlapping; to Carolyn*): . . . Get him out . . . get him out of here . . . (*He exits with Timmy*)

KEROUAC: . . . breakin' through . . . the Snake's breakin' through . . . (*Lights dim.*)

CAROLYN (*Crying softly*): . . . Jack . . . oh, Jack . . . I'm so sorry . . . so sorry . . . (*She exits*)

(*Kerouac remains alone in spot, sprawled at edge of the stage.*)

KEROUAC: . . . hissing . . . the Snake, hissing . . . When you die, you won't know . . . can't pretend you won't know . . .

(*Lights dim to out.*)

SCENE 4

(*Kerouac rises from the edge of the stage, where he was sprawled at the close of the previous scene. He is on a TV sound stage, New York City, 1958. In the middle of a station break. Those on stage include: Dan Cameron, moderator of the panel—youthful, bland, bright; Conrad Carver, an English novelist—about forty, pudgy, elegantly mannered, witty; and John Wiman, around forty-five, prototypical liberal—articulate and impassioned. Kerouac is wearing a checkered-plaid shirt, wrinkled pants, and lumberjack boots. He carries a large Dixie cup in one hand.*)

CAMERON (*Under, to Kerouac*): —Mr. Kerouac, if you'd resume your seat, please . . . we're about to go back on the air.

KEROUAC: Huh? . . . Oh yeah, sure . . .

(*A woman in the audience rises from first row and holds up an autograph book for Kerouac to sign.*)

WOMAN: Mr. Kerouac, I wonder if you would—

KEROUAC (*Smiling*): —oh sure, sure . . .

(*He signs autograph.*)

CAMERON: Mr. Kerouac—we're about to go on the air again—

(*Kerouac sits. Lights up full.*)

CAMERON (*Out to audience*): Welcome back to "Newsmakers." We've been discussing tonight Jack Kerouac's new novel, *On the Road*, which seems on its way to becoming *the* literary event of 1958. Just before the break, one of our distinguished panel members, Mr. John Wiman, made the point that—

KEROUAC *(Interrupting, sarcastic)*: —our distinguished political columnist John Wiman—otherwise known as *Broadway Sam*, showbiz city slicker—

WIMAN: —just a minute, Mr. Kerouac!

KEROUAC: —Rootless though permissible fools, who really don't know how to go on living—

CAMERON: —gentlemen, gentlemen!—*please!*

CARVER *(Arch)*: Do tell us about your rootedness, Mr. Kerouac. I'd be genuinely interested. It's hardly a style one associates with being "on the road."

KEROUAC: That tone, Carver . . . That's my chief complaint about the contemporary world you all inhabit so easily: the facetiousness of "respectable" people. . . . destroying old human feelings—older than *Time* magazine . . .

CARVER: That seems a remarkable turnabout. I associate the *Beats* with disdain for the "old human feelings," and now you talk reverently about retaining them. . . . I must say, Kerouac, I don't find your "vision" very—uh—*steady*.

WIMAN *(To Kerouac)*: Your people care deeply about one thing: *not* caring. It's the cult of *un*-think: asocial, apolitical, amoral.

KEROUAC: Well, walking on water wasn't built in a day.

WIMAN: I came here to have a rational discussion of the—

KEROUAC: —you wanna talk about the futility of Surrealism? That's always a good one. Or how about the loveliness of Mozart's flute? Who do you think the best jockey in America is today? Hah? And you betta say Turcotte!

CAMERON: Perhaps if we could—

WIMAN *(Angry)*: —our society faces two *serious* questions, Mr. Kerouac—two questions that responsible, rational human beings are addressing: something called the hydrogen bomb—I trust you've heard of it—

KEROUAC: —Oh yass, yass indeed . . .

WIMAN: And the *second* question is one of human equality, as exemplified by the current struggle among Negroes for civil rights. *These* are the dominant issues of our time.

KEROUAC: When God says, "I Am Lived," we'll have forgotten what all the shoutin' was about.

CARVER: Oh, my—aspirations of high piety. Much on the order of Billy Sunday. But I'm surprised, Jack—

KEROUAC: —Mr. Kerouac—

CARVER: —surprised that you seem to have lost your well-publicized enthusiasm for esoteric Eastern religions.

KEROUAC: "Beat" is like Saint Francis: a still center . . . an open heart . . .

CARVER: Ah—William Blake's little lambs, eh? "To see a World in a Grain of Sand / And Heaven in a Wild Flower."

KEROUAC: On your lips Blake sounds like donkey piss. *(TV monitor bleeps)*

CAMERON: The issues Mr. Wiman is trying to raise, Jack, are those that commonly dominate—

KEROUAC *(Growling)*: —don't give me all that shit. *(TV monitor bleeps)* Or I'll just walk my ass—*(TV monitor bleeps)*—right outta here . . .

WIMAN: As a political columnist, I have to write about Dwight D. Eisenhower every week—

KEROUAC: —he's very witty.

WIMAN: You interrupted me.

KEROUAC: Education is education.

WIMAN: For a man who claims to value kindness, you're not very polite.

KEROUAC: I'm polite, I'm not *politic*. You came here tonight to attack me!

CARVER: We came here to try to understand you. But I have to say, with due respect, Jack—

KEROUAC: —Mr. Kerouac—

CARVER: —that you don't make the task very easy.

KEROUAC: Why? Because I'm drunk? *(TV monitor bleeps)* Because I believe in ecstasy of the mind?

CARVER *(Dry)*: Because you seem to have no idea *what* you believe. Or if you do, you have limited ability to communicate it.

CAMERON: Gentlemen, gentlemen, please! Ours is, after all, a forum devoted to rational—

WIMAN: —it's clear you haven't heard a word I've said—What I believe in, Mr. Kerouac—

KEROUAC *(Yelling; overlapping)*:—while you're alive on earth the very hairs of your cats on your clothes are blessed—that's what I believe! What do you believe in, hah, Wiman?

WIMAN: —If you'll allow me to finish my sentence—

KEROUAC: —yeah, whadda you believe, Wiman, whaddaya believe? . . . I wanna know what you believe—

CAMERON: Gentlemen! Gentlemen!

KEROUAC: —we're all in *heaven*, that's what I believe—live your lives out . . . love your lives out . . . *(Kerouac goes off-camera for liquor bottle)*

WIMAN *("Dignified")*: If I might be allowed to finish a sentence . . . *I believe* in the capacity of human intelligence to change society, to create a world in which there is justice, freedom, love—

KEROUAC *(Yelling from offstage)*: —oh, yeah, I'll vote for love!

CARVER: As I said: furtive sexuality plus confused aspirations of piety.

WIMAN: We have to *fight* for that kind of world.

KEROUAC *(Returning to seat)*: *Fight* for love?!

WIMAN: You and your friends are trying to destroy this generation's instinct to *care* about the world.

CARVER *("High-toned")*: I find it astonishing to hear such flip, infantile remarks. Fortunately, the Boris Pasternaks of the world still live. Fortunately—

KEROUAC: —whadda you know about the world?—negative little paper-shuffling prissy—

CAMERON: —Mr. Kerouac, really! I think perhaps we may—

KEROUAC: —who are these men that insult men, these people who wear pants and sneer? What makes you all so clever in a meat grinder?

CAMERON: Mr. Kerouac, really! I think perhaps we may—

CARVER: —vulgar ravings, nothing more—

CAMERON: —perhaps if we proceed somewhat more systematically—

WIMAN: —responsibility means struggle.

KEROUAC: What are all your "decent" plans for "social change" when *you're ignorant of your own broken hearts?*

WIMAN: —self-indulgence—a convenient excuse for passivity, for selfish—

KEROUAC: —go to the lone plateau where you can hear the zing of the sound of *your broken hearts! That's* what "Beat" means, beaten down to a nakedness where you're able to see, you're deranged enough to see that the mind of nature is *intrinsically* insane! When will Billy Graham admit it?

CARVER *(To Cameron)*: Really, Cameron, I think this "exhibition" has gone far enough.

CAMERON: Yes, quite . . . Mr. Kerouac—Jack—I'll have to ask you—

KEROUAC *(Ignoring him)*: —no, you rather blame all troubles on a secretary of state or a white racist, lay the blame on such born victims of birth as that! Just 'cause you got white skin and ride in the front of the bus don't make you suffer less!

WIMAN *(Sardonic)*: In short, nothing, nothing can be changed. All equally guilty, equally helpless.

KEROUAC: I'll personally bullwhip the first bastard *(TV monitor bleeps)* who makes fun of human hopelessness!

CARVER: I think I've heard sufficient nonsense for one evening!

WIMAN: What we need is human courage!

KEROUAC *("W.C. Fields" voice)*: Um, yes, Jackson m'boy—human courage, the opiate. But opiates are human too. If God is an opiate, so am I. Therefore, *Mister* Wiman—*eat* me. Then we'll all laugh at the Second Coming!

CAMERON *(Jumping in)*: I want to thank our guests for joining us this evening on "Newsmakers." . . . The subject under discussion tonight was "Is There a Beat Generation?"

KEROUAC *(Out to audience)*: "Is there a *world?*"

(The lights dim on Cameron and the panelists. The Cameron, Carver, and Wiman speeches that follow overlap each other.)

CAMERON *(Voice gradually fades)*: . . . Our guests tonight were Mr. Jack Kerouac, author of the bestselling novel *On the Road*, John Wiman, political columnist and well-known civil libertarian . . .

CARVER *(Overlapping)*: . . . Barbarian antics . . .

WIMAN *(Overlapping)*: I had hoped for some civilized discourse, but apparently we've wandered into a downtown bar.

(As Cameron finishes up, Kerouac moves drunkenly down to edge of stage, starts yelling out at audience.)

KEROUAC: I go claim the bloody dolmens of Carnac, go claim the little cliff-castle at Kenidjack or Cornouialles itself near Quimper and Keroual . . . *(Peering out at audience)* Whoo . . . I'm the Phantom of the Opera, folks . . .

(Kerouac, in a spot, totters on the edge of the stage. TV crew, silhouetted behind him, starts to strip set.)

KEROUAC: . . .

Call themselves poets
Call themselves Kings
Call themselves Free
Call themselves
Hennis free
Calls themself . . .
Calls themself catshit!
Calls themself me . . .

What am I doin' here? . . . Is there some way I'm *supposed* to feel? . . .

(A woman, Ruth, appears just outside the circle of lights.)

RUTH *(tentatively)*: . . . Jack? . . .

KEROUAC: . . . Huh? Who's that?

(Ruth steps into the light.)

RUTH: It's me, Jack. . . . Ruthie.

KEROUAC: Ruthie?!—it must be them D.T.'s they keep warnin' me about . . .

RUTH *(Grinning)*: No, it's me. . . . How are you, Jack?

KEROUAC: But I don't—! I mean, what the hell are you doin' here in New York? I thought you lived in California . . .

RUTH: No, I'm back in New York again. I saw the program, Jack. I was in the studio audience . . .

KEROUAC: I showed those punks, huh? All those big professors burping with "rash-on-ality"!

RUTH: You made some good points, Jack.

KEROUAC: That Jewish Wiman guy's the biggest bastard. . . . *(Shakes his head with self-disgust)* Ooh . . . I'm getting' to sound as bigoted as the old man, cursin' out Jews and *Nègres*. . . . Shit, Saint Augustine was a *spade*—I know that? . . . Ah, Ruth, I usta like *every*body. . . . It's all happened for me too late. . . . The saints are gone, all gone. . . . I talk to waiters only now . . .

RUTH: Jack, you're *famous*! Everybody's talking about you! *On the Road* is the hit of the year.

KEROUAC: . . . Yeah, kids writin' me letters, knockin' on the door. . . . Scares Ma half to death—

RUTH: You still live with your mother?

KEROUAC *(Going right on)*: —they all think I'm twenty-five, set to hitchhike off with 'em, follow some great red line straight across America. . . . Shit, it's 1958, I'm lucky I can make it to the neighborhood bar. . . . I'm King of the Beats, but I ain't no Beatnik. *(Chuckles grimly)* There ain't no more Road . . . just like there ain't no more Neal . . . not so's *I'd* know, anyway . . . ever hear from 'im?

RUTH: Carolyn writes now and then. I think she's finally edging toward divorce, but keeps pulling back. . . . She says that Neal's getting wilder and wilder . . .

KEROUAC: Well, who the fuck wouldn't be wild, sittin' in the slammer! And all because she wouldn't sell the house for bail money. . . . Broke my heart when I heard that . . . lettin' Neal rot in jail . . . damn shame!

RUTH: It broke her heart, too, Jack. . . . But she had no choice, what with three young kids. If Neal skipped bail, she'd have lost the house and been thrown on the street. . . . I'm glad Carolyn stood her ground. *(Almost to herself)* . . . We let you guys get away with an awful lot, and for an awful long time . . .

KEROUAC *(Ranting)*: What's *that* supposta mean?! Can't you see, it's all a setup, a bum rap! Two to life for dealin'! Them fuckin' narcos! The reefers were for his friends, thas all, all for his friends. . . . I don't know what the hell there is to blame *me* for— huh? Huh?

RUTH: Nobody blames you, Jack.

KEROUAC: Don't tell me! I heard! I heard what those pricks in California are sayin'—that they picked up Neal because I had him takin' all that dope in the book! Shit!—they didn't pick *me* up, they didn't pick up Will or Allen! . . . *(Grinning)* I hear Neal gets lots of fan mail addressed to "Dean Moriarity, Hero of *On the Road.*" Ha! Put old Neal Cassady on the map, right? The goddamn book's a *hymn* to Neal!

RUTH *(Quietly)*: I guess he doesn't see it that way . . .

KEROUAC: Neal never knew any limits, that was his trouble. . . . You pay through the nose for short-lived shows. . . . Where's that ga-damn bottle?! Hadda stash the sauce back here, Ruthie, those old farts din wanna "shock the viewin' public"—hah!

(He staggers around looking for the bottle, then swigs from it.)

KEROUAC: Cauterize my wounds, Ruthie m'gal . . . Ma won't let me bring no gal back to the house—'less I *marry* her—ha! . . . Got her a nice li'l house. Used up all the bread, but what the hell—got *five* books comin' out this year and next, *five*! Wrote most of 'em years ago a'course. . . . Best one's *Doctor Sax*, though Allen don't think so—aw, what's he know, all wrapped up in Peter and takin' his clothes off every time he recites more'n two lines of his own poetry, and gettin' all political about the *bomb* and Joe McCarthy and—*(Repentant)* Aw, I don't mean that. Allen's the only loyal friend I got, even if he is a wolf in sheep's clothing. . . . *(Scornful; imitating)* Now we got that "cool" shit—"Oh, it's a wig, man . . . a real gas . . . like, you know, wow! Crazy!" *(Disgust)* . . . And claiming *me* as their spiritual father—that's a joke!

RUTH: Now come on, confess, Jack—

KEROUAC: Huh?

RUTH: Admit you like being famous *just a little!*

KEROUAC: Wanna know somethin', Ruthie? Hah? Hah?

RUTH: Sure, Jack . . .

KEROUAC *(Leaning down and "whispering")*: Truth is—I'd rather be *thin* than famous!

(They laugh.)

RUTH: You're not really fat.

KEROUAC: Wha—? You don't remember my fightin' Football Hero trim? Not an ounce of flesh on me . . . Now I couldn't even give ya a baby. . . . 'Cause of my thrombophlebitis—piss goin' the wrong way.

RUTH: Good lord—what makes you think I want a baby?!

KEROUAC: Oh, you always did. . . . Yup—I'm the end of a strong line . . .

RUTH: Jack, I'm happy just taking care of *me.* That's how I want it now. I love my work—*and* my life.

KEROUAC: Still snappin' pictures of everything?

RUTH *(Proudly)*: I've been in four consecutive issues of *LIFE.* They've even offered me a staff position. *(Pause)* No congratulations?

KEROUAC *(Perfunctorily)*: Oh—sure! Yeah, I think that's just swell, Ruthie . . .

RUTH *(Arch)*: I'm so glad you're pleased.

KEROUAC: You still got mad blue eyes, you know . . . little flutter to 'em, too. . . . Aw—it's all high school stuff anyway!

RUTH: . . . Jack, do you think you oughta go on drinking? I mean, you've—

KEROUAC: —I knew up in the mountains, Ruthie, when Gary took me up in the mountains. . . . I *knew* everything made sense, was *all right* just as it was. . . . *(Sad)* If I could only have held on to what I knew . . . *(Subdued)* Maybe I am drinkin' too much . . .

RUTH: My God, Jack, you haven't stopped . . .

KEROUAC: It keeps me from thinkin', like I'm doin' now. *(Flaring)* I think you were hung up on Neal—*that's* why you came between him and me.

RUTH: God, Jack, I couldn't have cared less about him! You're . . .
you're not making any sense. . . . *(She turns away, upset.)*

KEROUAC: Oh, Ruthie—oh, no, don't do that—Ruthie, no—what
did I *do?*—what did I do this time, huh—? *(He tries to comfort her. She
moves away)*

RUTH: . . . Leave me alone, Jack . . . please, just leave me alone. . . .
I shouldn't have come backstage.

KEROUAC: . . . I try not to hurt anything. . . . really, I try . . .

RUTH: Oh, Jack . . . you strange man . . . all these years, and I still
don't understand what—

KEROUAC: —would you feel better if you let me hold you, even
though I don't deserve it . . . ?

RUTH: "Don't deserve it"? . . . Who ever told you such a terrible
thing . . . ?

KEROUAC: I dunno . . . everybody, I guess. . . . I dunno what I did
wrong or when I did it . . .

RUTH: You withhold your love, Jack. That's what you do—what
you've always done.

KEROUAC: I guess I don't want it . . .

RUTH: But you *do.* Saying you don't is part of the same thing.

KEROUAC: You don't know. I'm a strange guy now . . .

RUTH: You could make some *effort*—instead of all those vague words,
big philosophies . . .

KEROUAC: . . . All my goddamn fault . . .

RUTH: . . . Oh, God . . .

KEROUAC: . . . Always sabotagin' great plans to be kind to livin'
things . . .

RUTH: No, Jack, it's not your fault. It's nobody's fault . . . nobody's
fault, darlin' . . .

KEROUAC: Why'd you call me "darlin'"?

RUTH: Because I . . . I still care about what happens to you . . .

KEROUAC: . . . Something's wrong with me. . . . I wanna go home
and die with my kittie . . . *(Ruth puts her arms around him, tries to
comfort him)* . . . Don't do it, Ruthie, don't do it, Ruthie, don't do
it, Ruthie . . .

RUTH: . . . Please, Jack . . . Please take it easy. . . . Let me help you a
little . . .

KEROUAC: . . . I can't. . . . There's no help . . . no-one to help . . .

RUTH: Just try to quiet down a little, Jack, then maybe you—

KEROUAC *(Blowing up):* —*I CAN'T!* . . . It's the secret poisoning society . . . big molecular comedown, like Allen warned back at Columbia . . . all the atoms fallin' apart . . .

RUTH *(Giving up):* . . . Okay . . . okay . . .

KEROUAC: What are you givin' me that bleak look for—like I was
dead?

RUTH: You *want* to be left out from everything . . . you always have.
. . . You'd rather stay royal drunk and feel sorry for yourself.

KEROUAC: That's right—cover the earth on, do the honors! . . . And
what'm I suppos'ta do with the terrors I see—huh? Huh? Got any
big Final Statements for that?

RUTH: You'll sleep them off, I hope.

KEROUAC: Ha!—shows what you know!

RUTH *(Flaring):* I've had my share, Jack. You've got no monopoly on
suffering.

KEROUAC: Ah, you're just mad 'cause I didn't stay with ya . . .

RUTH: No, I don't think so . . .

KEROUAC: Women own the earth, women own heaven, too. . . . It's a
tyranny . . .

RUTH: I'm going, Jack . . . going home . . .

KEROUAC: Why should you care, anyway . . . ?

RUTH: . . . Do what you like, I . . . I don't care . . .

KEROUAC: . . . Ma was right . . . It'll all drive me nuts. *(They're at the
exit)* So whatta we gonna do with our lives?

RUTH: Just watch 'em, I guess.

KEROUAC: You gonna be okay?

RUTH: I've been okay for some time.

KEROUAC: Salvation's only for little kitties, I s'pose . . . *(He starts to
cry. Ruth involuntarily starts toward him, then stops herself)* . . . *Oh ti
Tykey, aide mue* . . . Throwin' it all away, huh Ruthie? . . . Just
throwin' it away . . .

RUTH: Jack, I don't know what to say anymore. . . . I guess you and I said it all years ago . . .

KEROUAC: . . . Do you hate me?

RUTH: . . . No . . .

KEROUAC *(Doing a drunken little jig)*: . . . Well, do you still love me, then?

RUTH: I love the man who wants to know . . .

KEROUAC: Yeah, well . . . *(Raising the bottle)* Here's to the rosy Figury . . . that's what Neal usta call the Future . . .

RUTH: Goodbye, Jack . . . Take care of yourself . . .

(Blackout.)

SCENE 5

(Living room of Kerouac's house in Lowell, 1969. Twilight. Architecture and furnishings reminiscent of the living room of his boyhood home, but a "middle-class" Sears Roebuck version—plastic dinette set, maple and chintz. The same religious objects as in Act One. And one prominent new addition: a large oil painting of Pope Paul—almost in cartoon style, with huge blue eyes. A TV set in the corner is on, but not the sound.)

(Kerouac sits over his typewriter at the dining room table. He's aged consider-ably: his hair is thin and askew; he has a large paunch; his air is one of bewil-dered defeat; his tone bellowing, though sometimes in a self-mocking way. He wears a bright Hawaiian sport shirt. The top button on his pants is open, his belly hanging out. He takes the page out of the typewriter, throws it into the wastebasket in disgust, and goes to the refrigerator for a beer, limping slightly as he walks. He wears battered old work shoes. The doorbell rings. Kerouac looks confused, frightened, as if he might bolt. Then he gets angry.)

KEROUAC *(Muttering)*: . . . Motherfuckin' pest! I swear I'm gonna—!

(Tinkle of a handbell from the back room.)

KEROUAC *(Yelling upstage)*: —Yeah, Ma—I heard it! Probably the gro-ceries! Tell Stella I'll get it!

(He goes to the door and opens it. Joey Rose is standing there—young, bearded, wearing a jean jacket, ragged but elegant pants and fancy shoes; his manner is gentle and quiet. Allen is "hiding" behind him. Allen has changed a great deal physically: he's almost bald, is much heavier, has a full beard. His manner is far more settled and composed than when he was younger.)

JOEY *(As Allen whispers the words to him)*: Excuse me, but is this the home of Old El Jacko, Champeen Walking Saint? . . .

KEROUAC: What the hell do you—*(He catches sight of Allen)* Holy shit!—no, it can't be! *Allen!*—Good Christ! What in the hell are you—?

ALLEN *(Tenderly)*: —yes, it's me, Jack. *(Fingering his beard)* Didn't know if you'd recognize me . . .

KEROUAC: —you crazy bastard! *(Cocking his head toward the back room)* Don't you remember the near riot the last time you—

ALLEN: —we're on our way to a reading at Amherst . . . passed the highway sign for Lowell and thought, "Well, can't hurt to—" *(Kerouac gives him a huge bear hug.)*

KEROUAC: —you old cockroach . . . you old cockroach, you . . . *(They hang on to each other in a fierce embrace. Agitated tinkle of a hand- bell sounds from the back room. Kerouac jumps.)*

KEROUAC: Yeow! It's as if she could see right in here! Lissen—hang on!—I'll tell her it's Alex—Stella's brother—that we're gonna have a few beers and watch the Green Bay game—*don't you go away!* *(He hurries off to the back room.)*

ALLEN *(Teary)*: . . . Ol' Jack . . . God bless him . . .

JOEY *(Stunned)*: . . . That's . . . *that's* Jack Kerouac?

ALLEN: Yes . . . the legendary Beat himself . . . Ah, you should have seen him twenty years ago, Joey . . . handsomest man in America. . . . Fell in love with him at first sight . . .

JOEY: Wow! . . . I mean . . . he doesn't look at all like what I expected . . .

ALLEN: The years have been hard on him. . . . I'm a little shocked myself. . . . Be careful, Joey, he's a sensitive man, and his mother doesn't like me in the house. *(Chuckles)* Threw me out the last time!

(Kerouac comes bouncing back in.)

KEROUAC: All set! All set! She's listenin' to the *Beverly Hillbillies*. Come in, damnit, come in! You want a beer? Hah? Some whiskey?

ALLEN: Jack, this is Joey. He's a young poet from Oregon.

KEROUAC *(Glancingly)*: Yes, yes, hello, Joey . . . Well, sit down, damnit. . . . *(Beaming)* Allen Ginsberg—you old son of a bitch! *(Kerouac goes to the refrigerator and comes back with two six-packs of beer)* My God—how many years has it been?

ALLEN: Let's see, not counting the time your mother threw me out—? *(They laugh)* . . . Almost five years, in '64 when Neal came through New York with Kesey and the Pranksters . . . *(Kerouac scowls)*

KEROUAC: Some scene that was . . .

ALLEN *(Sad)*: I thought it would be a happy reunion . . .

KEROUAC *(Serious)*: Yeah, well, you didn't behave well, Allen, drapin' an American flag over my shoulders like that . . .

ALLEN: I meant it satirically . . . a mistake . . .

KEROUAC: That's no way to treat the flag, Allen. . . . It's not some old rag you play around with. . . . Never mind! Let's forget all that now. . . . Here, have some beer.

JOEY: No thanks, sir. I . . . I don't drink . . .

KEROUAC: Figures . . . Doesn't mix with the LSD, right?—the "higher consciousness"?

ALLEN: LSD's a useful tool, Jack. I've taken it many times myself.

KEROUAC: Oh, you—you'll do anything! Don't worry!—I tried it. Made me dippy with visions. I got enough visions. *(Winces)* Ow! *(Holds his stomach)* I got a goddamn hernia. . . . Belly button's poppin' out. That's why I'm dressed like this. . . . Well, I got no place to go. . . . I'm glad to see ya. . . . Gets kinda lonesome here sometimes . . . *(Joey reaches into his shoulder bag. Kerouac reacts angrily)* Listen, kid, you're not gonna take any pictures, are ya? 'Cause if you take any pictures of me, I'll kick your ass, you hear?

(Joey draws his hand out of the bag to reveal that it's holding a paperback.)

JOEY: I don't have a camera, Mr. Kerouac—

KEROUAC: —and don't call me *Mister*, see! *(Sees the paperback, repen-*

tant) Aw—I'm sorry! I don't even know ya, and here I am yellin' at ya already. . . . It's just that—you gotta understand—all kinds of people come by here pestering me. That's why we came back to Lowell. *(Growling)* I'm sick and tired of kids trying to pour out their lives into me so I'll jump up and down and say, "Yes, yes, that's right!" . . . Little farts of conformity. *(To Joey)* Pretty fancy shoes you got there . . . never seen a poet dressed like that before . . .

ALLEN: It's the new underground, Jack . . . they like soft and beautiful things.

KEROUAC: Yeah, I heard—Beat Dandies, like their rockstar heroes . . . those weird new eyes of the second part of the century . . . *(To Joey)* I'll bet you don't even know who won the Preakness this year, hah? Oh, I know—you got the military-industrial complex to worry about.

ALLEN: Their manners are gentle, too, Jack. You'd like them if you knew them better.

KEROUAC: Well, you always did keep up, Allen. I hear you've been *oming* your way from coast to coast. Me, I just stay the same, let all the fads wear themselves out around me. *(Gesturing toward the TV screen)* Everything gone in the mosaic mesh of television. . . . Can't stand the sound, but the images keep me company . . .

JOEY *(Embarrassed)*: I like *your* shoes, Mr. . . . uh . . . sir . . . I mean, well, they're like the ones I used to wear in high school. I don't suppose you'd want to, I mean, it would a real honor for me if you'd maybe want to exchange those for my—

KEROUAC *(Bellowing)*: —wha! You crazy? Can't you see me prancin' around Danny's Bar in pale leather *pumps!*—Whoa!

JOEY *(Crestfallen)*: . . . I'm sorry, I didn't mean to . . . It's just that I dug the—

ALLEN: —Joey was high-jump champ in college, Jack, once made a leap of six feet nine. Right, Joey?

KEROUAC: C'mon! Little fella like that? Who you tryin' to kid?

JOEY: Allen, I think I'll . . . why don't I wait in the car, or maybe walk around a little. . . . You two must have a lot to talk about, it's hard to do that with a stranger . . .

KEROUAC *(Softening)*: Oh, that's okay, Joey. *(Guffaws)* Strangers never shut *us* up, right, Allen?

ALLEN *(To Joey)*: Go ahead, Joey, if you'd feel more comfortable. I won't be long.

(Joey goes to the door.)

KEROUAC: Now, there's no call for that, Joey. Just sit down and have a beer!

JOEY *(Simple, unpetulant)*: No, I'd rather not . . . but thanks anyway. . . . *(At the door)* Your books have meant a lot to me, Mr. Kerouac . . . to my friends, too . . . I just wanted to thank you for writing them . . .

KEROUAC *(Softer)*: Oh, yeah? . . . Well, thanks, Joey, thanks . . . I'm always here, you know . . . don't have a phone, but . . . well, if you're in the area again sometime, drop in and say hello . . .

JOEY: Much appreciate that. Thank you. *(He exits)*

ALLEN: He means it—about your books, Jack. He's one of the sweetest guys I've ever known. A kind of joyful observer. Reminds me a lot of you, back at Columbia . . . on a sort of pilgrimage . . .

KEROUAC: Well, his eyes look clear . . . a lot of faith in his eyes. . . . Aw, Allen, tell him I'm sorry. . . . There's . . . there's so much bullshit everywhere . . .

(He reaches for a small medicine vial with a plastic cap, snaps it open and drinks from it.)

ALLEN: What's that?

KEROUAC: It's so I won't spill it. *(Shaking the vial)* Johnny Walker Red. Call me Mr. Boilermaker.

(Allen reaches down and picks up a magazine off the floor.)

ALLEN: *National Review*?! Your reading habits have changed.

KEROUAC: Buckley's saying *exactly* what we said twenty years ago: the sacredness of the *individual,* the—

ALLEN: —he means *some* individuals: whites, males, heterosexuals—

KEROUAC: —there's plenty to be said for the old America.

ALLEN: We challenged *all* the old pieties, Jack. And the kids today are, too.

KEROUAC: Yeah, yeah, I've heard ya on TV. You've always been a good talker, Allen, too good a talker—that's your trouble . . .

ALLEN *(Affectionately)*: You used to be a good listener.

KEROUAC: Well, I'll tell *you* something! The insane things being done in this country—riots, hoodlumism! It's enough to make Atlas drop his load!

ALLEN *(Good-natured)*: You always did need a hero. I guess Buckley's the new candidate. *(Charmingly)* I wish it could have been me.

KEROUAC: Aw—you're too accessible.

(They laugh together.)

ALLEN: It's funny, Jack: the words you say and the man inside don't match. And the louder you yell, the less they match.

KEROUAC: Still analyzing, huh? I'm glad some things don't change. Well, truth is, I'm a "Bippie"—the man in the middle. As I get older, I get more . . . genealogical.

ALLEN: Are you writing?

KEROUAC: Oh, sure. Gotta keep the Jewish literary mafia busy. . . . Still calling me a cut-rate Thomas Wolfe, the going phrase for mah "oeuvre." . . . *(Laughs)* Fuck 'em. *(Nodding towards the portrait of the Pope)* I still got those big blue eyes smilin' at me. Painted that myself, you know. May start a whole new career. Hah! Have some more beer . . .

ALLEN: No, Jack, thanks. *(Looks at his watch)* I have to go soon. The reading's at eight.

KEROUAC: Wait!—Whadda they all up to? Haven't heard from anybody in years.

ALLEN: Oh, we're practically the Establishment. They're starting to call Will one of the giants.

KEROUAC: Giant buggerer! Academy Award for Sodomy Significance!

ALLEN: Don't mimic your friends, Jack. It doesn't become you.

KEROUAC: Hah!—like what Will once said to me! "If I didn't know you," he said, "I'd swear you were the craziest piece of rough trade that ever walked." Hah!

ALLEN: Will was always pithy.

KEROUAC: You were both pretty *(Deliberately mispronouncing)* "pissy"
when you wanted me to be trade for you. *(Patting his belly)* Don't
want me now, do you. You got all those young high-jump champs
followin' you around . . .

ALLEN: You're still a handsome man, Jack. And I still love you.

KEROUAC: Neal, too, right?

ALLEN *(Surprised)*: Yes.

KEROUAC: I got my rhythm from Neal, my Okie rhythm, see. "Now,
look h'yar, boy. I'm gonna tell you what, see"—Neal, great Mid-
west poolroom saint alive . . .

ALLEN *(Gently)*: Jack, you *did* hear the news?

KEROUAC: Oh, yeah—Carolyn wrote me. They *say* he's dead . . .

ALLEN: In Mexico, by the railroad tracks . . . froze to death by the
tracks . . . booze and barbiturates . . .

KEROUAC *(Angry)*: Yeah, yeah, I heard all about it! Tell ya somethin',
Allen: it's bullshit—he's hidin', don't want to come back to the old
routine . . .

ALLEN: Jack, it's true. I know people who were with him when—
(Kerouac takes out the crystal.)

KEROUAC: —it's still glistening, see . . .

ALLEN: What is?

KEROUAC: . . . Present Neal once gimme when we were on a mountain road, hitchin' . . . a little crystal. Hmmm—near twenty-five
years ago! . . . I had the damnedest dream about him—just the
other night. We were takin' craps together side by side in a double
crapper. Neal is talkin' about an actor as I wipe myself with the
paper. "But you know he's queer," Neal says, "he blows the Kings."
And I have my part on my lap, and I can feel it swelling, so I hurry
to wipe up before it's a pole, but get all tangled in the wiping and
get some crap in my mouth. . . . Here I am trying to remove the
hunk of dreamcrap from my mouth which is also full of toilet
paper—I'd wiped *it*, instead of below—and Neal's talkin' away
about *(Breaks up with "laughter")* blow jobs! Crazy, huh? . . .

ALLEN: I have a feeling Neal would understand . . .

KEROUAC: 'Course he would! *(Starts singing)*

I'm romantic
And strictly frantic
I love those old-fashioned times.
(Pats his belly) Hah! Better lose some weight. . . . You ever see that
poem I wrote to you?

ALLEN: I think so . . .

KEROUAC: Ah! Didn't read it huh? Some old friend——! Well, I'm a
loyal person, too, and got nuthin' left to be loyal about . . . *(He
stumbles around, finds the poem)* Here——*(Reading)* "Poem dedicated to
Allen Ginsberg"——

ALLEN: I did. I *did* read it——I wrote to you about it!

KEROUAC: Oh——you did? Good! Then we can sing along together——
give it that real old-time feelin'. C'mon, Allen!

ALLEN: I forget it!

KEROUAC: Aw——and you swore you'd never forget me! Well——listen
then, and you tell me if you ever heard a better poem about gettin'
sucked off! *(Reading)*
. . . loll my windmill——roll my luck——
lay my cashier gone amuck——
suck my lamp pole, raise the bane,
hang the traitor
inside my brain
Fill my pail well,
ding my bell, smile for the ladies,
come from hell.
(He laughs uproariously, reaches for the vial of scotch.)

ALLEN: *Definitely* the best of its kind! I wish you had more competi-
tors.

KEROUAC: Most guys wanna hide that sorta experience. . . . Not me
. . . up front with everything . . . jes like Neal . . .

ALLEN: I'm glad you wrote about it. That took courage.

KEROUAC: Naw——I figured nobody would understand it. And if they
did, they wouldn't believe it!

ALLEN: Why the lines "hang the traitor/inside my brain"?

KEROUAC: Oh, no, you don't! I know what you're up to——want me to join Fags Anonymous—right? Alkie Anonymous, maybe, but that other stuff—no. You brought out all of that that was ever in me— maybe more than was in me.

ALLEN *(Smiling):* We all have an endless supply.

(Gabrielle suddenly appears from the back room. She walks with a cane and is able to force out only a word or two of speech. Stella Kerouac is trying to restrain her. Stella is a plain-looking woman about five years older than Kerouac; her manner is quiet, good-natured, determined. Gabrielle is ringing her handbell furiously, her eyes ablaze.)

GABRIELLE *(Strangled: hissing):* . . . Chien . . . chien en culotte . . . vas! . . . vas! . . . plein . . . d'merde! . . . vas! . . . Out! . . . vas! . . . FBI! Out! . . . FBI! . . . plein d'merde . . .

KEROUAC: Ma! Oh, fer krissakes! . . . Ma, it's okay. . . . Allen was in the neighborhood . . .

STELLA: Jack, I'm sorry. . . . She carried on so, I had to. . . . I tried to turn up the radio, but . . .

ALLEN: I'm sorry, Mrs. Kerouac. . . . I only stopped in for a minute. . . . I'll be going. . . . I'll be going now . . .

(Kerouac rushes up to Gabrielle, turns her toward the back room.)

KEROUAC: Stop, Ma! Stop! . . . You can't talk like that to Allen! Ma, he's my oldest friend! . . . The doctor, Ma, be calm! . . . It's all right, he's going, he's going! . . .

(Kerouac and Gabrielle exit.)

STELLA: I'm sorry, Mr. Ginsberg, but I think you'd better—

ALLEN: —yes, I was on my way anyway.

STELLA: She's been terribly ill.

ALLEN: I'd heard about the stroke. . . . You, of course, are Stella.

STELLA: Yes.

ALLEN: You . . . you and Jack weren't married, when I was here last time . . . but I'd heard about that, too.

STELLA: We were married right after Gabrielle's stroke.

ALLEN: I'm glad he—I'm glad they—have you, Stella. Please . . . please take good care of him . . .

STELLA: I waited thirty years to do just that. We knew each other in high school, you know . . . from a distance . . .

(Kerouac rushes back in.)

KEROUAC: —Allen! Ah! . . . I was afraid you'd gone. . . . What a mess! Boy, that old dame can still carry on, huh? It's true what they say: Canucks learn nuthin', forget nuthin'. . . . Stella, go back there to her. . . . I think she's okay. . . . Tell her Allen's gone . . . put her into the bed . . .

STELLA: All right . . .

ALLEN: Goodbye, Stella . . .

STELLA: . . . Goodbye Mr. Ginsberg. *(She exits)*

KEROUAC: Jesus, Allen, helluva way to end a reunion! What can I tell ya? She's a great old lady—a goddamn saint, lying back there, never complainin'. . . . But on the subject of you—well, we're all a little crazy, as I guess you know . . .

ALLEN: I understand. . . . I have to go anyway, Jack.

KEROUAC: Hey—wait! *(He pulls off his shoes and hands them to Allen.)* Here—give these to Joey. Tell him . . . aw, I dunno, tell him I think Oregon's terrific . . . that I love mountains . . . one place I ever felt at peace . . .

(They embrace and hold on tightly to each other.)

ALLEN: I love you, Jack. . . . If only you knew what a good man you are . . .

(Allen exits.)

KEROUAC *(Calling out through the screen door)*: . . . Come back and see me! . . . Please . . . You're a greater poet than ever!—you're really going now!—don't stop!—remember to write without stopping—I wanna hear *(Trailing off)* . . . wanna hear . . . what's at the bottom of your mind. . . . I love you, too, Allen . . . *(He starts to sob, Stella comes out of the back room. Kerouac doesn't see her)* . . . Can't go back . . . can't go forward . . . Our fathers raised us to . . . to sit on nails . . . *(Suddenly yelling)* Stella! *Hey!* Turn the goddamn mus—*(He turns and sees Stella standing there quietly)* Oh . . . turn the goddamn music up, will ya . . .

STELLA: I'm afraid it will wake her. She's quiet now. . . . Jack—he really mustn't come here again. That kind of excitement, she can't afford to—

KEROUAC: —lissen, who pays the rent here, damn it?! *I* pay the rent! I'm the guy who bought us *(Bitter laugh)* this thirty-thousand-dollar mansion, as Dorothy Kilgallen calls it in her column. Hah! If I paid thirty thousand for this shithole, I sure got cheated. . . .
(He gets the bottle of scotch.)

STELLA: It's time to eat, Jack. . . . I made a stew out of—

KEROUAC *(Lashing out)*: —you eat it! . . . *(Quieter)* I'm sad and I'm— *drunk!* I wanna see . . . For some reason I have a tremendous sad desire just to be with, just to see . . . *(Trails off)*

STELLA: See who, Jack?

KEROUAC: I dunno . . . civil wars of my mind and memory . . .

STELLA: Should I ask Alex to come over?

KEROUAC: Let's have us a little drink, hah? . . . Rop and dop, ligger lagger ligger . . .

STELLA: I wish you'd eat something . . .

KEROUAC: Wish I'd come sit sheepish at the table, huh? . . . Be like the wounded pioneer in the wagon train who's got to be fed . . . doesn't do anything to help the men, nuthin' to please the women . . . *(Quieter)* . . . Well, Stell, you knew what you were gettin' into . . .
(He swigs from the bottle.)

STELLA: If you're not going to eat, I won't bother to fix it . . .

KEROUAC: You eat, you eat! Gotta keep up your strength to take care of the idiot invalids—hah!

STELLA: I'm not hungry. I think I'll go to bed, read maybe . . .

KEROUAC: . . . Figured all I had to do was get a little home for me and Ma, read in the sun, pet my kitties. . . . Oh, damn it . . . Coulda been a big Zen Lunatic, sat under tangerine trees, shout in high voice at monk buddies, coulda lived in golden pavilion temple, coulda . . . coulda . . . Yeah—"coulda" . . . Forty-seven years old, Stell, and all I got's my . . . rage . . .
(The lights start to dim.)

STELLA *(Tentative, shy)*: . . . You have Gabrielle . . . and . . . and me . . .

KEROUAC *(Absorbed in himself)*: I've done irreparable harm—gar-

radarable narm! . . . So lies a moral—don't light your lanterns too
soon, it may be darker than you think . . .

STELLA: Jack . . . Jack, do—

KEROUAC: —irreparable harm—

STELLA: —do you . . . care for me?—

KEROUAC: —garradarable narm!

STELLA: Did you hear me, Jack?

KEROUAC: Huh?

STELLA: Do you . . . feel . . . affection for me?

KEROUAC: Whaddya mean? Of course I do! . . . Naturally, babe, naturally . . . *krissakes*—sure! *(He wanders over to the window)* My dog
Beauty died the night I discovered sex. They yelled it up to me—
"Ton chien est mort!"—at just that moment I was lying in bed finding
out my tool had sensations in the tip . . . *(He takes a deep swig, almost
finishing the bottle)*

STELLA: Jack, please . . . please take it easy. . . . Maybe if you go to
bed, if you try to sleep—

KEROUAC: . . . Put on the wrong regalia and you think you're somebody else. . . . Snake of the World . . . coiled out there, inchin' up
. . . hour by hour, all the ages of man . . . *(He points agitatedly out of
the window)* I—oh, Ruthie, *look!* LOOK! . . . blizzard's put a sheet
of snow on the pane!

STELLA *(Close to tears)*: Jacky . . . Jacky . . . it's—it's *spring!*

KEROUAC: God!—I oughta call home!—Pa had to go to work in this
muck!—I oughta call home—Maybe Pa's car got stuck. . . . *(He
turns to Stella)* Ruth . . . if we get to your house, Ruthie . . .
*(Stella starts to cry. She turns and runs into the back room. The lights
dim further; stage now in semidarkness. Kerouac finishes the bottle. Music
under, low.)*

KEROUAC: Easy, Ruthie, *easy!* *(Laughs)* . . . Sittin' on my hand like that!
(Jumps) Huh, Pa—what? . . . It was them coaches not lettin' me
smoke before breakfast, Pa, that's what I couldn't stand. . . . You
know I'm no quitter. . . . *(Sound of bats' wings beating in the dark. Kerouac jumps frantically, swoops and ducks)* Uh-oh . . . uh-oh, they're in

the room . . . they're in the ROOM! . . . NO! . . . NO-O-O!
. . . Don't think . . . mustn't think . . . rest . . . have to rest . . .
(He suddenly screams and ducks from the "swoop of a bat") Aiii!! . . .
Aaooww! . . . Big slurry lips . . . Beggars crappin' in burlap bags
. . . dead vests . . . *mémère* . . . drug . . . communist DRUG!Yawk
photograph VLORK of the Rooster! . . . steamin' mud . . . hot
boiled *(Screaming)* PORK BLOOD! . . . *MÉMÈRE! MÉMÈRE! (Lights
start to crisscross the stage, turning into white spots that pitilessly seek out
Kerouac as he tries to hide in a corner. He cowers with head in hand, whim-
pering and trembling)* . . . *Mon pousse* . . . *Mère de Dieu, priez pour nous
. . . pécheurs . . . maintenant et . . . á l'heure de notre mort . . .*
*(The lights scan out once toward the audience, then immediately go out.
Stage momentarily in darkness. Then a single shaft of light at the door. Neal
appears, looking as he did at his first entrance, aged nineteen, in Act One,
Scene 1. Music off.)*

NEAL *(Agitated; W.C. Fields accent)*: For cryin' out loud, Jacky *m'boy*,
how long you think that lil' ol' pussy's gonna sit out there? Can't
keep her goin' *all* by m'self, proud though I am of me comin'
attractions! TIME, boy, *TIME*! Got to get on the ball, darlin',
for a peaceful understandin' of pure love betwen us, all hassles
thrown *out*!

KEROUAC *(Weak)*: Neal . . . Neal . . . I . . .

NEAL: No need to *worry*, adamantine boy—

KEROUAC: . . . Where . . . where you been all this . . . time . . .

NEAL: Been all over the world, Jacky . . . inveiglin' wisdom, arms
hangin' low, lazy eyes sayin', " 'Tis a pimp, son, a pimp hides at the
secret heart of mystery . . ."

KEROUAC: . . . Maybe if I just stay here, Neal . . . just try to be quiet
and—kind . . .

NEAL: Well, yass, a' course, stare at the luminous Cross, watch the soft
fud come creepin' over the sand—I understand, ol' buddy, understand com-*pletely*. It's like that alto man we heard last night—up to
him to put down what everybody's feelin'. He starts the first chorus, rises to his fate, has to blow *equal* to it. All of a sudden somewhere in the middle he *gets* it—time *stops*! He's fillin' empty space

with the substance of our lives. Trumpet of the morning in America! . . . *(Pause)* And that's it. Neal, blank at last.

KEROUAC: . . . When . . . when will I see you again?

(Music builds until final blackout.)

NEAL: See me?! We got the same flesh and bone . . . *(Pause; gentle)* I saw, had a vision of you, handsome m'boy, walkin' across the top of America with your lantern-shadow—

KEROUAC *(crying)*: —Neal . . . I pray you . . . get back safe . . .

NEAL: Adios, you who watched the sun go down, smilin' at the rail, by my side. . . . We almost walked arm in arm. . . . Old fever Jack, goodbye. . . . *(Light out on Neal)*

KEROUAC *(Struggling to rise)*: . . . Wait—wait for me! . . . King . . . WAIT!!

(Kerouac's body slumps to the floor. Lights up full: natural daylight. Kerouac is lying on his back, eyes open in a glassy stare, palms turned upward, fingers locked. He's dead. Freeze for a moment. Then blackout.)

END OF PLAY

NOTES FOR *IN WHITE AMERICA*

ACT ONE

1. The opening statements, meant to suggest the spectrum of opinion when *In White America* was first produced (1964), are taken from letters to the editors and articles in *Time, Newsweek, The New York Times,* and *The Atlanta Constitution.*

2. Falconbridge, Alexander, *Account of the Slave Trade on the Coast of Africa* (London: 1788). The *Account,* a rare pamphlet, can be found more accessibly in George F. Dow, *Slave Ships and Slaving* (Salem: 1927), where it is reprinted on pp. 133–54. The last sentence in this scene is out of sequence; I have taken it from an earlier section of the pamphlet.

3. *Annals of Congress,* Vol. I, pp. 1224–29. The petition was not actually read to Congress by a Quaker woman, of course, but was introduced by a Representative. Also, the speeches themselves, which are here alternated between two actors, were in fact delivered by five separate Congressmen, and in different sequence from that presented in the scene.

4. The two opening sentences are from Jefferson's letter to Edward Coles, August 25, 1814; the remainder of the first paragraph is from Jefferson's *Autobiography* (1821). The rest of the speech is from his *Notes on Virginia* (1782). All are available in many editions: e.g., Adrienne Koch and William Peden, eds., *The Life and Selected Writings of Thomas Jefferson* (New York: 1944), in which the selection from the Coles letter is on pp. 641–42, from the *Autobiography* on p. 51, and that from the *Notes on Virginia,* on pp. 257–62.

5. Olmsted, Frederick Law, *A Journey in the Seaboard States* (New York: 1856), pp. 676–84. Olmsted's various travel accounts have been widely reprinted. The most comprehensive edition is Frederick Law Olmsted, *The Cotton Kingdom*, ed. Arthur M. Schlesinger (New York: 1953), in which the material used for this scene can be found on pp. 259–65.

6. A Federal Writers' Project in the 1930's interviewed ex-slaves and recorded their reminiscences. These were deposited in the Library of Congress in over 10,000 manuscript pages. From these, B.A. Botkin drew a representative sample which he published as *Lay My Burden Down* (Chicago: 1945). The material used in this scene can be found in the Botkin volume (in order of appearance) on pp. 125, 89, 123, 12, 84, 89–90, 25, 86, 122–23, 74, 73. In the second speech, I have combined reminiscences by two slaves into one narrative.

7. Jourdon Anderson's letter is in L. Maria Child, *The Freedmen's Book* (Boston: 1865), pp. 265–67; the Logue letters were printed in William Lloyd Garrison's newspaper, *The Liberator,* April 27, 1860. The Anderson letter has been reprinted more recently in *The Mind of the Negro as Reflected In Letters Written During the Crisis 1800–1860*, ed. Carter G. Woodson (Lancaster: 1926), pp. 537–39; and the Logue letters have been reprinted in Herbert Aptheker, *A Documentary History of the Negro People in the United States* (New York: 1951), pp. 449–51.

8. *The Confessions of Nat Turner . . .* , ed. Thomas R. Gray (Baltimore: 1831). This original edition is now rare; the *Confessions* is more readily available as reprinted in Aptheker, *op. cit.*, pp. 120–24.

9. May, Samuel J., *Some Recollections of Our Anti-Slavery Conflict* (Boston: 1869), pp. 40–50, 71–72.

10. Sojourner Truth's speech was first printed in *History of Woman Suffrage*, Elizabeth Cady Stanton, Susan B. Anthony, and Matilda Joslyn Gage, eds. (New York: 1881), I, 116. It has since been widely reprinted.

11. Sanborn, F. B., ed., *The Life and Letters of John Brown* (Boston: 1885). The speech to the court is printed on pp. 584–85; the final message to his guard, on p. 620.

12. Mary Boykin Chesnut, *A Diary from Dixie*, ed. Ben Ames Williams (Boston: 1949), pp. 31, 38, 292–93.

13. Thomas Wentworth Higginson, *Army Life in a Black Regiment* (Boston: 1870), in order of appearance, pp. 7–8, 22–23, 53–54, 26, 76–77, 40–41. In selecting excerpts, I have not kept entirely to chronology; I have put Higginson's discussion of the soldiers' religion (in his diary, Jan. 13, 1863) before their prayers (in the diary, Dec. 14, 1862), and I have used the celebration of the Emancipation Proclamation (diary, Jan. 1, 1863), to close the scene.

ACT TWO

1. Recollections of the impact of freedom are in Botkin, *op. cit.*, in order of appearance, pp. 223, 66, 236–37, 225, 231, 267. The second speech, delivered by a woman, is actually the reminiscence of a man.

2. Elizabeth Hyde Bothume, *First Days Among the Contraband* (Boston: 1893), pp. 22, 35, 68. In a few places, I have changed tenses from past to present, and in the first paragraph, I have rearranged the sequence of sentences.

3. Eliza Andrews, *The Wartime Journal of a Georgia Girl* (New York: 1908), pp. 316, 365, 373–75.

4. The interview with President Johnson is printed in Edward McPherson, *The Political History . . . of Reconstruction* (Washington: 1875), pp. 52–55.

After the Douglass delegation departed, Johnson, according to one of his private secretaries who was present at the interview, said: "Those d——d sons of b——s thought they had me in a trap! I know that d——d Douglass; he's just like any nigger, and he would sooner cut a white man's throat than not." (P. Ripley to Manton Marble, Feb. 8, 1866, Marble mss., as quoted in LaWanda Cox and John H. Cox, *Politics, Principle, and Prejudice, 1865–1866* [Glencoe: 1963], p. 163).

5. The KKK oath and first testimony are from *Official Report of the Proceedings in the Ku Klux Trials . . . Before United States Circuit Court . . .*

Held at Columbia, South Carolina, November Term, 1871 (Columbia: 1872), p. 61 (the oath), p. 69 (testimony).

Mrs. Tutson's account is in *Testimony Taken by the Joint Select Committee to Inquire into the Conditions of Affairs in the Late Insurrectionary States* (Wash.: 1872), II, 59–64.

6. Senator Tillman's speech is in the *Congressional Record*, 59th Cong. 2d Sess., Vol. XLI, pp. 1440–44.

7. This famous "Atlanta Exposition" speech of Booker T. Washington's was widely quoted at the time (e.g. *The New York Times*, Sept. 19, 1895), and has since been widely reprinted. It may be conveniently found in Rayford W. Logan, *The Negro in the United States* (New York: 1957), pp. 128–30.

8. W.E.B. DuBois, "Of Mr. Booker T. Washington and Others," *The Souls of Black Folk* (Chicago: 1903), pp. 43–44, 50–51, 54–55.

9. This is Monroe Trotter's account of the interview with Wilson, as published in *The Crisis*, 9:119–27 (January 1915). It should not be assumed that because the version is Trotter's, it is necessarily unfair to Wilson; in fact it agrees, in broad outline, with all other accounts of the interview I have been able to find (e.g. *The New York Times*, Nov. 13, 1914). The Trotter version, however, is the only one I know which gives extensive dialogue exchange between the two men, and so the accuracy of the actual words spoken cannot be entirely verified—an uncertainty which, though common to many (perhaps most) historical documents, makes this account something less than unimpeachable. Wilson's Secretary of the Navy, Josephus Daniels, visited Wilson the day after the Trotter interview, and later gave this account of the President's reaction:

"Daniels [Wilson said], never raise an incident into an issue. When the negro delegate threatened me, I was damn fool enough to lose my temper and to point them to the door. What I ought to have done would have been to have listened, restrained my resentment, and, when they had finished, to have said to them that, of course, their petition would receive consideration. They would then have withdrawn quietly and no more would have been heard about the matter. But I lost my temper and played the fool. I raised that incident into an issue that will be hard to down." (Daniels to Franklin D. Roosevelt, Mexico, June 10, 1933, Roosevelt Library, Official File 237. I am grateful to Arthur S. Link for this reference.)

The Trotter version occasionally switches from first person to third; wherever this happens, I have reconverted to first. The last line in the scene is a paraphrase taken from another account.

10. The French directive was originally discovered by W.E.B. DuBois on a trip to France following the Armistice. It was first printed in *The Crisis*, May 1919, pp. 16–18, and subsequently in Mary W. Ovington, *The Walls Came Tumbling Down* (New York: 1947), pp. 144–46. The directive was sent out at the request of the American Army by the French Committee, which was the official organ of communication between the American forces and the French. It represented American, not French opinion; when the French Ministry heard of the distribution of this document among the Prefects and Sous-Prefects of France, it apparently ordered copies of the directive to be collected and burned.

11. This composite speech of Marcus Garvey's is drawn from *The New York Times*, Aug. 3, 1920, and *The Independent*, Feb. 26, 1921, pp. 205–6, 218–19.

12. The Father Divine letters were printed in his weekly newspaper, *The New Day*, June 9, 1951.

13. The laborer's description is from an account written early in the century (Hamilton Holt, ed., *The Life Stories of Undistinguished Americans as Told by Themselves* [New York: 1906], pp. 186, 190–92, 194, 198–99). Since peonage continued largely unchanged until at least World War II, I have felt at liberty to place this scene in the 1930s.

The storekeeper's speech is a paraphrase, with the names and amounts invented. In the last paragraph I have switched the sequence of three sentences.

14. Walter White's wartime experiences are in his autobiography, *A Man Called White* (New York: 1948), pp. 278–82, 285, 293.

15. The fifteen-year-old girl described her ordeal to Daisy Bates, president of the Arkansas NAACP, who published the account in *Long*

Shadow of Little Rock (New York: 1962), pp. 72–76. The white man's reaction, also as told to Mrs. Bates, is on pp. 69–71 of her book. I have put the two descriptions together into one scene.

16. The short closing statements are taken from letters to the editors and articles in *Time, Newsweek*, and *The New York Times*.